Interior

Interior

Thomas Clerc

Translated from the French

by Jeffrey Zuckerman

Farrar, Straus and Giroux

New York

Farrar, Straus and Giroux
175 Varick Street, New York 10014

Library of Congress Cataloging-in-Publication Data
Names: Clerc, Thomas, 1965– author. | Zuckerman, Jeffrey,
   1987– translator.
Title: Interior : a novel / Thomas Clerc ; translated from the French
   by Jeffrey Zuckerman.
Other titles: Intérieur. English
Description: First American edition. | New York : Farrar, Straus
   and Giroux, [2018] | Originally published in French in 2013
   by Éditions Gallimard, Paris, as Intérieur.
Identifiers: LCCN 2017047962 | ISBN 9780374176860 (hardcover)
Subjects: LCSH: Clerc, Thomas, 1965—Homes and haunts.
Classification: LCC PQ2703.L47 I5813 2018 | DDC 843/.92—dc23
LC record available at https://lccn.loc.gov/2017047962

Designed by Jonathan D. Lippincott

www.fsgbooks.com
www.twitter.com/fsgbooks • www.facebook.com/fsgbooks

10 9 8 7 6 5 4 3 2 1

I dedicate this book to my great-grandfather Auguste Clerc, decorator, painter of religious objects, and orator—murdered by his wife on June 29, 1912, at the age of 48.

Decoration! Everything is in that word.

      —Mallarmé

Contents

Entryway 1

Bathroom 29

Toilet 61

Kitchen 75

Living Room 129

Office 181

Bedroom 257

Entryway

(4.35 m^2)

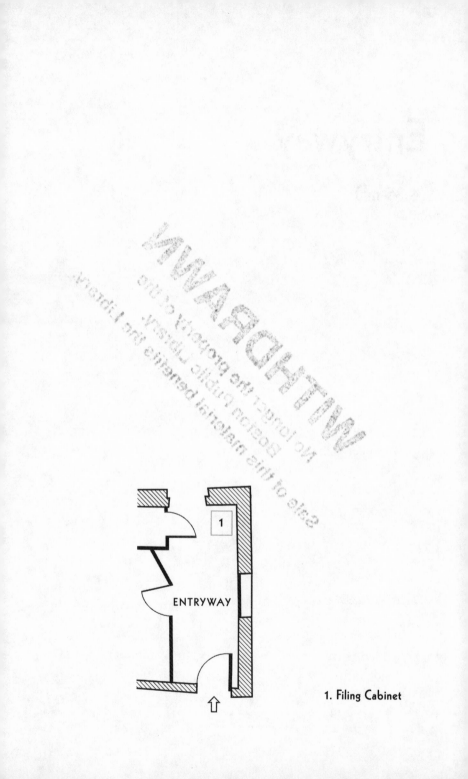

ENTRYWAY

1. Filing Cabinet

Doorbell

The doorbell rings. I go. Peephole. Nobody. I grab my keys. I open the door. The 3rd-floor hallway. Empty. A glance. The stairwell. "Anybody there?" I can't have been dreaming. I go up some steps. I go back down. I'm in front of my open door.

Hallway

This door isn't standard. Squat, shoved into its frame, it evokes some brutish epoch when people might have stood in front of caves, expecting monsters to poke their heads out. Its orange tinge is jarring, like primer paint before the final coat. It's old, it'll stay orange, with its uneven crust. Just looking at it, anyone would guess that the ceiling was low, the whole building too, this modest late 18th-century structure with 6 floors but only 2 façade windows. Ancient but inglorious: I live on 1 of those Paris streets Prefect Haussmann's equalizing regime left unrazed.

He Rings His Doorbell

If he wants to listen once again to that muted, shrill tone, which caught him by surprise, he'll press the little white disc embedded within its black plastic rectangle mounted on the right side of the doorjamb. He hears it rarely and rings it even more rarely still. His visitors generally don't notice the discreet button and so they knock on the door. Knocking on the door makes them seem more neighborly, since the doorbell's timbre is as impersonal as a luxury residence or a doctor's office. There's no name on the door. He enters.

He Enters His Home

I push open the door with the momentary twinge I always feel when coming back after some long absence or voyage: here's hoping nothing's happened. The molding on the inside panels makes it impossible to reinforce this door; only its old oak offers any bulwark against attacks. The Italian-style lock that I engaged with 1 double turn (€500) is really just makeshift: the vertical bar with multiple rivets wasn't properly sawn off at both ends, the screws are unevenly tightened along the doorframe, and the circle bored into the wooden floor for the bar to sink into is more hole than precisely cut ring. 1 small wooden doorstop wedged/jammed behind the bar is supposed to protect it from crowbars, but this rudimentary safeguard positively reeks of amateurishness, even though I let a specialist do it. I can't really say I regret doing so, considering that the burglary I suffered on February 8, 2006, was accomplished not by breaking through the door but rather by shattering the living room window, contrary to all those statistics indicating that 80% of burglars come through the front entrance. It was then, out of sheer precaution, that I had my lock changed. Even though the burglar entered through the living room window, I can't be sure that he didn't go back out through the door, relocking it with 1 of the keys I (idiotically) keep in the entryway, so that he could come back later. The scenario may be unlikely, but I can't rule it out entirely. If I'd known how many copies I'd made of my keys, I could have deduced whether he had stolen 1; but, like so many other people, I never pay attention to these sorts of things and so the theoretical stolen key is simultaneously present and absent: by describing my apartment as faithfully as I can, by presenting this detailed inventory to my reader, not only will I be in a position to calculate the number of keys in my possession, but I'll know how to correct the mistake of leaving my keys out for everybody to see. Isn't writing a form of material proof, an observation that collapses uncertainties? Since there was no way I could allow myself to go on living in fear of yet another break-in, even without forced entry, I hired 1 of those locksmiths that we in France call "Louis XVIs" (it's a long story) to come and change this undamaged lock that was now threatened by Schrödinger's key.

Locked Out

Keys make their power felt only in being lost, thereby turning doors into walls, if not outright barricades—as in the classic misadventure that befell me on October 5, 2005, just as I was heading out. Grabbing my set of keys and shutting the door as usual, with 1 firm yank, I immediately realized on the landing that I had thoughtlessly taken along the keys for my Nanterre office instead of the keys for my apartment and was now *locked out*. Without my wallet or phone or anything more than 1 pair of office keys, I very quickly descended into frustration, worry, despondency, and self-hatred. No question about it: my day had been ruined.

This mistake has 1 identifiable cause: that same morning, I had learned of my dear friend the writer Guillaume Dustan's death at 39 (I, too, was that age). Perturbed as I was by this news, which I'd heard just before leaving to teach, on the threshold of my apartment, unsettled by the idea that someone of my own generation could die so early and so brutally, I found myself, immediately after my lunch at home, in the situation I have described, alone on the landing, helpless, reeling dizzily, heading toward the 1st café I could find and using their phone so someone could get me out of this mess.

Entering

Having crossed the doorway and shut the door with its 2 massive hinges so reminiscent of primitivist works of art in their 13-centimeter height and diameter that they aroused whistles of admiration from my locksmith (compliments carry 0 value save when delivered by experts), I step into the entryway. At the moment I enter my place, I reflexively slam the door: the burglary I've just described doesn't have any bearing on that action, since I'm not obsessed with security the way my colleagues are. The breach of my domicile, as unpleasant as it may have been, didn't drive me to reinforce my home with heavy-duty security doors, alarms, surveillance cameras, door chains, bars over the windows, or any other such paranoiac apparatuses. No, it's more my desire to remain hermetically sealed from the outside that prompts me to twist my wrist and shut myself in. This sanctuary in the heart of the city, this warm or cool oasis standing sentinel against the street. With that essential gesture, I dam the deluge: I enter my kingdom. The key's metallic click as it turns 2 times in the lock prefigures my passage into this other world. I do so even when some visitor leaves: as soon as he's out, he can hear me turning the key right behind him, setting off laughter on both sides of the door: the loon is locking himself in.

The Key to All Keys

At which point I leave the key in the lock, in its natural place. While my eyes stay fixed on the cluster of keys hanging and swinging like a clock's pendulum, in regular undulations that soon slow and come to a stop, I look for other elements bearing this double function (both organization and utilization). These keys are 3 in number: the largest 1 governs the entrance to my apartment and opens 2 doors—the door leading to the street, for which it isn't really needed, since punching the code (54 B 68) does the trick; and the door leading to the courtyard, for which it is very much necessary—while the 2nd key, with a black plastic cover on its bow and its short, crenellated shaft, is used for the apartment door; the last, very small key opens the mailbox. In 1 sense, these keys aren't mine; I'll have to return them when I get to the end of this book and I've left this apartment. These keys, weighted not so much by their volume as by their symbolism, signify ownership without wholly embodying it. The persistence of keys through history astonishes me: unlocking a door remains a terribly human, antiquated gesture forever haunted by the risk of failure.

In the Poe House

The 1 ideal, enduring key chain design I've always sought is now finally in my possession: a miniature book made of silvery metal and about 2 cm by 2.5 cm, with ring attached, the book's cover reading EDGAR ALLAN POE, the 3 words arranged vertically. The "book" has a spine also debossed with POE, and on the back cover, in small engraved letters, is the sentence I BECAME INSANE WITH LONG INTERVALS OF HORRIBLE SANITY. I bought this superb key chain in New York on July 26, 2009, while visiting the Poe Cottage, an antiquated wooden house tucked into some corner of the Bronx, on 1 small square right between 2 massive unwelcoming avenues, and which I found only through sheer perseverance, even as my queries to passersby went unheeded; nobody in the population of poor black people and working-class white people milling around that neighborhood had any apparent knowledge of *Edgar Allan Poe's house*.

The book's $1.50 gleam, weighting the fetters of my small key ring, is testament to my reverence for the author of "The Philosophy of Furniture."

Old Oak

A door, like a sheet of paper, has 2 sides, and on the verso of mine I see unappealing wood. Deceptive ornamentation barely hides its defects, which I've tried to cover up with wood filler. A useless undertaking: gaps and bumps still hint at the oak's paradoxical fragility, which my slipshod job only accentuated. When I feel it with my hands, the door seems knobbly, but not solid; it's more screen than proper door. Like a cardboard cutout of a knight that I could simply knock over.

A Peephole Named Judas

The peephole is at neck height for me, so I have to bend down slightly to use it. A position rarely employed: few and far between are those who seek to breach the boundaries of my apartment, fewer and farther still are those who arrive unexpectedly, and fewest and farthest are those occasions when the 2 categories meet and warrant a preventive glance, which is to say the moments when strangers present themselves at my door. The peephole's rounded magnifying lens creates a visual distortion, an effect I would say approximates anamorphosis. Since the French word for peephole is *judas*, sometimes I decide to play the betrayer and use this tiny panopticon as a base from which to spy on all the people going up or down the stairs— and when I'm also able to hear their voices too, then all that's left would be for me to scribble down their conversations here . . . But at heart I can't bear to be a backstabber. The only secrets I'll betray are my own.

Portière

Having slammed the door, I double my foyer's defenses in the winter with a portière that keeps the draft out. It's always cold in my entryway since the stairwell leads directly to the courtyard and outside air: a defect perhaps due as much to its builders'

indifference as to the modesty of means at their disposal. (I
wonder who actually built my building? Some artisan who left
no signed work behind, as opposed to those great architect-
engineers who took pride in forever engraving the letters of
their last names into the flesh of bourgeois stone . . .) In the
19th century, interiors started being insulated from the elements; but in my apartment I have to do this work myself,
stuffing the door's crevices with foam and hanging a rod
above the doorframe for holding 1 thick green velvet curtain
bought at the Saint-Pierre Market and hemmed by a Kurdish
tailor at Château d'Eau. The length of the cloth is incorrect—a
flaw that continues to annoy me, since I was the 1 who miscal-
culated the door's dimensions, as well as those for hemming
the portière and then the relationship between the 2: the velvet
lets cold air trickle out the left and right sides, while most of
the wintry chill sits in 1 big heavy mass down low, held in by
all the extra velvet on the floor. Sometimes, when I'm bored in
the winter, I wave my hand around to enjoy those faint currents of cold air that, despite these defense systems, permeate
my apartment; I sweep them from place to place as, with a slight
frisson, I savor the carelessness of the unmodern world and of
France itself, with its centuries-old architecture so ill adapted
to the needs of the present day.

Rod

I note the small rod's awkward position: to get out, I have to
push the curtain to the left, but because it isn't set on the
door but above it, the cloth's thickness prevents the door from
opening all the way. Of course there's no real need to open
the door all the way, but at certain moments (several people
coming in at once, or the sheer width of a new piece of furniture being brought in), this causes a huge pile-up, as we might
say on the road. The curtain's way of hampering the door is

an affront to the natural order of things: cloth somehow being elevated above wood. If by chance someone insisted on pushing the door all the way open, the curtain's thickness would, as it resisted, drag down the all-too-light rod holding it up, and so pull its screws out of their wall mounts, bringing the curtain and everything else attached crashing down to the floor. The internal limits of a system are endlessly fascinating. Luckily, nothing and nobody ever reaches 100%.

Fiat Luxury

1 wall switch mounted on the left controls the room's lighting, so that anyone entering the apartment is temporarily refused entry to the kingdom of light. This instrument, which manages to merge technology and poetry, execution and idea, is, in French, called an *interrupteur*: it interrupts the Darkness in which we dwell, and within which we must search for the Light. A little pressure from 1's finger and the hallway appears: 3.3 luxurious meters by 1 narrow meter—its white walls, its window on the right, its wooden floor, its 2 doors side by side on the left, and the egress at its end, obscured by another cloth.

Falling Light

Illumination comes from an oblong, white glass ceiling light—the only real 1 in the apartment—light falling gently down from above. Its shape, somewhat softened by the thin layer of dust coating its globe, hardly interests me, but beneath this lack of interest is outright deception: this fixture is merely a far less sophisticated substitute for the beautiful restaurant chandelier I lost in tragic circumstances. 1 afternoon, bound to my desk, I hear an enormous noise tear through the quiet of my interior. I leave my seat, I go to the entryway: the chandelier lies, shattered, in the middle of the hall, in a jumble of glass shards. Propelled by its own weight to the floor, it had subsequently flown into 1,000 pieces. The metal sconce, its poorly anchored weight having been underestimated, had abruptly come loose, bringing down the massive glass rotunda as well. What a shame that it couldn't have fallen on some burglar's head, knocking him out in the act, committing a crime of its own as it was destroyed. The thief laid low by inanimate objects, a tale too tall to be true, lit up my caricaturing imagination for an instant as I used a dustpan to collect the fixture's scattered glass slivers and its orphaned metal base. I've hardly ever suffered any similar domestic accidents, but this 1 shed light on the 2 major problems with ceiling lights: the blinding risk of just such brutal drops, which I've never let myself forget since, and the sinister gleam they cast over a room, crushing it with light forced downward rather than gently spread in all directions.

I can't stop fixating on an odd thing about my replacement light: it's cracked. But it could only have become so subsequent to contact with some object or else some violent individual, which wouldn't have been me. Upon reflection, it must be a legacy of my (actual) burglar, whether because he was looking for something hidden in the fixture (as in *Family Plot*, Hitchcock's final film, where a diamond is secreted in a crystal chandelier) and then broke it out of spite, or else, more likely, he simply collided with it, somehow, in his haste. As such, the 2 ceiling lights in my entryway (past and present) have each suffered damage, total or partial—as if their position overhead paradoxically doomed them both to injury.

Window on the Walls
In this light, it's possible to walk into this hallway-entryway and appreciate the natural illumination streaming from the right thanks to the window looking onto the building's courtyard. As the sight of this small, walled-in courtyard strikes me as depressing, if not sordid, considering the 10th arrondissement's relative paucity of lavish courtyards, the original inhabitants' relative modesty of social status, and the 3rd floor's relative

inadequacy of panoramic views, I've draped some large white cotton curtains in front of these double casement windows. Thus filtered, their light adds to the space's serene ambiance. Held in place by 1 gray brass rod identical to the portière's, along which several small ring-clips slide, this curtain is always kept shut, even when I open the window for some air. Its natural-fiber cotton, acquired at the Roissy IKEA, protects me from the walls of facing buildings and the windows of fussing neighbors.

Optic/Haptic
I'm caressing the curtain's slightly quilted texture; I'd like not only to give my readers a guided tour of the museum-of-sorts that I consider my apartment, but also to make them rub their fingers over every inch of it; literature moves me because it respects nothing.

Concierge Services
Around the sides of the white curtain I peer out at the courtyard. I bring my eye to the lateral gap and, like a silent spy, I let my gaze take in the slow, lugubrious rhythm of this interior space, largely uneventful, but not always—as when snow falls.

Modern White
Like all the other rooms of my apartment, the entryway is painted white, and while I do happen to have a personal preference for all that is bright, I'm also following the current cultural taste, which has established white as the color par excellence, and which divides interiors into 2 hermetic categories: "contemporary" spaces, and everything else. Pared-down classical styles have become equal to modernist interiors that disdain all decorative and chromatic excess. As I welcome Adolf Loos into my place, he whispers *Ornament is a crime* while

sipping a Mauresque aperitif. In fact, all this whiteness only reinforces the greenery-bereft-greenhouse or charmless-clinic effect of my little entryway.

On the Ground

Continuing to creep forward, on the left wall of the hallway-entryway (which will lead us to the main room in due time) we'll find the bathroom and, immediately thereafter, the toilet. But taking in the whole space means we mustn't ignore the floor.

Buffet Down Low

With any luck, nobody's toes will get stubbed on the low Buffet on the right wall; and I don't mean buffet as in side table, but rather as in this painting by Bernard Buffet (or, at least, this reproduction thereof) set on the floor, depicting some harbor town I've never managed to identify on a canvas measuring 94 × 58 cm and in a sickly green typical for this painter. It's not actually all that serious if I accidentally kick this daub I found on the street, thrown out from the by-the-hour hotel under renovation nearby, because the attachment I feel toward it is uncertain at best. It's not this wall decoration's woeful state of preservation (its upper left corner is damaged; the picture is just glued onto hardboard) so much as the sheer fact of its existence, owing to Buffet's style—alluring due to its horrendousness—that's brought it low; allowing all who walk past to appreciate just how necessary some famously bad artists may be: their radically poor taste serves as a reprimand to our hubristic self-confidence. We can all be brought low.

Terra Infirma

As for the floor itself, the entryway's is adorned, like pretty much the rest of the apartment (aside from the bathroom and the toilet), with old oak parquet, once covered by linoleum, a bequest of the previous owner, which then had to be sanded and varnished away. The beautiful wood paneling's pattern unfortunately does little to hide its structural problem: sloping slightly from the entrance to the bathroom, the floor forms 1 small depression over 10 cm^2. Determining the origin of this indentation is fairly easy for anyone well versed in the colossal amount of structural work that my home has required: it's likely that the floorboards beneath the parquet are in terrible shape and that, as with the bathroom, before I had it completely redone, the rafters holding the ceiling of the floor below have rotted away. Since repairing this trench would be far beyond my financial means, I tend to avoid this area . . . and yet, when I'm at my most anxious, visions of this sinkhole yawning open beneath me tend to plague my mind, and I see myself falling through the floor and landing in my 2nd-floor neighbor's apartment. At the same time, I can't deny the positive *appel du vide* this potential rift holds for me. When I feel the floorboards sag beneath the pressure of my toes, I relish the act of pushing deeper, testing the physical integrity of the entryway, an action that terrifies and excites me all at once, or maybe like a sore in my mouth or toothache that I can't keep from probing with my tongue. Reducing the problem by fortifying the floor with a massive injection of concrete would certainly be 1 practical solution; but, then, shouldn't these structural problems be solved with a complete and proper overhaul? I leave the sagging area for terra firma.

Charted Territory

The only furniture in the entryway stands at its end, filling the right-hand wall, sneering at everyone who enters. It's no more or less than a gray metal filing cabinet with 4 drawers, its height 1.32 meters, its width 41 cm. This piece of furniture, blandly functional in style, and hard to date precisely—just think of all the "modern" eras it must have endured over the course of its reign—adds to the room's understated tone. Its bureaucratic grayness accentuates its bulk, which provides a gentle reminder of the Balzacian fortitude I had to summon in order to capture it: during a stroll down the rue du Dahomey in my old neighborhood, I stopped in front of a social security office under renovation and, seeing this filing cabinet among a heap of discarded furniture, I decided to claim it for myself. As its weight and my inability to get a good grip on it would have made this a backbreaking prospect for me, I went to the Kiloutou equipment-rental company nearby and got 1 of those things that delivery people use all the time and that we simply call a "dolly," to cart this filing cabinet 500 meters. I managed, with much huffing and puffing, to get it up to the 4th floor, thanks to the furniture mover I had no idea was buried deep within my muscles. This is how people form attachments to their belongings: by paying the price with their own bodies.

Serendipity

The delight I take in my accidental discovery of this monolith, a phenomenon called *serendipity*, is compounded by the pleasure of having salvaged it myself from the junkyard, by the spontaneous nature of such urban redistributions, and by their near-total unexpectedness. This fortuitous furnishing therefore bears witness to my self's particular tendencies, my self's agency within this urban ecosystem.

Functionalismus

1 has to reckon with an ingenious constraint when opening the cabinet's drawers: only 1 of them can be drawn out along its runners at any given time, because having 1 open locks all the others shut, which in turn makes it possible to concentrate solely on the open drawer. Coherent and authoritarian: functionalism

follows the form of its function. In the 1st drawer from the top
are all my school papers in color-coded folders: these are, in the
main, handouts for the classes I attended at various points in
my education and which I kept because they were so well done—
some are so good, in fact, that I reuse portions of them, thereby
reinforcing the stereotype that teachers just copy their work
from each other ad nauseam. But, really, what else could a class
(or a book) be, anyway, if not a patchwork of other, older material, served up with some personal flair? Everything's here in
this 63-cm-deep reserve that I like to open all the way, pulling
the drawer out to its fullest extent so as to appreciate the metal's
resistance against the weight of so much paper and to hear the
click! as the runners hit their limits.

Drawer 2

In the 2nd drawer are my financial files (bills, bank statements, pay slips, tax forms, etc.), kept in an ever-changing order, because I can never decide whether it's easier to reach a
folder closer to the inside or the outside of the drawer. I like
the shifting positions. Anyway, the red folder specifically dedicated to my 2nd job as *maître-conférencier*, or lecturer, labeled
ADMINISTRATION NANTERRE, is usually easily accessible, so
it's simple enough for me to produce whatever documents are
needed for everything to go smoothly in that sphere. The requirements of social life force me to open this drawer often:
all in all, the irritation most people feel when confronted with
"paperwork" is unfamiliar to me; on the contrary, I like the
idea that a life could be summarized thus, could be made to
fit into a single envelope. I once knew a famous actress who told
me about a member of her family who had brandished an old
yellow envelope bearing, in black letters, the word JUIF: documents conferring upon her an identity at once fundamental and
contemptuous, as seen through 1 particular administrative

lens—giving her life substance even while putting it under threat. There's a bit of the archivist in me, after all; I'd never have undertaken this massive documentation of myself if I weren't convinced that archives, like capital *L* Literature, tell the truth. And while it's true that a conversational approach might do more justice to a person's biography than a dry presentation of all the evidence pertaining to it, the problem is that this argument has so often led to our being made to gloss over the material conditions of these lives—as if the "soul" were more noble than a tax form!—that I find it's completely out of the question for me to pass over these documents and even the least element of my interior in silence.

Money

The money file contains all my statements from the Banque populaire Nord de Paris, which I've kept since I opened my account there in February 2002—the beginning of a new stage in my life. The pitiful state of my finances deserves a novel of its own, but I am barred from belaboring those details here owing to the self-imposed constraint that there be 0 discussion in these pages of any subject that might be the focus of some future literary work. In effect, talking about money—rich vein that it is—would wind up producing a hypertext to this project contrary in spirit to the surfacist descriptions intended for it. All the same, anybody perusing this drawer could easily see that my €3,000 per month suffices to rank me among the 20% best-off French people, which in fact grants me the right to buy this 50 m² 2-/3-room apartment in Strasbourg–Saint-Denis that you're visiting in absentia.

While looking over my bank statements, 1 overpaid consultant noted that, for the year so far, my monthly mortgage payment of €925 hadn't changed, nor had my €150 in maintenance fees, whereas my taxes had gone from €645 to 715, suggesting that my financial situation is improving. As this apartment's owner knows all too well what it costs to own, and especially not to own anything, it can be concluded that the tranquility any apartment provides its owner is a preview of social transformation: a room of 1's own, that's the start of the Revolution. The thick cardboard box bound with a strap and holding smaller folders related to the apartment (files pertaining to the property deed, fees, insurance, and so on) is the administrative counterpart to these lines I've sketched out here on my computer. A folder titled "miscellaneous pay slips" specifies the various supplementary payments I receive that allow me to improve my daily life: alongside my main métier in academia, I practice the thankless art of criticism, the unappreciated art of being a columnist, and the scenic art of performance.

Model Home

Leaning against these folders (unless it's the folders that are leaning against them—with any 2 objects in relation there can be at least 2 relationships) is a shoebox into which is welcomed all evidence of my recent outings: invitations, programs, prospectuses. "Recent outings" isn't exactly right, because it's only when the box has been filled, which might take several months or even years, that it's moved to another part of my apartment (→ BEDROOM) and a new box takes its place. Given their multitude, it's impossible to inventory all these pieces authoritatively. My need to preserve these traces of my activities shouldn't surprise any reader aware of my propensity for building monuments to myself. The only rule I have for conservation is this: I have to have been physically present at the event thus memorialized (plays, concerts, soccer games, etc.), so that the evidence might figure in this social cartography of my existence.

Examining the older shoeboxes of this sort reveals that I spent 1 particular stretch of time carving out a cultural life for myself: if I hadn't attended my share of films, performances, and other such outings, I wouldn't really have felt as though I'd truly "lived" . . . a stance that could only ever be considered contemptible by such despisers of worldliness as those socialites who seem to believe that the pleasure of beholding anything other than their own selves each day must be some sort of vice. In their presence, standing all alone in a corner just looks pathetic—whereas escaping just feeds into their system of exclusion. Nothing could be more unsavory than these false hermits striving to proclaim their insularity—but I can sidestep the dangers of such disagreeable duplicity if I just make use of my strong, incontestable propensity to sit watching the entire French Open on TV without feeling the least discomfort. Leaving my apartment, as will be clear by the end of the book, is something I believe I must *earn*.

Foolbox
The 3rd drawer is where I keep everything needed for home maintenance: tools, light bulbs, extension cords, etc.—piled up in no order, stashed out of sight thanks to this furnishing's setup, which, by concealing items of 0 aesthetic interest as easily as it does the choicest baubles, thereby fulfills its egalitarian design. I open this drawer, which I equate with misfortune, as little as possible: it's not just that I have so little equipment in here, but also that I feel nothing but dread and terror as regards this array of tools. Since utopia, in my mind, would be a place where machines work quietly all by themselves, devoting so restricted a space to this "toolbox" of mine follows from 1 secret strategy: deep within myself is the foolhardy belief that "I don't need what I don't have," and that accumulating more and better tools would simply increase, almost reflexively, the reasons to use them . . . In other words, that things anticipate the needs they serve, and as I don't know how to make any sort of minor improvement to my apartment, or indeed how

to fix anything, I have instead succumbed to this especially fragile superstition: that catastrophes may be averted by divesting myself of their remedies (a tactic equally useful for the medicine cabinet→BATHROOM).

Hammer Without Smith

This hammer, my only real tool, was stolen from the worker who came to fix the hot water tank in my bathroom, and who absentmindedly left it behind on the tile (the advantage of having practically 0 furniture is evident here): as an unpremeditated theft, an appropriation by omission, a countertax levied against the exorbitant rates charged by a category of professionals intent on plumbing home-repair budgets to their fullest, this vengeance exacted by an intellectual against a technician delights me. As much as I'm in favor of homeownership necessarily being private, I'm also in favor of sharing tools, consistent with a communist ethos. The semicommunism I aspire to consists of collectivizing everything that's uninteresting. Mr. Green, in the entryway, with the wrench, would thoroughly approve.

Shambles

The sheer lack of space granted to tools in this drawer results in general disorder, since I keep numerous wholly unrelated things there, thereby giving this shambles an atmosphere much like the 1 the surrealists attributed to flea markets: 1 map of France assembled out of cut-up pink carpet (a gift from my friend Bruno Gibert during his "contemporary art" phase); 1 Polaroid camera, unused for eons; 1 water gun for attacking rhetoricians; 1 flashlight sans battery; some spare light bulbs; 1 cassette labeled THOMAS CLERC DEFENDS HIS THESIS; 1 disk drive; 39 road maps; 1 rectangular metal lampshade in which I've stuffed the box for 1 Montblanc pen that I've never used; 1 3-meter tape measure the same size and color as a wasp; elegant copper nameplates meant to make 1's front door look especially sophisticated; 1 Lip watch, definitively stopped; some cables; and a cookie tin full of nails—all in all a mass of what people from the Pays de Loire region might refer to with that odd regionalism *la jaille* and what we here just call junk. There's also 1 travel chess set, the memento of a bygone era when I was obsessed with this game for months, before eventually giving it up as violently as I'd taken to it, obeying a particular corollary of the law of caprice, namely, that 1 can avoid exhausting a primary enthusiasm by trying out some alternate dilections, the better to go back to the original with fresh eyes—just as a trip to a foreign country makes it easier to love 1's home upon returning. Chief among these manias would be soccer, for which I save my televisual fervor, or the used bookstore that occupies the Sunday mornings of whosoever agrees to accompany me there.

The Past

Finally, in the lowest drawer, the humblest 1, shoved there for convenience's sake, are all the old folders underscoring the geological strata of my past: the residue of bread-and-butter work for various publishing houses, trip tickets and other travel papers kept in manila envelopes, souvenirs of my time as a student, and other now distant activities I could easily call to mind, but rarely do, like the particulars of a book read out of obligation. These papers, and the memories they summon up, have to be laid out horizontally: roles both on- and offstage at the Artistic Athévains theater (1983–1996); the archives of the literary magazine *Le Mérou* (14 issues), which I founded along with some young Turks in 1986 and which fell apart in 1995; the minutes from a secret society—Les 4 Fages—founded that same year and scuttled in 1996. 3 activities (the theater, the literary magazine, and the secret society) that only call for 1 brief description, the point they share in common—aside from a delight in life's pleasures—being that of communal living: I don't live in a house but in an apartment. Apartments contain rooms that contain some furniture that contain folders wherein a life has been stored away; life isn't a simple directory of personal belongings. Life overpowers death.

Sliding Along the Runners
As I pull open the heavy drawer, I'm amazed by how smoothly it comes out of its recess. The system of sliding runners surpasses the rough friction of wooden drawers. It simplifies the process of managing memories.

Downside Up
Each drawer bears 1 small rectangle where 1 small piece of card stock is supposed to indicate its contents. Only the 1 on top— WARNING PLEASE READ SAFETY INSTRUCTION PROVIDED IN TOP DRAWER—has been kept. I've handwritten CONFIDEN- TIEL on the other 3, which makes 0 sense because Literature only pretends to be secret.

Tray
I keep 2 types of objects on top of this cabinet: category 1 contains such objects as 1 round ashtray, which I've repurposed (I don't smoke) as a key holder—it's deep enough for the job. This tinplate ashtray, stolen from a waterfront café on some Saint-Raphaël beach in 1994, under the disapproving gaze of my friend, who at the time had a business relationship with the café's owners, is midnight blue with a world-map design, and holds 1 copy each of the keys to my apartment, the keys to my Nanterre office, and the key to my cellar space: keys, keys, keys. I've put this key tray here specifically to be within arm's reach whenever I enter or leave my apartment, so that I won't have

to go through the same ludicrous experience that drives me nuts every time I see it happen to other people: trying to find their keys before heading out; but this seeming convenience could pose serious problems should there be another burglary. Keeping my keys in full sight is a security risk; it would be better to hide them away, far from their respective locks, in a place known only to myself (I've now done so).

Keys to the Kingdom
Rusty like tombstones, lonely like men, chilly like corpses.

Made in Cogolin
The other item belonging to the 1st category, here, however, was *purchased*—from the Romanies in the flea market at Cogolin, a town in Var well known for its pipes and rugs: this 26 cm metalloid rectangle composed of trapezoidal shafts, with 4 black rubber-coated feet and a row of 36 engraved numbers—or, if it's better for each item to be given a name, this record rack (for vinyl singles)—can also be used to organize mail; even so, I leave its beautiful structure devoid of all paper.

Édouard I
The item on top of my filing cabinet belonging to the 2nd category transcends its status as a mere object to achieve the status of "work of art": it pertains to 1 52 cm × 52 cm color photograph that my vice-friend Édouard Levé gave me in thanks for a piece I wrote on his work. This photo, in a pine frame, is part of his *Homonyms* series, and depicts *The Homonym of Raymond Roussel*; it was shot in 1998, back when he and I were very close; I chose Raymond Roussel's homonym, among the other possibilities on offer (Emmanuel Bove, André Breton, Eugène Delacroix, Georges Bataille, and Yves Klein) in a coded homage to the identity of the man who gave it to me, rather than any aesthetic reason, which would in any case be antithetical to

this work's conceptual nature. Conceptual art is, in my view, the most beautiful of all the arts, and if I had to choose here, for myself, the sort of classification that, as a critic, I easily impose on some of my colleagues, I'd consider myself a post-conceptual writer.

Inalienable Objects
1 last glance brings to the fore those items that no apartment dweller could possibly forget: that aggregate of *inalienable objects* preceding 1's own presence and in time succeeding it— objects belonging not to the resident, as such, but rather, being necessary to the apartment's proper functioning, acting as its real masters: pipes, outlets, meters, drains, etc. 2 different elements are most prominent in this array of wholly impersonal objects that the law calls *property in mortmain*: 1st, on the right wall of the entryway, the electrical panel, made up of the fuse box, the circuit breakers, and 2nd, the gas meter itself. This equipment is so visually interesting because it's mounted on 1 slab of extremely old dark wood, which contrasts with the plastic switches. Out of this block of backcountry wood come 4 thick wires sheathed in fraying cloth, which once caught the eye of an extremely French electrician from Électricité de France: "You're running a risk," this electrician sighed, reinforcing the dilapidated setup with some black tape. This patch, as touching as a beggar's rags, sets these other details in harsh, cold relief.

Breakage
The impressive number of fuses (15) in my fuse box causes me some anxiety: I don't see why there should be so many, and I only ever touch the 4 main 1s, which I only consider "main" because they're labeled on a single placard listing the names of their corresponding rooms: I assigned the role of "bedroom"

and "office" to their respective rooms only because of these preexisting labels. Fortunately, the fuses almost never blow, but when they do it's in the winter, because having 3 heaters, the lights, and the washing machine all running at once (I don't count the computer because it's practically always on) inevitably results in blown fuses. Restoring power by flipping the breaker from 0 to 1 is the only act of technical proficiency that—once I've gotten the better of my paralyzing fear of being stuck without any heat through the worst of January—I am able to carry out.

Gas on Every Floor

The 2nd inalienable object demanding our attention is on the opposite wall, facing the 1st: the gas meter, 1 small brass block hanging from 2 pipes that run the entire length of the room. Only its grommet touches the wall, so subtly that the pipe almost seems to be floating. At the moment I'm writing these lines, the reading on the counter has gone up to 22/04, which is nearly my birth date. The last official to have taken an official reading from this piece of unseizable property was 1 fairly butch woman who, perched on a stool, kept praising my taste in music as the strains of Amy Winehouse's *Back to Black* reached our ears, mere days after the news of the singer's death.

Intercom

The 3rd impersonal object, a white-corded intercom, which unlocks the courtyard door, is fixed to the wall. It was manufactured by the Acet company, and presents me with 1 unlock button and a 2nd button bearing a logogram I simply can't decipher. I don't know what this 2nd button does when I press it (maybe it's producing an unexpected effect at this very moment, with consequences that affect me only later—such as flashing my name on the intercom screen downstairs?), but I've been forced to accept that this supposed intercommunication device doesn't allow any actual communication to occur. In some cases, its function has even been overpowered by the unadorned human voice: certainly, in the summer, when my window is open and someone rings downstairs, if the door doesn't unlock automatically, as is supposed to happen when I utilize the object under discussion, my visitor will yell "It's not working!" and I'll yell "Wait!" It feels particularly absurd to shout a capella what should have been intoned through the intervening intercom; but this noncoincidence between handset and entrance, and thus between my visitor and myself, generates a small yet fascinating physical tension.

Object Failure

Several scenarios draw attention to this object's shortcomings: the impatient visitor who, ringing and not getting any immediate response, simply presumes the proprietor absent (though I remember that when I used to ring at the door of the massive bourgeois apartments of my childhood, I always had to wait a fairly long while before anyone opened the door, indicating the affluence of the owners thus summoned, forced to cross not only a succession of rooms but a hallway and an entryway before being able to answer my call, wealth being measurable in both space and time); the timorous ringer who, not having pushed the intercom button long enough, waits in vain for me to respond when a 2nd, longer press is all that's required; not to mention the frequent hysteria resulting from the 2 parties involved simultaneously doing contradictory things and so preventing the door from properly unlocking, for example X giving it a shove before I've even been able to unlock it. 1 of the most bizarre cases I can relate was that of my friend who, impatient to see me, pushed the lowermost button so hard that the entryway buzzer's subsequent blare knocked the handset off its perch, with only the tangled braid of its cord preventing it from hitting the ground; the doorbell's violence had been so extreme that the momentarily unusable device had barred me from buzzing in my dear friend. Still, this minor domestic downfall at least underscored just how all our domestic telephonic devices struggle in vain to mediate our overflowing humanness—the object in question being brought low by the simple transmission of desire.

Édouard II

It's time to leave this room, but not before looking back and noticing, on the floor, against the wall separating the entryway from the bathroom, the 2nd artwork I own; it's also by Édouard Levé and also framed under glass. This 35 cm × 18 cm black-and-white photograph, dating from 1998, is titled *Thomas Clerc refuse le prix Goncourt* and depicts me during a conference at the Canadian embassy on the topic of failure. I would have liked to appeal to Édouard Levé to take another photo with a different caption. This possibility having unfortunately been made impossible, I've set this lucky charm out of harm's way.

Piecework

As I turn around to glance 1 last time at my entryway, seeing this room as more of a patchwork than an artwork, the synthesis of its elements (the green portière, the parquet, the white cotton over the window, and the glass-brick wall of the bathroom, which we'll get to in due time) communicating a distinctive sparseness resulting in a "light, chic feeling" . . . I have to say I do like it. Considering its modest objective qualities, I've tried to make the best—or anyway the least worst—of it. Playing the presumably-minimalist-but-not-radically-so card, what I wanted was to set up the rest of my apartment along a

qualitative slope leading toward contrasting, increasingly impressive effects. My life's work!

But then it hits me. The room's very name is a deception,
because even though 1 must certainly *enter* an apartment in
order to be inside it, dedicating a whole room to that function
isn't strictly necessary: 1 has either entered or 1 hasn't (indeed,
some small apartments without front steps don't even have an
entryway). And yet, though its congruity with the hallway
partially deprives it of any specific identity, my entryway exists
a bit all the same. Some days, I'm touched by this effort it
makes to exist; others, its smallness annoys me as it would any
beleaguered bourgeois.

In-Actions

There's nothing to do in the entryway but enter or exit: interior architecture hasn't managed to invent any other functions
for the space, though I sometimes dream of adding a sliding
glass door that might somehow sanctify it. But what else is
there to do here? Head in. Open the door. Walk through. Turn
on the light. I never linger there.

The Doorbell Rings Again

There's the sound of the doorbell ringing again. This time,
since I'm right by the door, I open it more quickly. Nobody. I
glance through the peephole again. I slam the door shut, then
take 2 steps from the entryway into the 2nd room.

Bathroom

(3.78 m^2)

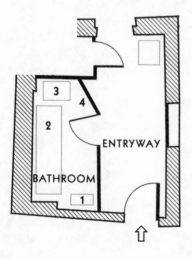

1. Sink
2. Bathtub
3. Washing Machine
4. Glass-Brick Wall

Just on the left upon entering, after taking 2 or 3 steps into the hallway-entryway, we push open the bathroom door: 1 tiny room 2.15 m long and 1.76 m wide.

Inferior Mirage

The most striking thing at 1st, aside from its smallness, is the fact that it's not a room in and of itself, but actually a part of the entryway, demarcated from the latter by means of a Sheetrock partition wall that 1 solid ax blow could easily bring down: a room added onto, or rather, carved out of, another. At this point in Paris's history, when the standard of living has caught up with rising sea levels, this fairly necessary room often has to be cobbled together from nothing, since it's long been common in apartments both old and modest for the advertised "bathroom" to be as substantial as those "inferior" mirages of oases thirsty travelers believe they see in deserts. In my personal hierarchy of rooms, however, my bathroom ranks very high. (Which might not be the case for the majority of Parisians, in whose homes the bathroom is usually the black sheep, a black mark against the supposed superiority of Western civilization . . .) Even though I've had to downscale my ambitions in this space, as in so many others, the fact that my bathroom actually has a bathtub elevates the room to the upper ranks of its class. In French, real estate vocabulary has invented the term *salle d'eau*—a phrase revelatory in its sheer plainness—to distinguish bathrooms actually containing a bathtub from those that don't. The literalness of the appellation "water room" is so bereft of dignity that it bestows upon its rival, the bathtub-laden *salle de bains*, or "baths room," an automatic prestige.

Camera Fluida

As a counteroffensive against the room's persistent dampness, the bathroom door is always left open. Situated more or less across from the hallway-entryway's window, opening the 1 allows the other to air out—an ingenious arrangement, as those all too familiar with the Parisian obsession for ventilation will agree. My bathroom is fairly shabby, but at least it can be aerated. After all, there are bathrooms, even in some luxury apartments, devoid of all ventilation: an absolute heresy. A proper bathroom presupposes at least 1 airway for the eradication of offensiveness. Every stench must wither and die in this camera lucida, in the full light of day.

The Glass House

To make the room as bright as possible, I've had the rest of the entryway-hallway's dividing wall built with glass bricks. The effect of this transparency, although moderate or practically nil as seen from the hallway side, is arresting from inside in the bathroom. My original hope had been to wall up the entire room with glass bricks, so as to establish a sort of correspondence between this glass and the water flowing within, but the Romanian workers in charge of renovating my apartment talked me out of this, because of the danger inherent in the bricks' increased weight relative to the plaster wall they'd be embedded in. I learned that to hold them in place, iron bars would have to be installed to reinforce the wall around them. These bricks total 36 (4 across × 9 down): Michel Leiris's age when he put the finishing touches on *Manhood*, as well as the year in the 20th century when the French won the right to have weekends.

As is always the case for the glass bricks used in bathrooms, these so-called transparent blocks are clouded so as to avoid prying eyes. It may seem strange for a bachelor to resort to such methods of concealment, more germane to communal life, but this useless effort pleases me, contravening as it does glass's original virtue. In fact, the faces and bodies deformed by this system seem all the more suggestive. A nude body visible behind a square of distorting glass engenders a sort of ecstasy: a deformation not unrelated to the 1 that occurs during sexual congress, when the tumult that takes hold of all features seems to bring them back to a rawer level of humanity.

International Klein Room

Being a part of the artwork I've hoped to turn my apartment into, the bathroom hews to my conception of a disconcerting, outrageous minimalism: it's covered almost entirely in white tile, the bathtub and 1 small stretch of blue wall notably excepted. It exudes a sort of emptiness that, given its function, I wanted to affirm, resisting all needless ornamentation, all superfluous adornment, finding it unthinkable to overpower such a sober space. A bathroom is a bathroom; it is, more legitimately than any other room, tautological. Only the blue/white binary bears witness to any chromatic ambition: of the 36 glass bricks, 2 are the same blue as that of the bathtub's tiles and the section of wall. This shade of blue verges on International Klein Blue (IKB), and I like to think that this 2-toned room accordingly calls to mind 1 of those modernist artists who considered color and design of equal value. Klein was very much a pro artist, but his con-artist side does make me smile slightly; there's 0 question that he made art purely for the art world and so purely as a means of building up his reputation, which makes him an authentic impostor. Which means my bathroom is more authentic than Klein ever was.

Raynaud White Tiles

But in this watery space it's Jean-Pierre Raynaud's influence that's most keenly felt, through those 15 cm × 15 cm white tiles, selected in homage to his "Maison" in La Celle-Saint-Cloud, to which he devoted some 24 years of artistic labor before destroying it. On the floor, the whitish tiles clash slightly with the purer white of the walls and the indefinite color of the baseboards, which contribute to the room's tonal coherence— its chief asset (augmented by the grout's light gray). Because I did an imperfect job of resealing them recently, these floor tiles are separated by a grout that differs from the white-silicone caulk that's always edged the bathtub. Refilling the spaces between such tiles is an essential element of decorative art: in effect, 1 very beautiful tile's effect can be marred by the mere presence of some useless grout or, on the contrary, diminished by the lack of any clear divide separating its brothers and itself: between the 2 schools (visible grout or 0 grout), I lean toward a distinct grout and a color that meshes with that of the tiles; this grout isn't tinted, however, so a sad dullness keeps the tiles' color from standing out, because the mortar is too dirty to form a distinct boundary. This attention to seemingly insignificant details is nothing more than the syllabic rhythm of a period or the transition between 2 sentences. Carefully considering this question of seams between tiles, I end up pondering those discreet aesthetic principles of demarcating words, shapes, and things. In painting as well, the thick contours of Manet or Léger stand out equally as much.

Unsealed

Persistent humidity has ruined the floor tiling. 3 or 4 of the tiles are in place thanks only to sheer miracle, considering that so many puddles of water have dissolved the caulk that once held them in place. The loosened tiles' pattern brings to mind muddled memories of unpleasant dreams, visions of falls or treacherous slips or tooth extractions. The detached tile, testament to the inherent frailty of the human species, underscores the half-abject, half-touching erosion against which the art of permanence constantly struggles. The fear and disgust that degradation, breakage, and detached fingernails stir within me all find resonance in this room, as if this particular space I tread daily were more of a threat than any of the others. Unlike their counterparts on the wall, which attract the connoisseur's eye in their perfection, my floor tiles are humble. My incompetence with tools is astounding; it took me 2 hours to straighten them out with a special compound that now holds them a bit better.

Even without squatting for closer inspection, it's easy to see that the 1st tile by the room's entrance is broken. The only way I can explain this damage is as the result of a woman's heel, and I suspect it's 1 of my friends, who always wears high heels, and who ignored my explicit rule to only ever walk barefoot in the bathroom, although that's a decree even I don't always follow. As such, this cracked square stands as evidence of the inevitable failure of every prohibition.

The Hyacinth Tapestry

To combat the floor's dampness, I've put down a little dark-purple mat that keeps the floor around the bathtub dry. I picked out this beautiful deep violet color as a way to elevate the floor rug's humble function: aside from the touch it adds to the room's bluish components (which it outclasses in true blueness), this color manages to redeem a cloth meant for 1's feet. The

problem with such minor objects, diminished by their designated uses, merits serious thought: I would be lying if I claimed
that all the objects I own have equal value to me. I can't accord
as much weight to this floor covering as I do to my computer
(→OFFICE) or my pink-and-white-striped shirt (→BEDROOM),
but I don't hold it in such contempt that I can't take note of
its qualities. So I've done my best to highlight its assets, and
its amethyst tone is the predominant 1 in my eyes—I care far
less about its cottony softness, frankly. I try to give each object
a chance.

Pedology

There may not be much room to walk around in here, but being
barefoot does offer me some paltry few extra centimeters, and
those of fairly small proportions would get even more. *Pedol-
ogy* refers to both the study of soil and the study of children: this
mat, having endured plenty of abuse, has also been subjected
to overuse at the hand (or, rather, foot) of a particular child,
who swished it swiftly over my tiles, as if it were a mop: 2
uses in 1.

2 Sources Are Better Than 1

Illumination comes from 2 sources: 1 wired ceiling light that
diffuses a yellowish light, and 1 little fluorescent light over the
sink, which diffuses a whitish light: despite the "ish" suffixes,
I'm not unpleased by the result. Even with their respective
ugliness, the 2 lights together result in something much more
agreeable than their separate uses would have hinted at. Whitish
and yellowish, in effect, cancel each other out; using only 1 of
these light sources chills 1 side of the room, accentuating the
tiles' formalism and the health-spa ambiance. From this I can
deduce a theorem: 2 austere light sources, fighting against each
other, result in 1 successful illumination. Of course, the range

of theories about proper illumination is almost as complex as
their real-world application. It's rare to find 1 lighting setup
that satisfies all parties present. But the truth is that I've successfully subdued my bathroom's clinical tone.

Water Damage

The ceiling is a fake 1 that, in addition to its light fixture,
boasts 1 small air vent. This barrier was recently sabotaged by
my 4th-floor neighbors, who, intending to fix their bathtub
themselves, sent such huge quantities of water raining down
that the bathroom's white wood-tone paneling buckled. Although these neighbors do annoy me for various reasons that
I'll get into in due time (→LIVING ROOM, OFFICE), I don't
consider their attack on my bathroom to be their worst of-
fense. And I do bear in mind that there are 4 of them up
there living in the same amount of space I do, and that their
limited means have forced them to do without the services of
those fellows who can turn shit into gold (that is, plumbers,
not writers).

Bathorama

Due to the room's space constraints (shutting the door again
after entering means squeezing around said door while sucking
in your gut and pulling in your butt, as if the room were doing
double duty as a gym), a walking tour is out of the question,
so a gawking tour will have to do. 1st, on the left, there's the
old-style sink that I bought the day I moved in (September 11,
2001) for the modest sum of ₣100 at the Vanves flea market.
As a retro counterpoint to the room's general modernism, this
ceramic piece has a picturesque charm, but it has 2 objective
disadvantages that I did not foresee at the time, and which, if I
were granted the chance to make the purchase over again, would
keep me from repeating my mistake, misconstruing these flaws

as exciting features: namely, 1st, that such sinks are set on a single tapered foot, whereas modern-day sinks tend to come with wide bases in which 1 finds a little cabinet for storing bathroom accessories. This extra space, which would have solved the problem faced by every Parisian, was in my case wasted by acquiring this ancient model that, privileging a columnar form for the sake of 1 sink's singular function qua sink, forces me to keep as few items here as possible, leaving the area fairly empty.

Original Nudity
In its non-erotic sense, nudity is natural in bathrooms and bedrooms; possible in the toilet; furtive in the living room and the entryway, when these need to be crossed in order to enter the bathroom; incongruous in the kitchen and the office; and simply disagreeable in the cellar. The pleasure of being naked at home is that of unrehearsed performance. The nightmare: a nudist colony, already an attack against eroticism, reaching its nadir in the form of a convenience store where people must run their errands in the nude.

Mixing Faucet
The 2nd and chief disadvantage of this ex-1-star-hotel sink, which reminds 1 of Marcel Carné's films (and an era when the pure whiteness of laundry paired nicely with a particularly French degree of physical and moral filthiness), was, for a long while, its lack of a mixing faucet. Its 2 wholly separate taps made it impossible to get comfortably warm water except by filling the sink, a problem made most acute in winter when the cold water was incredibly cold and the hot water boiling hot: brushing my teeth called for a tooth mug, an object I eventually had to get rid of because its ultimate uselessness annoyed me. The more satisfactory solution was to install a mixing faucet, which I put off, for financial reasons (€200), as long as I could, and which, in the end, when I finally took the plunge, only served

to underscore further the manifold disappointments inherent in owning what had once been a thing of beauty. Thus do so many objects that seduced us at 1st come, over time, to betray us.

Opening the drain, set in the white enamel, is done by means of a central powdery-gray bump that, when I squint my eyes, looks like an old squat inkwell, or maybe a tiny mountain, topped by its latch, which I push from left to right to empty the sink and vice versa to hold in the water. By contrast, the dizzying complexity of modern plumbing's mechanisms tends to be completely hidden behind the sink itself. Sometimes so completely that even the latch is eliminated outright. How does anyone stopper their sink in such cases? I was once confronted by just this problem at a luxury hotel, and subsequently spent 5 exasperated minutes trying and failing to solve it.

Enamel

As befits the structure of this type of sink, its soap holders are characterized by grooves etched in its enamel as well as all the dirty remnants of collective sanitation. I use the 1 on the left to hold my toothbrush and toothpaste, while the 1 on the right holds liquid soap in a bottle, which I prefer for hygienic reasons to bar soap, which always leaves scummy traces. My favorite toothpaste brand has long been Fluocaril, owing to its medicinal flavor, its green & white packaging, the "fluor" of its name implying both fluidity and fluoride, the "car" perfectly suited to carefully fighting dental caries. Since the practice of occasionally changing toothpaste brands is recommended so that 1's teeth don't become habituated to the same product, I've opted for Elmex as my alternate, whether the usual orange tube or the green 1 for sensitive teeth. French people, on average, buy 1 toothbrush each year, and I take pride in being above average relative to this population apparently so skeptical of dental care as to be downright suspicious.

The Tooth-and-Footman

The toothbrush calls for a vertical holder I cannot provide; therefore, it reclines horizontally on the sink, a disappointing pose given its form, but less so than when I try to keep it upright by wedging it behind 1 of the taps; its thin profile keeps it from staying put and it falls down like a bony dancer. I'm reminded of the photos in Eric Madeleine's project *Made in Eric*, in which the artist lends his body to various household uses, at 1 point offering up his foot so as to utilize the space between 2 of his toes as a toothbrush holder.

Water Supply

Sometimes I run the water and watch it benevolently, and the urge to praise Paris's water supply, which seems so ordinary to us today as to occlude the practically unearthly difficulties of its implementation, runs through my veins. Marveling at the technological world is as fine a way as any to while away some time waiting for death, though it would be stretching a cliché into the realm of hyperbole to say that the taps "sing out" with water (in similarly hyperbolic terms, when I ascend in an elevator, I tell myself that maybe I'll meet the gods on Olympus; when I descend into a parking lot, maybe I'll meet Orpheus). The water's flow, a source of tranquility, never ceases to intrigue me: I'm astonished that there's always enough, and if I were a mad scientist, I'd keep the faucet open ad libitum to see if and when this infinitude ended. This prospect of extravagant waste both delights and terrifies me; I've also learned that Paris's water is now under public management again, and that makes me happy. Even if I praise private property (as a status symbol), the idea of privatizing water seems idiotic to me. Nothing could be more ominous than nationalizing personal effects, as in the Poland of bygone days, but nothing could be more idiotic than putting basic necessities under private management. I'll shut off the faucet of my speech here.

The Mirror Amplifies

Above the sink, I've hung 1 large mirror that's 1.05 m wide and 75 cm tall and makes the room look bigger while also attesting to the strength of my upper body. Due to hot water vapor, this mirror has gone white in its lower-right corner; but its bright, clean surface is the 1 spatial amplification I'm most proud of. My dwarf bathroom has its "Versailles" side. In the mirror where he gazes at his reflection, Narcissus multiplies: Mao × Marilyn = Mishima.

He Gets Bored

I'm bare-chested. I'm in front of the mirror. I fill the sink. The water is warm. I flick on the little fluorescent light. I splash water on my cheeks. I rinse the blade of the Bic razor. I take some shaving cream. I pat it on my cheeks. I rub it under my jawbone, around my mouth. The shaving cream covers the bottom of my face. I spread it on both sides. I draw the razor over my skin. I hold its handle with my left hand. The cream squishes slightly as it's scraped away. I look in the mirror. The stubble puts up a fight. I dip the blade in the water. Hair floats on the surface. I begin again. I take extra care around any moles. I rinse myself off.

The Haze of Forgetfulness

Hot water vapor has clouded the mirror. Shaving must cease. The door has to be opened, as well as the hallway window, in order to let in some fresh air, so the operation can resume. During this interregnum, he traces words with his finger on the glass. What words? He's forgotten.

Bath/Shower

The bathtub's superiority over a mere shower is in its double function—and the converse is not true. Shower stalls resist horizontality, but bathtubs don't forbid verticality. Shower advocates have their justifications (generally spatial constraints), but are rarely consistent: their fundamentalism will never succeed in supplanting the bathtub. A bathroom without a bathtub, no matter how well appointed it might be, is merely a *salle d'eau*. Luxury bathes; poverty showers. The most broad-minded of aqueous solutions is to combine both shower hose and bathtub.

Standing to shower, I feel all too keenly the inadequacy of my sanitary setup, since I don't have any place to hang the shower head. Either I'm forced to soap myself up while holding the nozzle against my hip or my thigh, a posture that results in wasteful sprays of water, or if I set the hose at the bottom of the basin, the water's pressure makes it twist and spew everywhere. So I hold its damp head down with my foot, a gesture that I always accompany with the verse of a great poet: "My foot on some serpent where our love fires the coals."

A Room for All Seasons

All arguments in favor of a bathtub prove useless in the summer, when the shower rejected by wintertime finally wins out, just as southern France, where creature comforts aren't much valued, wins out over the north. No other room is so relative, or so sensitive, to the changing seasons. Time wins out over space.

Shower Psycho

A significant absence explains all the water overflowing onto my tiles: I've always refused to hang up a shower curtain here, as though a lack of separation between body and room would give this space a greater feeling of openness, confer onto the act of washing a greater degree of innocence. The inherent ugliness of shower curtains serves to contradict their intended purpose, whether we're talking about a clinical white model or some fantasia, although especially in the 1st case, where the whiteness will inevitably, over time, come to struggle against a grime just as likely to have originated from its own plastic as from contact with humans; I can't shake the thought of certain curtains in certain sordid pension showers whose flowing folds shelter nothing so much as their own teeming germ life. No, the shower curtain—that disingenuous object emblematized by its use in Hitchcock's *Psycho*, where it was made to serve as censor as well as mise en scène—may be fantastically interesting, in its way, but is quite, quite impossible in reality.

The Bathtub

Sad surrogate for a happy childhood, salvation of many a depressingly cold winter day, material and moral balm for all of life's ills, the bathtub is the site of a pleasure so pure that an adult film actress once insisted in an interview that her 1 absolute requirement after a day of filming was a *good hot bath with a sweet vermouth on the rocks*—I can quote those words verbatim. Bought at the Batkor warehouse in the northern suburbs, for the price of F1,500, this 1.58-m-long bathtub has an optimal 65 cm depth (the Ritz's bathtubs, by comparison, are 69 cm). I am constitutionally unable to take seriously the financial argument that the "cost" of a bath is 3 times that of a shower, even less to pay heed to the ecological necessity of restricting water usage to save the planet. I can't imagine living in a house without a bathtub, much less living in a capital city devoid of such balneal pleasures. My tub is open from October to May, daily during the winter, always in the evenings.

Drawing the Bath

In the delight it causes, somewhat similar to the anticipation preceding the commingling of bodies, filling up 1's bathtub is 1 of the most comforting forms of passivity to exist. While

the water pours into the bathtub, 1's interim activities, circumscribed within the time needed for the bath to fill (13
minutes), take on a particular charm: defecating, completing
some administrative task, putting on some music, taking off
1's clothes. Though it used to be the purview of servants, this
is precisely the sort of task that makes for a legitimate argument in favor of each person's autonomy: I wouldn't like it if
someone else dealt with my bath; I want to check the water
temperature myself and adjust the hot and cold knobs without having to appear in a bathrobe before some subaltern.
Drawing 1's bath is an intimate affair, and a subjective 1 too,
speaking physically: should my counterpart catch me drawing
my bath, she would undoubtedly be alarmed by the (according
to her norms) near-boiling temperature of the water.

Special Effects
My superhot bathwater produces a heavy mist that spreads
almost into the hallway, just like a special effect: penetrating
the bathroom, the explorer comes across a new land, where he
might find the creature from the black lagoon or the still-warm
body of Elvis Presley.

Yonder Water
When I'm in the bathtub, I always leave the bathroom door
open to take in the view of the entryway-hallway. In this way I
can increase my prospects to infinity. There are 2 possible ways
to orient the bathtub in this room, corresponding to each side
of the bath, and having the drain positioned closer to the back
practically forbids me from orienting it on its right side; so I've
positioned the head of the bathtub closer to the open end of the
room, where the view is more agreeable, but I don't remember
whether I made that decision consciously or whether the plumbers themselves, in their duty-bound professionalism, did.

In the bathtub, through a sort of poor man's telescope, I can see 2 rooms at the same time, the doorframe perfectly narrowing my field of vision. There's a sort of satisfaction in looking at 1 room while I'm in another, as if at a painted panorama: and what I see is, as a matter of fact, the wide-open hallway window overlooking the courtyard, veiled by its white curtain. The greatest pleasure, when it's beautiful out, is in leaving this window open while I'm bathing; then I can enjoy the fresh air that plays off the warm water and the near-invisible whiteness of the sheet gently billowing in the breeze. The idea of taking a bath thus exposed while still hidden from the outside world delights me, as if I were secretly flouting public decency: this horizontal immobility is conducive to a delicate sort of intoxicating and innocuous contemplation of 1's surrounding environment, wherein the bath's aqueous caresses summon up mental constructs verging on phantasmagoria. Sea baths don't have this same steadiness due to the boundaries of 1's compartment: in them you're swallowed up by living matter, which wears you out with all the physical exertion necessary to keep from being overwhelmed; swimming pools, by contrast, must yield to the collective, to sports, to bathing suits.

In Focus

If I slowly raise my dripping hand to occlude the rectangle of the door 50 centimeters in front of it, I can reach a 3rd visual level. I focus on the stretch of wall perpendicular to the floor, I spread out my fingers, and I imagine, behind the curtain's opaque cloth, a landscape that is not my mediocre courtyard but nature in full bloom. 1 other element visible from the moment in space-time that is the bath (and which might strike a chord with other aficionados of this simple domestic pleasure) is the electricity meter described *supra*.

Placidity Meter

It's unnerving to focus on this meter from an aquatic position; it's a constant reminder of death's dominion over life, as any contact between water currents and electric currents produces effects we know all too well. Rocking in this warm water and looking at this apparatus, I ponder how the thread of my life is bound to a fictive space: barely 1 meter separates me from a potential suicide, but this definitive divide between 2 antagonistic worlds is life itself, in a nutshell. This interval is sufficient. And I'm delighted, if only slightly, to know that I'll remain untouched by any electric currents as I splash around in a watery current, even as my thoughts steep in a horrific scene: a masked woman breaking in with an electric hand mixer that she throws into the water to electrocute me! Ever since I saw it as a teenager, the *Columbo* episode that depicts this murder has stayed traumatically intact in my mind.

Immersion

Bathtime is clearly my time for contemplation, for losing myself in dreams, feelings, and sensations, in flights of fancy, abortive theories, and recollections of overheard remarks, in memories, prospects, furtive sentences, thoughts, or obsessions generated by this calm immersion of my entire body. I've set the world to rights less often over coffee than in bathtubs, all by myself, scrubbing my skin and my soul, meditating on this small, warm horizon. Taking a bath is 1 of those rare passive activities during which synesthesia occurs with almost 0 effort: touch, clear sight, 1's own smell, the taste of the water, and the soft sound of waves lapping or flowing all unite in a Gesamtkunstwerk that has, I think, practically no equivalent. Even my bathroom itself is changed by bathing: the glass wall finds its ultimate raison d'être, the water in all its fluidity heralds a suspended instant, during which the bather may enjoy true freedom.

4 Sides of 1 Bathtub
I attribute 4 qualities to the bathing rectangle—Well-Being, Placidity, Immobility, Nonexistence—which are not the same as those of the bed (→BEDROOM).

Cleanliness Is Next to What?
My left foot, when I'm in the water, rests on the far edge and jostles against 2 plastic containers: 1 is normal Klorane shampoo, with a consistency akin to sperm or, more innocuously, thick coconut milk; the other is an organic chamomile shampoo, Cattier brand, which looks like honey. Nearby, my soap, which I've chosen for its transparency—the better to keep any detrimental colors from sneaking into the bathroom and harming its overall harmony—is called Neutralia. According to its label, it's acid-free. Like anyone else with mildly obsessive-compulsive tendencies, I've joined the cult of cleanliness, and if I had it my way I'd wash myself several times each day, which I do in summer, since I can barely stand the smell of my own sweat—except for when it's from a romantic tryst, since then it carries an added spice, and is resolved, eventually, by a shower. Like Mayakovsky, who reportedly scrubbed himself many times daily because he couldn't bear his own scent, I've progressively moved from a reasonable standard of hygienic care to 1 that's far more extreme, even though the adverse effects of this have already become clear: skin washed too often will lose its sweat-regulating cells, and even though I never used to sweat, now, as a result of all my repeated scrubbing, my frequent showers, and my successive baths, I do. Between French hyperfilthiness and American overcleanliness, I'm trying to find a happy medium.

Interesting Stench
Every room has its own stench; the bathroom's smell doubtlessly comes from some hidden standing water. It's a putrid

roasted-cauliflower smell that's revolting, sporadic, but ultimately interesting because it's untraceable.

Door + Towel

I don't have a towel rack. So I use the door as a rack, by hanging my towel over the top. The inconvenience in this is that
the paint flakes under the humidity; the advantage is that by
putting the towel in contact with the door, it's clear that no
object is autonomous: the towel has to have a place to hang just
as the door has to serve its greater use. So I've overcome the
purported uniqueness of objects, which had been annoyingly
insistent: I've expanded this 1's range of possible uses. And
in the excitement of this revelation, naked in the shower that's
also a bathtub, I'll just grab the huge red towel (which I'll end
up using again and again over the course of my life) with a
swift, rapid, athletic yank.

Washing Machine

Past the bathtub, on the right, the washing machine sits snugly
between the tub and the wall separating it from the toilet. I
know that for safety reasons it's not advisable to have a plugged-
in washing machine too close to a water source, but these safety
standards, a vexed social issue, make safety a mere pretext for
extorting more money: electrocution, despite being a far greater
risk than termites or strangers, isn't averted by these "safety
standards," because Paris's apartments are so small that there'll
never be enough space in between everything to guarantee
safety.

For anyone who's interested, I own a Vedette washing machine that I bought in 2008, having acquired the preceding
1 in 1989, purchases that ought to have offended my stated
aims of quality and multifunctionality, but space constraints
conspired to allow this monomaniacal triumph of poor work-

manship into my home. All things considered, though, the machine's performance has been perfectly acceptable—unless of course we measure its effective life not in terms of how many years I've owned it but in terms of how many hours or days it's actually spent doing its job. The latter metric, unfortunately, is horribly suboptimal. I do only about 1 load of laundry per week, and 1 every 10 days would be 36 wash cycles per year (let's say 40 with the summer). The machine works for 1 hour 40 minutes as many as 40 times a year, which is a risible performance by Kapitalism's standards.

And Then My Umbrella Ella Ella Eh Eh Eh

Between the bathtub and the washing machine is a very narrow gap (2.80 cm wide) filled by 1 off-brown umbrella that I found in a movie theater and that, as is usually the case when it comes to petty theft, I've retained instead of attempting to return to its inattentive, unlucky owner. This umbrella, which I almost never use (I feel like it rains less than it used to), has found its natural resting place here; besides which, it's so ugly I never bother taking it with me when I go outside—I'd practically be inviting thunder and lightning if I did! So I've buried it in this nook, where it often falls over from sheer inactivity. The disdain that Bloch, Proust's minor friend, often demonstrated toward such belongings is certainly justified here; still, I feel as though it would be about as easy to get rid of this thing that happens not to belong to me as to get rid of my entire worldview.

Awkward Little Nook

Behind the washing machine, a small nook serves to hide laundry detergent and the sponges I keep for cleaning the apartment. These awkward little nooks, these low-lying areas, murky and forgettable, found in every apartment, are mostly inhabited by dust bunnies, which don't really belong in a pristine bath-room. A rubber-gloved hand (mine) sometimes ventures into these depths, assisted by a vacuum cleaner's nozzle.

Advertising

My preferred laundry detergent has always been Ariel, the brand that my mother used, and that's far from the only way in which I'm my mother's son. Ariel's excellent advertising campaigns, as some of my cohort may remember, consisted of insisting that 2 packs of traditional laundry detergent didn't hold a candle to a single pack of Ariel—resulting in a housewife refusing what should have been a good deal (2 for the price of 1!) thanks to the irrefutable justification of quality over quantity. But the other reason I've been loyal to this brand for so long is because, a very long time ago indeed, I had a girlfriend who went by the same beautiful Shakespearean name, and I've always clung to that memory, because, in my heart, eroticism endures less through images than through names. Detergent can't work on the toughest of stains, and this subtle propaganda has set permanently; these days, I use a powder that may be less expensive than Ariel, but no less effective: in terms of actual ingredients, I don't see any qualitative difference. Publicists, even for literature, are the least interesting people in the world.

What Dryer?

Among the room's other prominent components, there's a clothesline attached to the wall, its full length (3 m) vastly ex-ceeding the room's span, which is why I bothered to get a wash-ing machine with a built-in drying function (€800), although it doesn't dry terribly well, which means I end up pulling out the retractable clothesline anyway. Like so many city slickers I dread the fishy scent of clothes still damp for lack of space to dry. Sometimes my thoughts linger on a laundry room of a size

I could only wish for; but for laundry there's nothing like the countryside. Hanging it all to dry on 1 line strung between 2 tree trunks will always be a priceless luxury; in French, the kinship between the word for laundry, *linge*, and the word for line, *ligne*, is a perfect reason to insist that 1's *linge* should always dry on a taut *ligne*. Even now, though, manually hanging clothes up to dry offers to this launderer's eye such unforgettable imagery: clustered hillsides and clouded skies of cloth swept by crisp air, textured textiles of every color billowing in an April breeze.

In Praise of Design

The simple gray plastic of this retractable clothesline—and, after all, every object has to be designed completely, from its colors and materials to its mechanisms, before it can be produced in the real world—succeeds because it was so well thought through: I have all the more respect for these sorts of functionally satisfying items, being formally perfect, than I do for objets d'art that are astonishing in their sheer pointlessness. Here, German industry (especially the Leifheit brand, the airy, twinned syllables of its name rolling right off my tongue) unites aesthetics and standards, in contrast to a France that remains cloven between these spheres. The horizontal white base serves to support a sliding plastic bar, which I pull to unwind the string; once the laundry is dry, all I have to do is unhook the clips and loosen the base's lock so that the no-longer-taut clothesline is yanked back into the case. It's child's play to let the line reel back into its cave, and sometimes I have a bit of fun; instead of keeping hold of the apparatus as it winds tight, I let go of the plastic strip and watch it flail around at top speed as though in a panic. But I'm always scared that the mechanism will break or the line will get tangled up, so I generally hold the reins at least until the halfway point. I'm an adult, after all.

Neapolitan Misery

The retractable clothesline is most often in repose, curled up, and therefore invisible. When it's not, the bathroom sags under all my laundry's weight and looks like some overloaded Neapolitan street scene. The room may fulfill its function with brio at such times, but the feeling it most clearly exudes as it disappears beneath that sopping mass is misery, a misery I would never feel if these clothes were strung from windows . . .

Pharmacopoeia

As in all the bathrooms in all the world, there's a little cabinet amounting to a little pharmacy, its name evoking both *remedy & poison*. Positioned on the right wall, above the Vedette washing machine, this red metal box, 45 cm high and 35 cm wide, its depth fairly shallow (15 cm), is perfect for the moderate use I make of it, correlating to my quasi-pathological antipathy toward the very notion of illness. Bought at IKEA, featuring an embedded lock—a fairly useless precaution since I don't have any children or any sticky-fingered maids—this piece of furniture delights me with its unabashed redness, a red that screams "Danger!" As Roland Barthes notes in his *Lecture Course at the Collège de France*, edited by my homonym, "an individual is defined by his *Pharmacopoeia* . . . a little medicine cabinet." Having already made a similar remark about practically all my earthly possessions, and being faithful to the topographical rule that I've imposed upon myself in this inventory, I won't shy away from performing such an exposition of my own interior.

In 1 part of the cabinet I store my various all-purpose products (Band-Aids, nail clippers, Q-tips, rubbing alcohol), single-use packages of soap and shampoo taken from various hotels (a legal form of plunder), protective items (earplugs, condoms, etc.), and so forth. Actual medicines are in a separate area.

There aren't very many, thanks to my general good health—
I can't help but knock on an oaken corner of my desk (→ OF-
FICE) as I write that. The concoctions that take shelter in this
red refuge are 1st and foremost the sorts of simple thing
found in an infirmary, such as aspirin and antiseptics. I don't
have many telltale medicines; what's most telling is, again,
and above all, my wholehearted defiance toward illness, toward
the state of being ill, and most of all toward the overwhelming
attention granted to the bedridden these days, particularly
in the media, like those daily broadcast "wellness features" in
which people won't shut up about their most horrifying health
scares, certain at least that they'll be heard by their resentful
compatriots who, too, have repurposed their misfortunes into
reasons to live. But illness hasn't spared me thanks to any sort
of divine grace—my only gods are the household sort—and I
regularly suffer from gastrointestinal distress, which has necessitated a remedy by the name of Spasfon; I even underwent
an operation 7 years ago to discern the exact reason for this
complaint, following the €300 recommendation of a doctor
named Boboc who, finding nothing more than a *diverticular
lymphoid hyperplasia*, a benign issue that he encouraged me to
treat with some Bédélix, a small brown powder with an agreeable taste that would "solidify it all," drove me in the end to
simply tell people that I had a touch of lactose intolerance.
As my 1st name rhymes, in French, with "stomach" (*Thomas/
estomac*—I'm afraid I do tend to put stock in coincidences like
that), this tummy ache of mine has only served to convince me
that ailments, all too often, are bound to their homophones—
whence my reason for preferring psychiatry over conventional
doctoring. The other ailments that I suffer, without any real
regularity, are headaches: I have a bottle of Doliprane with a
reassuringly yellow label; yellow is a color that wholly suits medicine. What I most appreciate about my pills is the objectivist

poetry of their names, providing relief before I even need it: migraine sufferers swear by Doliprane's kinship to *mal au crane*, a French term for headache. When I've had too much to drink, I wipe out my feelings of bleariness with some betaine citrate, a miracle remedy I swear by and always take on trips or before nights out since it's especially effective when it's taken preventatively. Deeper in my cabinet are some antifungal creams, since I sometimes get athlete's foot, a reward for frequenting my gym, and some Pansoral (formerly Borostyrol) too, since sometimes I get canker sores, albeit not as a reward for frequenting other people's mouths. And then I do come down with conjunctivitis from time to time, so I keep a bottle of eyewash and some saline pods in there for treating discharge: an all-too-justified judgment upon my scopophilic impulses, perhaps, interfering with the vision of a voyeur whose pseudonym could well be Peeping Tom.

Anti-Antidepressants

Despite my perennial hypochondria, my phobia of illness has managed to protect me from the full brunt of this disorder, my body's sheer insistence on being well proving a far more powerful remedy than anybody could anticipate. Thus, if I'm not sick, it's due as much to my mental fortitude as it is to some Nietzschean choice in favor of life; a choice, after all, that 1 can't avoid making: for my part, if I'm obliged to suffer the illness of my neurosis, I've decided that I simply don't have room for any others. My existence proceeds on the plane of magical thinking, as it were: since I have the impression that talking about an illness is the surest way to catch it, I avoid all conversation on the subject, inasmuch as this is possible, since this would otherwise and immediately plunge me into a convulsive state of disease. Still, the only kinds of medicine I'd never take are antidepressants. If absolutely necessary, I'd recommend the poetry of Pessoa or Lacan instead.

Probing the Wound

He's in front of the mirror again. He takes a moistened Q-tip and thrusts it into a red vial. He knows that it'll hurt, then he pulls down his lower lip and swabs the cotton tip along the gumline until he finds, in the furthest region of his jaw, the small open wound that's been irritating him for days. He rubs in the Q-tip insistently, the gingival area swells and burns, the mucous membrane stings, an indescribable odor wafts through the dental valley. He cries, but deep within his pain he feels a tiny pleasure, and his tears wind up a bit ambiguous.

Patermysterias

Behind the door, a chrome rack from my maternal grand-mother is mounted on the wall. In the golden days of my childhood, chrome signified wealth; to my adult eyes, it's just typical of every bathroom, all the more so in the case of this particular object, 1 of the most inconspicuous in my apart-ment, despite its gleaming surface; I don't take half as much pleasure in admiring its 4 wobbly pegs as I do its essential in-visibility whenever I gaze upon these reflective railroad ties bound to chrome-plated tracks: nailed to the back of the door, and cloaked by all the clothes it bears, this wall rack is covered by 1 teal bathrobe as well as 1 pair of pajamas, which I don't wear all that often. As I touch this rack, the only 1 I have—when guests give me their coats and bags, I plop them down on my bed—I can't help but be overcome by memories of a childhood prank called *patère-mystère* that crops up in French versions of the *Junior Woodchucks' Guide*, and never failed to get a laugh out of me: this party trick consisted of sawing off part of a wooden coatrack and swapping it with 1 decoy strip of wood that would cause all the coats to fall right to the ground. These racks being called *patères* in French and this impossible gadget being especially mesmerizing because of the effect it would have had on my paterfamilias, I took to calling my father *patermyster*, convinced that this singular man was hiding some secret from me; I didn't understand back then, even if I did suspect it, the mystery underlying all paternity, a mystery that took on extreme forms in my childhood home: I've never been able to accept the idea of procreation, and I'm delighted that Malthus, a historical figure I admire (in direct proportion to the inexplicable contempt so many narrow-minded people hold for him), shares my 1st name. For me, procreation is the opposite of Venice—*verbum sat*, of course.

Coughrobe

The cotton bathrobe hanging from that rack somehow finds its way into all the rooms of my apartment. Its (omni)presence sometimes befuddles me . . . but its beauty offsets the glumness of being home sick. Whenever I do put it on, it's for a good while: it means I'll be home recovering for several days.

Unshareable

Since no shelves have been installed in this room, which is far too small for widespread disorder, I have no choice but to submit to its spatial constraints, which would never meet the needs of life *en couple*. The bathroom is the most unshareable room. Since I must be satisfied with its bareness, I adopt the spirit of the ascetic, making a virtue of necessity by way of the rhetorical figure known as *hysteron proteron*: not planning on coming down with a fever, I didn't bother to get a thermometer; not intending to be disorganized, I didn't bother to get a cabinet; not intending to develop diabetes, I didn't buy any sugar . . . I don't have x so I didn't need y. This apartment is a totality of subtractions.

Jaunty Doorknob

The door that opens this chapter will close on it after I've explained that it's made of plywood and not actual wood, a cost-cutting measure I had 0 say in because the decision preceded me. I've already seen ridiculous conversions undertaken to turn these hideous doors into trestle tables in cottages or garages. This shoddy excuse for a door is made less so by its doorknob from the Bazar de l'Hôtel de Ville, a translucent handle topped by a gleaming black billiard ball. Thanks to this jaunty detail, I'm able to focus on my little doorknob to the exclusion of the big door it adorns.

Inalienable Object No. 4
Here's the water heater, tall and stout. I had it put in while renovating and installing various other things for the exorbitant sum of ₣6,500 (€991). 1 way or another, extortion inevitably ends up tainting the technical components of my life, but the problem is especially acute whenever I interact with technicians whose expertise is so wholly superior to mine as to prove that amateurs like me can wreak as much havoc as self-satisfied bureaucrats. This white tank with a capacity of 100 liters, standing upright, eats up plenty of the bathroom's space, completely throwing off the room's visual equilibrium. Here is its handle, here is its spout; mounted on the wall with 2 solid (I would hope) rivets, it has to be emptied for maintenance, which I never do, thanks to a combination of ignorance, laziness, and incompetence. When it gets all backed up, hear me shout! It's already stopped functioning once, for 17 wintry days during which I stewed without any hot water, torn between demoralization and fatalism, stoicism and a fiery desire to wipe out the working class (well, the electrical and plumbing sectors). Fortunately, 2 Portuguese emissaries saved me from carrying out this plot, and if I gloss over the €250 fine levied upon those of us incapable of replacing just 1 resistor ourselves, I can take some pride in knowing they didn't reap any extra dividends in the end—dislodging all the built-up sediment in my Fleck-brand heater took 1.5 hours (.5 for the water to drain,

1 for the hard-water deposits to be scraped out and the resistor replaced): they said they'd never in their careers seen a water heater in such a state of internal disrepair, its reservoir corroded by 5 years of neglect. But what could I have done? Just tip it over and pour it out?

Science Fiction
Some plumbers excavating a water heater unearth the perfectly preserved memoirs of the man who invented the water heater.

Invisible Volume
Though I might, like Bernd and Hilla Becher and their singular photographs, admire the form of this industrial object, so perfectly suited to its function, I'm keener to isolate the qualities that, despite its size, are less clearly seen: or, to be more precise, that I've ceased to see. It's a spatial paradox: the object taking up the most space in this room doesn't stand out at all. Its purpose justifies its mass, which means that any attempt to hide it (with a cover, for example) would prove to be a risky operation likely drawing far more attention to the object in question than no camouflage at all would.

The Belle of the Baths
I know that my bathroom isn't beautiful; it's not as comfortable or spacious or reassuring or pleasant or even practical as a woman might wish. I willingly associate the bathroom (and not the kitchen) with the realm of femininity, because of the connotations of luxury, modern beauty, and gentle sophistication inherent in a particular image I hold of that sex. By contrast, my bathroom hews to a Spartan aesthetic: lacking any warmth, it exists in a perpetual winter whose only advantage is allowing me to indulge on occasion in a fantasy of being a

stoic Greek soldier possessed of absolute self-control. Of course, I could always spend a little money to summon the technological goddess known as Space Heater, but—though I do pine for her!—I give her the cold shoulder.

Hot/Cold

I hope I might be permitted to draw 1 inference from this lack of heating, with which I'll be concluding this chapter and this room: what I'd most regret would be to learn that my readers were drawing no heat from this book, that my words neither warm your heart nor chill your blood . . . Still, the autobiography of a home must inevitably touch on the farthest reaches of the thermal prism, cold succeeding heat, burning following freezing, each room revealing those treasures dictated by its identity. My bathroom's lack of any sort of radiator, hardly offset by the bathtub that heats it occasionally, is full evidence of how shabby my life here really is.

Toilet

(1 m²)

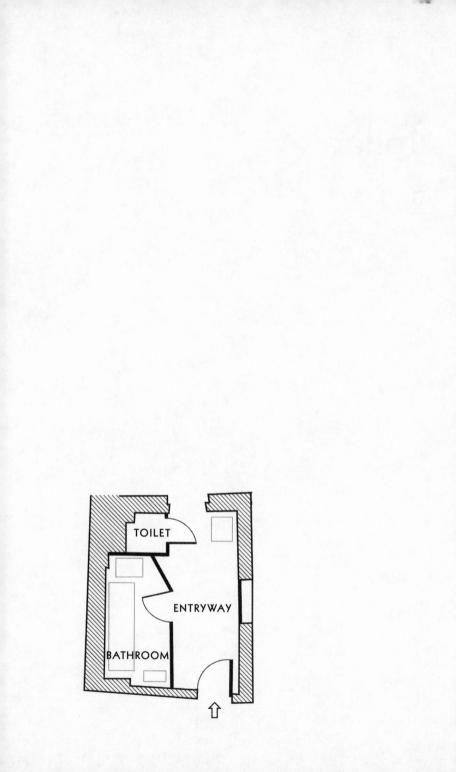

Room or Nonroom

The toilet is logically the smallest room in the house. It's part of the hallway-entryway, past the bathroom but on the cusp of the main room, and constitutes a distinct room, the 3rd in the apartment: like most of the apartment, the room was completely redone when I moved in. Despite being terribly cramped (built for a dwarf who would have measured 36 or 38 on a tailor's tape), it's still completely separate from the bathroom. It's a spatial question, deciding whether to keep the toilet area separate from the bathroom, so as to reinforce the idea of its being an autonomous zone, as it were; or rather to open up the space (however slightly) by removing the wall in question, at the risk of robbing the toilet of its precious independence, vis-à-vis the specific function of the area in question. I've opted for the 1st solution, following the well-known principle— to which I'm attached for reasons beyond the purely architectural—of the division of labor.

It Takes 1 Door . . .

In contrast to the bathroom door, the toilet door is shut more often than not; not completely shut, but rather ajar, in order to hide a room that's only ever entered on 1 specific pretext. Moreover, it's not easy to shut the door, which, like its neighbor, is made of a plywood so flimsy that it doesn't quite click into its latch, undeserving of the name. No discerning eye could miss the cheapness here, though the more aesthetically inclined would note that, besides their poor quality, the other trait shared by these 2 doors is their translucent door handles capped by billiard-ball knobs (this 1 being red). This is how I've conferred a modern, cheerful note to the hallway-entryway where these 2 successive balls of color flourish. But considering that the 1st door is always open and the 2nd always closed, if I want to create this particular effect, I have to "prepare" the room by closing the 1st door, which happens mainly when I receive visitors, which isn't often. Any apartment's mise-en-scène depends on just this sort of tiny detail, but in such profusion that the profession of interior decorator (which I would find wholly intolerable) was thereby called into existence.

Potty Mouth

The white-tile floor is the same 1 that covers the bathroom; everything is white here, aside from the black toilet seat (an intentional decision), and the small kitschy orangey '70s-style ceiling light I bought at the Vanves flea market, which disseminates a soft gleam favorable to a seated posture. This tricolor ensign (white/black/orange) designates a country that doesn't exist: as a child, I used to draw made-up territories (islands, usually) that I relished reigning over, designing flags for them bearing rare or appealing color combinations, hoping to get as far away as possible from the French model. Did I already have "shitty taste" even then?

Inalienable Object No. 5

The toilet is the only room in my apartment wholly and impeccably governed by the *inalienable object* that gives it its name. A social distinction can be marked by the toilet's space or layout, but the fact remains that it's constituted by a unique and central element that makes this the most democratic room of all: extra space or a clever layout would be ridiculous, and so this room grants both the richest and the craftiest homeowners no advantage whatsoever.

Head/Ass Wipe

An alcove in the wall—on my left, once I'm situated properly—allows for 4 shelves that serve to elevate, a bit, this room otherwise marked by the baseness of its purpose. Starting at the bottom, the 1 within closest reach is intended for cleaning products, toilet paper, and bleach. I use a pink, soft toilet tissue that serves as a corrective for the beige, rough paper of my childhood, which I've never encountered anywhere else—not in prison, not in hospitals, not in the USSR.

Reading Room

The 3 other shelves serve to hold magazines, and I have to concede that their presence here in this room constitutes an homage—although a dubious 1—to their literary quality. If I keep them, it's either because I've contributed some texts to them or because I'm interested in the latest news and the toilet is a good place to take that in—besides which, I do have a tendency to hoard. Shelf no. 3 is full of store catalogs, cultural-event programs, and various memorabilia like the April 1965 issue of *Elle* corresponding to the week I was born, found in an empty house in La Creuse and which I couldn't not consider a sign—but a sign of what? Shelf no. 4, the uppermost 1, is bracketed on its left end by an old special issue of *Libération* titled "Why Do You Write?" and includes, among various orphaned issues of general-interest magazines, copies of cultural journals, which I read more or less attentively, such as *Cahiers du cinéma*, *Art press*, or *02*, but also artist catalogs, entertainment listings, and interesting or didactic books about history or science, all of which points to 1 of my fundamental tendencies: polymathy. This passion, of course, runs into spatial limitations, due to its expansionist nature, and I have to struggle not to accumulate even more texts so that this semi-library of ephemerae stays reasonably organized.

A close look at these collections would show that most of their contents are not too recent; some are several years old. I have a particular absurd fascination for old news, not as in the historical past, but as in slightly outdated, even completely disconnected from the present moment, already gone stale. I've developed a rhythm of sitting down with a magazine from 2 or 3 years ago, neither ancient history nor wholly up-to-date, as befits these sorts of publications. Both my inclination to gloss over the here and now, and my moral disinclination to abide the friction of incessant information, are perfectly suited to the toilet.

No Context

Considering their heterogeneity, I've utterly failed in all my attempts to organize these magazines. Their wildly different origins and foci, and the fact that many of them are represented by only a single issue, resulted in a visual pandemonium that culminated in their being summarily stacked, vertically and horizontally, with neither rhyme nor reason: since I have no more space to keep them all together, I've been forced to clump some of them by height and cap those with heaps of other books laid flat in order to stuff the shelves completely. It doesn't look at all nice, but what else can I do?

Bathroom Learning

It would be difficult not to draw some sort of connection between my desire to digest every form of knowledge and that other, less noble form of digestion to which this room is dedicated. Certainly there's something anal about encyclopedism, is there not, and perhaps that's the reason I've stocked my toilet with these indigestible scraps better known as periodicals. There are 0 real books in here, unless they've come in on short-term visas, like the *Guide to Rugs* or the *Gospels in Slang*.

The Smallest Room

In the left corner, 1 broom and 1 cleaning cloth coiling around it both stand sentry, doubling the toilet's sense of closetness. A good home would store these miscellaneous items in an actual closet. By leaving these in plain sight, I'm simply reinforcing the room's thanklessness.

Underbrush

More discreetly, at the toilet's base, 1 small scrub brush stuck vertically in its small pail serves as a tiny echo of my push broom. Toilet brushes are the sorts of instrument that, in an ideal world, where neither urine nor excrement would remind us of our native condition by forcing a rhythm to our days, we would wish wholly absent, and yet they still insist on making their presence known. There's 0 question that this toilet brush is the most disliked object in my entire apartment. There's nothing I can do about that, but it's nonetheless possible to raise its profile a bit, whether by repurposing it—a huge army of brand-new scrub brushes set in 1 of those white cubes that we call an art gallery—or by prettifying it. Having a lower-end model that I'm perfectly happy with, I refuse to invest in 1 of those fancier versions (you can even get them in Monobloc designs, with chrome bases that hide their bristles) that call to mind the sort of people who say "Shoot!" instead of "Shit!" when they curse—which only, by the way, draws more attention to their vulgarity. I prefer to embrace the total crumminess of this object; too much of an untouchable to be slyly prettified, too touching to be wholly worthless. Like an uninspiring C-list actor worthier of pity than of contempt, the toilet brush plays its role . . . diligently.

Down in the Hole
Every afternoon I throw my coffee grounds into the toilet: 1 of those rare moments when a specialty food (Sul de Minas from Brazil, €3.80 for 250 grams) comes into contact with the toxic. The basin turns black with the coffee's dregs, and I could probably see the future in there, if I only knew the 1st thing about tasseography.

Eco-Friendly Economics
As I position the toilet-bowl cleaner block beneath the seat, beneath the bowl's rim, in the exact spot where it'll get the most water from the tank as it flows in irregular cascades, I consider that I am governing my kingdom as best I can. What a cruel irony it is, though, that this "eco-friendly" toilet should release a volume of water so paltry that I end up having to flush it 2 or 3 times!

Trompe l'Oeil
The utilitarianism of the items *supra* are countered by several attempts at an artistic completion of this scene setting, a locale I feel I've brought into perfect harmony by affixing, on the door's inner face, 1 trompe l'oeil, a sheet of reflective aluminum measuring 24 cm × 25 cm in which I can't even make out my own reflection. I'm fond of setting, alongside the rare official artworks I own, such occasional personal creations or decorations of uncertain status. For a while I kept a double photocopy of 1 photograph of Pier Paolo Pasolini's bespectacled face on the door instead. I don't know why I felt the need to attach this reproduction of a reproduction in duplicate. The

question every clearheaded decorator inevitably asks: Am I making art or shit?

Vietato Fumare

When I leave the toilet door shut, those walking by always comment on 1 adhesive pictogram depicting 1 cigarette barred by 1 red line, which I adore for its simplicity. Its message doesn't matter to me, because I don't really care whether people smoke in my place, and/or whether they do it in my toilet. Smokers transform my apartment into a semipublic place, enacting a conversion between inside and outside: as on the street, I tolerate it. Isn't the smoker my guest? In fact, my vinyl "no smoking" sticker makes the prohibited cigarette possible: all it takes is to mention a thing's nonexistence to conjure up its ashes.

In Flagrante Decoratione

I believe I've made clear that my toilet has been the object of a certain aesthetic attention, but, aside from cases of willful decorative insanity, such as in des Esseintes's or D'Annunzio's home, I detest overdone apartments, and instead am haunted by the idea of an economy of means that might help me better recognize art for what it is. I can't stand residences decked out in 1 single overbearing style, where everything's been selected according to social and aesthetic imperatives, where everything is supposed to represent "good taste" even though that always just means "bad taste" in the 2nd degree (i.e., involuntary), or, worse yet, outright snobbery. Tastes change even faster than fashions, so I prefer the hazy concept of "creating an ambiance," which befits a space that's already had its use described by Théophile Gautier in his famous phrase: "The most useful place in a house is the water-closet." Evidently, it's because of this room's most emphatic and unequivocal mission that I've felt the need to enhance its more welcoming qualities (in moderation).

Purely functional toilets are a bit harsh for a private apartment; they're meant for public spaces with a high standard of cleanliness, as we might find in the United States or in some Nordic countries (but not in France, where institutions allow toilets to remain filthy because it's unacceptable to so much as mention "filthy things"). Their crudeness is actually determined by their owners' attention to cleanliness. And yet, trying to polish a turd, in the good old Freudian tradition, doesn't require sanitary facilities to be adorned with glitter and sequins—I've even seen traditional toilets replaced with faux carved-wood "thrones," better known as the "Throne of Dagobert," with various built-in accessories (ashtray, music box)—quite the opposite: too much ornamental compensation for the fecal risks drawing 1 extreme toward the other. In essence, luxury flirting with the very shit it intends to mask. No, the toilet itself must remain underdecorated. Better to hew to the simplicity of contrast.

Shit Happens

True to my minimalism, I have no wooden or plastic toilet paper dispenser attached to the wall—implements in the design of which those trends I've already mentioned (ceramic flowers, painted pine, deodorant, printed designs, etc.) are by no means uncommon. On the contrary, reducing the container to its contents, meaning just the toilet paper, seems far wiser, if not far healthier: getting rid of frivolities means paying full homage to the paper itself: the barbaric sight of a bare roll set on the tank says: *Here is the truth and nothing but the truth*—which fits to a T my own definition of that method of excretion we call Literature.

Twin Towers

I grab 2 new toilet paper rolls; I hold them up and peer through them like binoculars. Then I set the 2 on the tank, 1 on top of the other, and I add 2 on the other side, then 3, then 4 more rolls, and the 2 towers rise in shitty sculpture, teetering ever closer to their undoing, just like 40 years ago, in those ads where my childhood doppelgängers brazenly unrolled toilet paper over an entire house.

Piss

There are 3 activities that give these sanitary facilities their purpose. 1st, being polydipsic, I urinate very regularly and with the relief inherent in all that is part and parcel of emptying myself organically, physically, and otherwise: I enjoy emptying my pockets of all the objects weighing them down, enjoy undressing quickly before making love, enjoy extracting various contents from all sorts of containers. When it comes to urination, there are 2 distinct schools of thought: the 1 that recommends doing so as noisily as possible, aiming directly into the basin, and then the contrary theory, expounding muted micturition: aiming for the porcelain sides of the bowl rather than the water it contains. Attached as I am to the corporeal inclination to exultantly liberate 1's self from 1's humors, I adhere to the 1st, thoroughly Rabelaisian, course of action. Nevertheless, I still feel some shame, and so, occasionally, for 1 reason or another—in polite society, for example—I curb my pleasure. Making noise while pissing—raining down with 1's capacious watering can upon the water waiting below— releases a vertical tone that practically can't be muffled. Public urinals in particular displease me, especially in France where they're filthy, small, and designed for a promiscuity that's not at all my style. Defecation and micturition should be carried out in absolute solitude—the 1st especially—and certainly of all the communal activities that would have to be undertaken in the phalanstery I sometimes imagine living in, it's that 1 I feel the most resistance to doing in public. 1 of the most repugnant spectacles I've ever had the displeasure of witnessing (or rather, not witnessing, as I was so disgusted that I had to run away from the very prospect of having anything to do with it) took place in the public washrooms of a neighborhood in Canton. When I realized, upon seeing the long row of men's heads sticking out over a low mud wall, that I would have to squat next to them in order to relieve myself, I practically heaved up all my organs.

Shit

Far too little has been written about the 2nd vocation, defecation: this rupture with our ordinarily upright posture, this isolation and concentration on the substances of which we are consubstantially made, deserves an appropriate setting. Ideally, 1 with a small window looking out onto nature, which homes in the countryside do offer. There's something both touching and soothing about the idea of ridding myself of shit: a sweet death that leads to rebirth, a discreet desertion, a necessary evil that isn't all that evil. In the toilet, where I usually pair physical actions with more cerebral 1s, I like to take my time. This makes me the perfect incarnation of man's dual nature (corporeal and mental): reading here reconciles the highbrow and lowbrow functions of this space without any conflict. Though, sometimes, out of pure love for the thing, I don't read anything at all, seeking no more than to enjoy the slow, intimate descent, in an illusion of torpor, of what Rimbaud immortalized in verse as "the heavenly praline."

Cum

The 3rd vocation, masturbation, may be in thorough disrepute—yet shouldn't it be considered a kissing cousin of writing, given that both practices see the practitioner ejaculating alone while thinking of others?—but it's certainly enjoyed on the toilet, despite the fact that 1 could hardly think of 2 less complementary forms of matter than cum and shit: the 1, a component of life itself, arises from love, just as its scent arises from the chestnut tree, thanks to the miraculous accident that has graced its foliage with that same damp, fresh smell; shit, on the contrary, even in its name, reeks of foul compactness: it's born in falling, whereas spunk comes in beautiful geyser-like spurts. (Granted that there's some perverse joy to be found in its low character: shit is a burlesque of cum.) Onanism, despite being efficient and solitary, is participatory, the imagination running across a panoply of beloved faces during the process— bodies both clearly remembered and merely imagined. Still, its libidinal economy results in an additional small but unique pleasure: that of an erotic self-control verging on total mastery, whereas copulation always carries the risk of fiasco or deception. Masturbation is, by definition, minimalist: reduced and certainly reductive, but also reductionist in the way it avoids dragging in any other participants; humble, by no means a spectacle of note within the theater of the body, but full of a concealed intensity. Besides, those who consider aesthetic minimalism a simple "nothing" labor under a misapprehension, because *nothing* isn't far from being *everything*: minor occurrences often producing effects far more devastating than purportedly and stridently "great" events; the art called "minor" often proving far more discreetly singular than the most celebrated works; subtle gestures generally superseding grand proclamations by virtue of their simplicity. And, by the way, the term "intellectual masturbation" is a pleonasm that doesn't bother me in the least.

Too Fraught to Handle

I'm phobic when I'm in other washrooms, especially public 1s; I can't bear to touch a door handle that 1,000s of other hands have already touched. I've gotten in the habit of opening my door at home from the inside by using my elbow. It's tricky, but it's doable (it requires some leather elbow patches → BED-ROOM).

Up/Down/Fragile

Shutting the toilet door behind me, I'd like to reiterate that in my conception of life and literature nothing is above or beneath anything else, just as there's no room in my apartment more essential than any other: the most contradictory intentions can result from the toilet's being on the very threshold of the main room. Just as the Buñuel of *The Phantom of Liberty* swaps the proper places to eat and to shit, so I will now make my way to the kitchen, which is also the main room.

The Bell's Ringing!

But now the doorbell's ringing again. Still happy that I'm not about to see a man about a horse, I rush out of the toilet and open my front door, where of course there's 0 sign of any human presence. Since I'm already there, I wipe my feet on the door-mat (60 cm × 39 cm) before heading into the heart of my home.

Kitchen

(5.95 m^2)

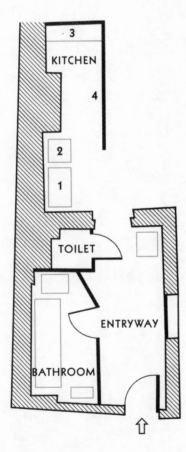

3

KITCHEN

4

2

1

TOILET

ENTRYWAY

BATHROOM

1. Sink
2. Stove
3. Countertop
4. Half Wall

Perched on the Threshold

The only way to enter the main room is through 1 small doorway of proportions so narrow (80 cm wide) and low (1.85 m) that the obese and the gigantic are essentially barred from entry: those above a certain height have to bend their heads down to slip through this air lock of sorts. Ideally, most rooms found in private dwellings would have 1 such vestibule that impedes access. The air of mystery conjured up by such thresholds, which don't open into the room itself so much as they arouse a desire to enter, would make our cramped homes far more attractive. Once I have the space to do so, I take a deep breath—and it really does matter to me that this space not be crude, accessible at a glance, like modern and industrial lofts; rather, it should be curved, meandering, circular, winding, oblique, sophisticated, sinuous. The ideal apartment (I can't say "dream apartment" because I rarely dream) would be just such a false labyrinth.

This streamlined portico, framed by artificial lintels to hide wiring, lacks a door. It's essential to suggest some demarcation between the apartment's 1st section, with its thoroughly utilitarian rooms (entryway + bathroom + toilet), and its 2nd, more "personal," even more social section (kitchen + living room + office), so I've resorted to my loyal curtain. Thus, 1 simple piece of beige linen marks this point of passage, like the indent beginning a new paragraph, a line break lineating a poem, the outline shaping a floor plan. In winter, I bolster the curtain with a 2nd piece of fabric tacked directly to both sides of the threshold, as a way of keeping out the drafts that would otherwise set the cloth fluttering as they blow through. This barrier also splits my home nicely in 2 in terms of temperature: zone 1, bereft of all heating, plummets to arctic atmospheres, while sector 2, accorded several electric radiators, enjoys regulation temperatures. The rest of the year, just 1 of these "precious" cloths (€2.25 each) remains so as to function as a divider; and when, inevitably, I lose interest in them entirely, I take down both curtains, these movable screens that appeal more to my theatrical sensibilities than to any compartmentalizing tendency. The curtains function as a cheap yet convincing way to imply an illusory grandeur; their true value is in providing a backdrop even as they reinforce each room's autonomy: I can't help but compare their usage to that habit some aristocrats of centuries past had of concealing their paintings and their scandals—most notoriously *The Origin of the World*—behind curtains.

I admit I dislike this linen cloth's coarse, cut-rate look—its rough texture, its beige color akin to canvas stretcher bars or couch frames. Shoddily hung to make its removal easier, it's folded over on top and on each side; down at floor level it lets through some centimeters' worth of air, giving the whole setup the feel of a campground. Actually, giving my apartment a "vacation home" feel is 1 of my secret goals . . . I'd insist on my imaginary country home being a grand work of art, but the work of building it from the ground up will always have to remain a fantasy, a pipe dream, even as I must come to terms with the fact that all the work of renovating my actual apartment has only made it, in my mind, a 2ndary, anterior work of art.

If I don't have the means to alter the underlying structure, then I'll just indulge my daydreams by dressing it up a bit.

The Stone Lion

Push aside the cloth, step across the threshold, and on your left, at shoulder height, there's no missing the stone lion's head nailed to the jamb. Formerly part of an ancient fountain, wherein jets of water spurted through its leonine maw, this regal lion presides over the entrance to the inner circle of my apartment, it roars its welcome to visitors just as mezuzot on the doorposts of Jews' houses and on their gates decree the divine blessing over their homes. Meeting the stony stare of this ocher-brown lion, whose eyes seem to bore through time, yet whose cruelty has 0 effect, strips me of all character. It scowls at me, no matter what I do; I leave it to its wall. I know it's there. Watching. Nailed to 1 white pillar, it feels fairly remote to me, like the statues in a park or on some estate. A cousin to the archetypal Metro-Goldwyn-Mayer lion, it delimits my living room with a frozen roar: *ars gratia artis.* He who dares cross the doorway under such favorable auspices reaches the 2nd part of the apartment, the largest in surface area, some ⅔ of the total square meterage.

The Mainness of the Room

The main room stretches from the open-plan kitchen (in French we call them *américaine*) on the left to the living room on the right. Its size is arresting. The doubling here swiftly offsets the narrowness of the apartment's 1st part in 1 way that reminds me of . . . a sonnet! The sonnet is a poem that, in moving from quatrains to tercets, decreases its number of lines (from 8 to 6) as it increases its number of rhymes: its palette of sounds expands (3 instead of 2). My apartment is configured in such a way that 1 moves directly from the narrow realm of the hallway-entryway canyon to the expansive living-room-kitchen-office-bedroom prairie.

I've often noticed an appreciable satisfaction on the faces of visitors entering this space, as must have been the case for myself as well on the lucky day I saw it for the 1st time. Whereas crossing the hallway-entryway provokes little reaction, considering the site's narrowness (accentuated by the fact that everyone has to walk behind each other, sometimes even in single file)—my visitors have completely different looks on their faces when they enter the living room, expressions revealing their realization of my apartment's true potential. This reversal of fortune, this raising of spirits along with the apartment's square meterage informs visitors that they've reached a world far more welcoming than anticipated.

The Multivalence of the Space

This sudden abundance of space that comes into sight, much like the sky opening up, or a plain, or some other perspective long obstructed by whatever obstacle, is the result of many conditions, chief among them the fact that 1 single glance now encompasses 4 areas at once (the kitchen and the living room, and opening onto the bedroom and the office): 1's field of vision is widened by the configuration of these rooms, by the depths they suggest, as well as the relatively immense lines and surfaces now on display—the walls, for example, and the wooden floor, and the broad and perfectly smooth white ceiling. Here, at last, it's possible to walk, to take 100 steps, to venture across a territory that may not be objectively large but which "becomes" large perceptually—here I can cross the room diagonally, cut a path toward my office, stretch out on the floor, or reenact the best moments of the 1982 France–West Germany soccer semifinal using some crumpled-up paper as a ball.

CH (2.45 m)
Ceiling height is a measure of our psychological strength; it determines our hopes.

By Design
Since this book's design follows my apartment's, I'll start with the left side of the room, which is taken up by the open-plan kitchen.

Where the Problem Lies
Open-plan kitchens are found in so many Parisian apartments not because people want them, as such, but because space here comes at such a premium: our paltry square meterage doesn't allow for a stand-alone room devoted to cooking—notwithstanding those especially bourgeois apartments I have now abjured—so plopping down all the components of 1 kitchen in 1's living room takes care of both spaces in 1 fell swoop. And yes, perhaps the space usually reserved for the kitchen gets opened up in certain lofts for camaraderie's sake, rather than by necessity—the ancient Greek *megaron* must have had its charms; similarly, I can't deny the potential attraction of open-plan kitchens—but this was by no means the intention I had in mind when I agreed to put all my appliances in my living room. Speaking for myself, I'd rather not have an open-plan kitchen at all. Originally intended for working-class housing, such arrangements have now taken on positive and state-of-the-art and even posh connotations, spurring their implementation in apartments where the concept really only serves to mask the reality of being ridiculously cramped. Thus, what began as a purely practical measure is now presented to us, through linguistic legerdemain, as an incontrovertible advantage. Distorted by this trickery, what ought to be simple, utilitarian kitchens see their most obvious quality, their paucity

of space, become their least acknowledged 1: true luxury, then, must be space itself—space pure and simple.

In a Station of the Métro

The apparition of these ads in the crowd at the massive Auber métro station, in which we see a minuscule studio apartment transformed into a palatial residence with the wave of a wand, the Murphy bed unfolding into a mezzanine, the living room apportioned into a loggia . . . But modularity is a lie, particularly there. How patronizing to advertise furniture for small spaces in such an enormous 1!

Hallway on the Chopping Block

Likewise, real estate agents showing off these teensy-weensy mouseholes like to trot out hackneyed reassurances to the tune of "No hallway, no wasted space!" despite the fact that a nice hallway offers enough perspective to create lovely foreshortenings and illusions of vastness . . .

Modernist Prayer

My Le Corbusier, give us square meters,
Lead us not into the rabbit-hole of temptation
And deliver us from plywood.

Defeat, American Style

Having forgone a self-contained kitchen—which would have had the advantage of sparing my apartment and my guests all the odors as well as the other more or less respectable components of culinary preparation—I find myself forced to admit that open-plan kitchens do indeed offer certain practical advantages. The irony being that, while we call such setups "American," in French, I've suffered a painfully un-American defeat in acquiescing to this state of affairs: that is, America has invaded my space both culturally and actually, all the while insisting that it's perfectly natural for consumption to occur on the site of production; indeed, just as natural as taking a bath in a bathroom and going to bed in a bedroom: a narrow logic that draws 0 distinction between *eating* and *dining*. Still, considering that I'm not so much a domestic theoretician as a man with a (very flimsy) sense of practicality, I cannot help but admit, too, that pragmatism should always win out over principles that, even if I had the means to realize them, would ultimately prove indefensible. In short, I'm stuck with my "American kitchen" not because I've been forced to surrender to any concrete reality but because I think it's actually quite a successful innovation, in its own way. 1 of the things I was most excited about when I acquired this apartment was just this opportunity to take full advantage of the conditions it would impose upon my natural inclinations: this, anyway, was how a philosopher who lived in a horrible '70s-era residence in Montparnasse defined a free man.

Problems and Solutions: The Wall

1 way of demonstrating my reverence for keeping functions discrete may be seen immediately in the *separating half wall* that so clearly delimits this space. The wall, distinctly horizontal and 60 cm tall, starts just 2 paces beyond the entryway and runs 3 meters long, till it abuts the perpendicular wall of the bedroom. In this way the kitchen and the living room are, despite being in the same room, distinctly separate, the "corner-kitchen" (if we want to use such idiotic terminology) being restricted to 1 large rectangle on the left. The idea of this half wall, inspired by a junk-mail interior-decorating catalog, satisfied my taste for clear boundaries and limits, an awfully uncommon predilection these days, since the prevailing tendency, conversely, is to commingle everything in accordance with that peculiar cocktail-party hypocrisy that crowds together all manner of dissimilar things. By contrast, a surrealist

apartment where the bathroom is the entryway, where the
toilet takes up most of the floor space, and where the bedroom also functions as the living room—that certainly seems
like a far more radical challenge than yet another "convivial"
kitchen fostering a false sense of community.

To Conceal or to Reveal

Even by myself, being subjected to a perpetual view of my dish
rack or dry goods doesn't rank high on my list of desiderata.
Those "sleepers"—the professional term for those kitchen
items that usually stay on their shelves, such as ingredients, or,
as needed, sponges, dishes, or the toaster—already outnum-
ber those items on permanent display. Far more important is
this white plasterboard half wall crowned by a small wood cap
(also white), which proves its value in the way it conceals, horizontally speaking, most of my kitchen's mundane secrets.
This half wall's secret-compartment effect is especially manifest viewed from the living room side, when people are sitting
on the couch, for example, and so can only see, from that angle,
the kitchen's prettiest or, anyway, least offensive elements—for
example the white wall, the dark backsplash tiles, the glass
objects. All questions about the organization of an open kitchen
can therefore be simplified to a single question: to conceal or
to reveal? Is it better to deck out 1's kitchen in grand style,
even if that means overpowering 1's living room space, or to
try to hide every trace of its true purpose? I've opted to lean
toward the latter solution, which in my case means depending on 2 primary tactics: 1st, to flagrantly refuse kitchen
furnishings up above the half-wall line, such as hanging
cabinets, which would advertise the space's purpose far too
violently; and 2nd, to keep all those high and so visible surfaces scrupulously tidy. This last point clearly depends on an
exacting lifestyle.

Spatial Progression

Immediately to the left of the doorsill 1 small wall extends
107 cm, perpendicular to the long main wall forming 1 of the
room's sides. That's the corner of the sink and its dish rack.
Along this wall runs 1 copper gas pipe (painted white) in an
eccentric, geometric, yet free-form path of vertical drops and
hairpin turns. Visible pipework has long been an eyesore for
neoconservative aesthetes and other idolaters of art for art's
sake, according to whom all indication of materiality, all exposition of underlying structures, ought to be banned. There's
never been any shortage of vituperative jeremiads against the
Eiffel Tower and the Centre Pompidou, which make a splendid exhibition of their organs and iron piping, offending the
classical credo that "true art is in the concealment of art." My
eccentric pipe is, in its own way, a culmination of those very
qualities of both Eiffel's edifice and that of Piano and Rogers.
Protruding out of the wall from the air vent up above, it disappears into the depths behind the sink.

Out of the Odornary

This shadowy mouth, which dissipates odors, is outfitted with
1 electrical fan that can be turned on by flipping a particular
switch. I practically never take advantage of this suctioning
function, considering that my kitchen is unenclosed and easily
ventilated by the 2 nearby living room windows, which do a
far better job of evacuating smells than this "ordinary" appliance ever could. To chase aromas away, all I have to do is open
a window; banishing such absurd "ordinary" conveniences is
far more difficult. Whenever I get close enough to the fan's
square rocker switch, I can see that its dirty white plastic cover
bears several partial inscriptions, like the 1s on Cy Twombly's
canvases: ARRËT [sic], VITESS [sic], and VMC, an acronym
standing for who knows what.

Fascinating!

Below this switch is another 1, controlling the light on the wall just above the sink. This wall plate is upside down, a detail that would be invisible to the naked eye but for a small, flipped Legrand logo. I would deduce that the electrician who redid my wiring had bad eyesight.

Mastering the Art of French Tiling

Coming back down to eye level, 1 of the most beautiful decorative achievements in my apartment emerges: the bottle-green tiling that surrounds the sink. These tiles, made elegant by their slightly indented texture and bearing all the tiny defects inherent in artisanal craftsmanship that mass production unfeelingly stamps out, were installed incrementally as I made successive visits to the tile factories over by the boulevard Richard-Lenoir, itself named after that grand 1st-Empire manufacturer. This deep, dark, practically black green, called bottle green, is quite unlike any of the colors usually found in kitchens. Selecting tiles is 1 of the many exhilarating decisions to make when putting together a room. The hatred I harbor for all those sandstone or pastel-colored (melba pink) tiles with disgusting floral patterns 1 finds arrayed in kitchens is perfectly offset by this dark green with its dull reflections and manifold irregular gleams. All it takes is a scratch to show that the veins of faux marble pattern are merely painted on, but nothing of the sort occurs here: my tiles in "Edgar Allan Poe" green (as I've christened it) have all the mystery and depth of an anti-kitchen. The tilers I hired scoffed at my choice of color, but that simply proves how right I was. Underscored and overscored and sidescored by 1 white grout, these 125 squares measuring 10 cm × 10 cm each adorn the wall in such a perfect and artistic way that I never tire of looking at them, of devoting all the care I can to keeping them as lovingly clean as they deserve to be: wiping a damp sponge soaked in cleaning products over their appreciative faces puts me in a state approaching ecstasy.

Neutralize Your Kitchen

Neutralizing my kitchen's effect on my apartment was my goal in conceptualizing this room on account of which I feel equal parts disdain and impotence. Disdain because I'd say eating is pretty low in my personal ranking of essential daily activities; impotence because I barely know how to cook, and, well, this explains that. Since the room already has to fulfill 2 functions, there's no chance I'd ever give precedence to the more parasitical function. Which is exactly why everything, or just about, is hidden away by my fantastic half wall.

Imperial Kitchen

I actually wonder if the phrase *cuisine américaine*, which already hints at some kind of vast, untamed territory, doesn't conceal, behind its apparent conviviality, the implicit aim of invading our living rooms, the better to colonize them. If so, these American kitchens chew up and spit out all Gallic attempts at hospitality— just as the Wild West pioneers hunted down "redskins" to impose their own spatial, culinary, and domestic dominion.

Thomas Cooking

And this is how 1's apartment proves to be discreetly political, its layout dictated by social processes practically carved into its very moldings. I've known bachelors so wholly enthralled by life outside their apartments' walls that they don't even have a way to heat up a little snack at home, and then the converse situation, bourgeoisie who've sanctified their salons to the point that no exterminating angels are needed to keep them at home, or else social climbers so drunk on sheer space they don't bother to install a single bookshelf. Nothing is more enlightening than those TV shows about people's houses, where everybody

can see how the "déco" only reveals the cosmic emptiness beneath all interior adornment. This kitchen I've cooked up, a
massive failure as far as sophisticated layouts go, dashes all domestic hopes; it's as much a blight on human dignity as those
package tours on which Thomas Cook built his name.

Site Comments

"So, you prefer bourgeois closed-off kitchens to American
open-plan kitchens?"

"Pass me the navarin of lamb, please."

4 Subspaces

If we follow the side wall that forms the apartment's (and even
the building's) outer boundary, we can delineate 4 successive
subspaces: the sink unit, the stove, the shelves along the chimney shaft, and the perpendicular countertop at the back, all of
which I pass, again and again, pacing, like a starving man or a
waiter.

Basal Knowledge

The sink area, 60 cm deep by 1.10 m wide, is made out of a
white waterproof plastic material that puts up with all sorts
of culinary abuse. In this block sits the sink itself, carved out
of white enamel, 1 strip of plastic countertop on its left and 1
larger swath on its right, which accommodates my metallic dish
rack. A sink's depth, derived from the measurements of the body
washing the dishes or preparing food, is calculated thanks to a
rationalist program that determines the dimensions of furniture based on the activities for which they were intended: in
this case, 86 cm deep. But just as literature always escapes the
paper on which it's written, life escapes mere geometry. These
measurements navigate the discrepancy between upright and
downbent postures by putting the sink at lower-abdomen
level—which only means that our nurturing sinks wind up, for

men and women alike, at the level of our genitals, which are protected here by the curve of the rim, the raised lip of the plastic superstructure. No doubt it's an act of sublimation when kitchen counters and human crotches rub against 1 another— but what of dishwashing? Can dishwashing be sensual? Sleazy old macho caricatures depict working women as instruments of pleasure, aprons covering their fronts but leaving their derrières bare . . . (As for me, I always leave my cotton apron draped on the half wall, ready to use.) Washing dishes certainly doesn't strike me as particularly erotic, but, then again, isn't eroticism precisely the abrupt explosion of tedium into passion?

Little Doubles

Having been deprived of 1 of those double sinks made available by our society of abundance, I find myself imagining, again, that material comfort must take the form of a general duplication of space (double bedroom, 2nd office, 2nd bathroom, etc.). The only doubles to be found in my apartment, however, are of things that, themselves, take up no space at all (pens, USB drives, nail scissors, etc.).

Realist Dish Rack

To the right of the sink, all open space has been fully occupied by my dish rack. As far as is possible, I try to keep my dish rack free of dishes, just as I try to avoid leaving any of them to steep in my sink, as it looks far more beautiful when bereft of all encumbrance, its tines blanched like my teeth and gleaming like the small amount of moisture in my mouth. If the dish rack were allowed to become overloaded—and it does often threaten to reach that stage, since, even though I live alone, I use an inexplicably large number of dishes each day, pulling out plate after plate, going through all my cutlery again and again, using the equivalent of a restaurant's entire tableware stock over the course of 4 daily meals—the heap of dishes there would form a mound of at least 30 cm in height and thereby obscure my beautiful bottle-green wall. (Thus do we find ourselves hurtling relentlessly into 1 of those hyperrealist interiors Huysmans so relished in his 1st period.)

Swamplands

But let's deal with the dish rack properly. It lies on a plastic plateau inlaid with psychedelic blue patterns, its edges raised above the shallow depth of its interior, usually filled with the water dripping from my piled-up dishes. This parallelepiped's chrome frame and rounded feet look passable enough when the apparatus is empty and thus visible, but the effect is wholly lost when it's full of dishes. And, actually, the swampy bottom of the plastic plateau beneath it is 1 of the most fascinating areas of my territory. The liquid filth that reigns there is a notorious exception to my predilection for cleanliness: this moldering water, no matter how many times I pour it out into the sink, reappears incessantly, a brownish sediment that corrodes both the chrome on the rack and the plastic beneath. It's hard for me to properly explain this swamp that apparently congeals out of clean water dripping off of clean dishes, but clearly all it takes is a little time for stagnation, for depurification to set in, and then, in this stagnation, the slow rusting of the dish rack's metal, dyeing it a repugnant rubiginous color. Even when the plateau is dry, for example after I've come back from a vacation, I'll find it covered with a sort of earthy layer, like some Mexican mesa or timeworn sierra, while the dish rack's feet have been partly eaten away. Furthermore, the entire ensemble wobbles on my plastic countertop, which originally wasn't the case, but as humidity has deformed the plastic to the point of indentation, it's now lopsided.

So, sometimes, when the plateau is full of standing dishwater, I stir it gently at its edges to watch the stale swamp sludge around. To me this mini-marsh evokes, of all things, the Vietnam War, a troop of marines making laborious progress through a horrific morass that any right-thinking civil servant would have insisted be cleared away immediately; but not I: the potential for a clean dish coming into contact with this fetid mass seems just dangerous enough to intrigue and excite me, like a beautiful shirt's sleeve dragging through some sauce without its wearer realizing it; and it's so hard to make out, when the rack is full, this zone threatening to contaminate all that touches it unwittingly. Plates and silverware set in the dish rack never really touch this brackish water, but they do graze it, like prisoners in a cage hanging just above the river where they'll be drowned.

I know I should act: even so, I remain stupefied, stuck in this domestic quagmire. I've let the whole situation deteriorate. In this once-clear water, resignation steeps and stagnates. A just-barely-acceptable filthiness holds sway. Just as my bathroom is a failed Mondrian, so my dish rack is a rotting Le Corbusier.

Lateral Spaces

There's so little counter space to the left of the sink that it's impossible to prepare a dish there or even set down food for a moment; everything has to go 3 meters to the right, past the sink, on the perpendicular countertop at the far end of the kitchen. This sheer lack of logic, which forces me to circum-navigate my kitchen just to set down a plate, is physically man-ifest in this mess to the right of the sink, which, rather than being rectilinear, is askew, shoddily cut by amateur artisans. But I can't hold this against them: I could hardly have done better in their place (total disdain for handiwork is 1 of those little things that set me apart from all other Frenchmen), and I'm a terrible cook to boot (likewise). And yet, the tiny strip on the left of the sink—counterpart to the dish rack—welcomes, despite its narrowness, my 2 electric-kettle components, its plug-in base and its reservoir, which make up a whole but are easily separable.

I Boil

The kettle, being white, contributes to the room's chromatic unity; it presents simplicity of form (it resembles a bird's beak); it's undeniably cost-effective. In short, it's 1 of the kitchen utensils I use most often, several times each day, every morning for coffee, most afternoons for tea, and many evenings for infusions. All I have to do is to insert the male plug connected to the base to the female outlet along the wall: in 11 seconds—yes!—the water goes from a weak hiss to a hydroelectric surge, culminating in a torrent of huge bubbles that I annul by unplugging the cord. (Otherwise even my thoughts would start boiling.)

La Phalle

The slender curve of the tap's shaft—longer, of course, than it is wide—arcs high above the basin, extended at its terminus by the flared mouth from which my potable water flows. Flanked by 2 handles, *la phalle* is feminine in gender yet masculine in shape, and its hermaphroditism renders it utterly self-sufficient. Due to an installation error, however, my 2 faucet handles have been reversed: the hot water—indicated here by the color red—is on the right, and the cold water—blue—on the left; a harmless mistake, all in all—it would be far more problematic if the red and blue markings were to contradict their universal semiotic usage. *La phalle* drips; the tap, improperly set in the countertop, wobbles. If the 2 side-by-side handles aren't twisted firmly shut, 1 teardrop falls into the sink every 8 seconds. Defective objects are often wellsprings of disproportionate rage; a horrible crease contorts my mouth as soon as they threaten to break.

The Cure

But what would the cure be? A plumber? *And I'm sitting in the kitchen sink / And the tap drips, drip drip drip drip drip . . .* (from the Cure's 1st album, 1979, its cover showcasing, on a candy pink background, 1 lit floor lamp, 1 Frigidaire, and 1 vacuum cleaner).

2 Sponges

Situated around *la phalle*, there's no missing my sponge and dish soap, the latter as transparent as clear water. The moment when I have to replace a worn-out sponge is a solemn 1: I set the new and the old next to each other and instantly feel my eugenic tendencies playing up. The old, wizened, thread-bare, hunchbacked sponge, its scrubbing side gone completely smooth, its hardened yellow pad begging for 1 last use—well, it's heartbreaking.

Sole Light

60 cm above the sink, perched on the wide swath of white wall, is 1 beautiful rectangular gray aluminum fixture, whose 2 downward-pointing bulbs cast light through 1 translucent plate on what lies below. This modernist adornment, unearthed at a pawn shop that's since disappeared, is actually 1 of a pair, and usually sold in 2s; at the time, my limited means (I lived with practically 0 money for 15 years) prevented me from ac-quiring both halves of the diptych. Still, the pawnbroker agreed to break up the set. Only the owner of such an object can be conscious of that missing other half; personally, I've never felt the least regret about splitting up the pair. Granted, I can't see all that well in my kitchen–living room because of this uncoupling, but what is, by contrast, perfectly illuminated is how this purportedly sacrilegious rupture between 2 objects that always come in a pair pulses within me as a sort of sancti-fication of solitude. This orphan shines enough for 2.

Horror Flick

Whenever I flip the switch, I'm scared of frying my optical nerves. The whole apartment connected to my body, like a laboratory of contraptions all run by a mad scientist.

Lights Out

The fixture's only failing is that it's open on the top and so vulnerable to dust falling in from above, which frequently causes the bipin bulbs to short-circuit. When that happens, I have to get up on a chair to pluck them out with a firm but careful yank; and, come to think of it, the dust that I just now blamed is far less likely to be the cause of these frequent burn-outs than the installation's obsolescence—enough so that there's no use in my trying to blame the shoddy quality of the bulbs themselves, which have lifetimes as short as the candles they're supposed to replace. When I change them, I take my time about it: inspecting their small oval bubbles of glass, their thin filaments blackened and useless (officially supplanted by energy-efficient light bulbs, nowadays); after which I go to the living room table and set out all the replacement bulbs I have on hand (←ENTRYWAY), small and large, screw-in and pin, 15 and 25 and 75 and 100 watts. Before choosing and installing their replacements, I take 1 last look at these corpses, and I take pictures of them, giving back to them the light they've lost.

Cabinetness

Under the sink is 1 double-door, 84-cm-tall cabinet that houses all my dishes. The door handles, 2 small translucent pegs the same green color as my tiles, reinforce the green/white dichotomy of this area, which is echoed by 1 vertical band of tiles on the right-hand side. When the cabinet doors are shut (as is their wont), this setup has an undeniable appeal, much as 1 might see in a midrange interior decoration magazine. My kitchen, clean and tidy, does very well for itself in terms of aesthetics.

Elle Décore
The work of interior decoration magazines consists of presenting houses without any trace of the actual work that must have gone into them. Figures emerge from décors already perfect and whole. Grinning.

Homemaker
The lady of the house used to live in a magazine. When it went out of business, she jumped out the window.

Left
Upon opening the left-hand cabinet door, 2 shelves appear: beyond lies the domain of dullness. In the foreground of the upper shelf 1 set of deep bowls and salad bowls are piled on top of each other, as well as 2 colanders, 1 in hard gray plastic, the other in red stainless steel, the pair not so much adversarial as complementary. On the lower shelf are my plates, stacked in the most logical order: in front are the 1s I use the most, small plates (mismatched, purloined from various sets) as well as the larger flat and deep plates; behind these are towers of oversize 2-toned mauve-and-cream plates in a nouvelle cuisine style, notable mainly for being too inconveniently heavy for my dish rack and too inconveniently big to hold actual food which, once plated, would be as lonely as a castaway on a desert island. In its owner's hands, of course, the matter of weight isn't inconsequential, since every plate is a semisculpture. Rather than the groaning weight of sandstone or the alarming fragility of Sèvres china, I like the sturdy texture of traditional ceramic. And, from a decorative point of view, I happen to adore mismatched dishes, which tug at my heartstrings just as much

as any historical fresco. There's something a bit bourgie about having a perfectly matched set of dishes: Guy Degrenne, Christofle, you're as boring as a handicrafts museum! The bulk of my 12-plate battalion is 19th-century Sarreguemines dishware with a blue-green floral border, found in a Breton flea market (€30). Getting back to the cabinet, all the way in the rear, hidden in 2 boxes and completely inaccessible unless I get on my knees are champagne flutes that I pull out for "special occasions" only: kneeling down for some champagne seems both utterly Protestant and slightly blasphemous, which is why I keep my other glasses, for less Jesuitically unattainable pleasures, closer at hand.

Right
Upon opening the right door, 3 shelves are revealed, each 1 deeper than it is wide. On the middle 1, in a tattered box, is my silverware: forks, spoons, and knives, bought from a penniless family that I suppose must now be silverless. The threat of tarnish always looms: oh, wretched promiscuity! This vast range of flatware, which also includes peelers, kitchen knives, wooden spoons, and 1 spatula, makes me think of the backwoods. (This thicket's polar opposite, the flat arctic landscape of the stovetop cover, can be found further down in the text and in the → KITCHEN.) Next to the silverware box sit various utensils: 1 rotary cheese grater, 1 meat cleaver, and 1 citrus juicer all higgledy-piggledy in a cake mold, which also happens to hold the instruments needed to make cake. Sometimes I grate cheese using this stainless-steel Mouli grater with handle + small grip that fits nicely in my hand—even back when I was born, in the '60s, there was already a Mouli grater in the house. Whenever I see someone grating cheese, History loses all its solemnity, its shape, and its logic. Cheese, nostalgia, and modernism melt together in a fondue pot.

Unemployed Knife

As for my meat cleaver (and its custom-molded plastic sheath), only the occasional reappearance of roast beef in my kitchen re-awakens it from its torpor each year. Rancière may propose a "distribution of the sensible" in which the dividing line is drawn between binaries, but the number of household items never actually used by their owners would surely overwhelm any such principles if our indissoluble feeling of ownership didn't already do so. The socialist idea of loaning out 1's meat cleaver, in particular, is somewhat discomfiting, disturbing, and outright disgusting. Perhaps it's because of our revulsion toward other people and their bodies that capitalism has proposed an infinite production of individual objects. And thanks to capitalism, this cleaver has joined the ranks of the unemployed, and I can count the number of times I've had to use it on the fingers of 1 hand. If I didn't have it, would I even miss it?

Danger

To my knowledge, this butcher knife is the only real weapon I own; or, rather, considering that it's possible to weaponize practically any object, it's the most dangerous. Since I have a certain predilection for weapons (going all the way back to my childhood, when I liked to play with my father's Browning), I tend to worry about domestic accidents, which are apparently responsible for the deaths of 19,000 people per year, meaning 52 a day, not to mention the 11,000,000 accidents resulting from 1's surroundings, all of which leads the author of the report I'm copying these statistics from to conclude that "the house is a very dangerous place." This knife's 33 cm length (20 alone for the blade) adds to its elegance; all the same, it's not terribly sharp, and won't break the skin even when I run my finger along its cutting edge. Its black handle with 3 silver rivets made in the French capital of cutlery (Thiers) is far more imposing than threatening, and although the object's quality is unimpeachable, it does strike me as rather anodyne, just like the city where it was forged—a city no more renowned than any other given wasteland in the industrial wasteland that is France; and on recognizing how this knife's only power is in being seen, I worry that Thiers, much like France itself, is nothing more than a knife without a blade—and without a handle too.

Anti-Starck

The 3rd and last specimen in the cake mold, my plastic citrus juicer, is 1 of those things every family in the world owns, consisting of a protruding cone where 1 can press down an orange or a lemon half, and then a reservoir in which to collect the juice. The simplicity of a €2.50 object is fascinating less because of its actual function—I'm lazy and generally drink premade fruit juices—and more because of its negatory aspect: this citrus juicer is *anti-Starck*. In essence, designer Philippe Starck's famous Juicy Salif (which costs €19), a sort of aluminum tripod buttressing a metal reamer that's been made to look like the fruit it's meant to penetrate, is both pretentious and impractical. With its long, monstrous, mannequin-like legs, it's vastly inferior to simple family juicers. Every object has its sort of anti-counterpart, its triumphant or failed countermodel—just as this book is an overinflated re-creation of *Voyage Around My Room*. I'm the anti–Xavier de Maistre!

Eremitism

Above the central shelf, the upper shelf holds coffee cups and teacups, as well as saucers, which are pointless accessories because I don't need sugar or, consequently, a spoon. Useless objects seem destined, above all, for other people. (Could 1's eremitic tendencies be flushed out by throwing a proper party?)

Fictive Egg-Holder

My little ceramic egg-holder is green and chipped. As it doesn't include a wide enough base or rim to hold the egg's top or the shards of its shell, those inevitably have to be set on 1 plate. I need it despite its inadequacy because it's the only 1 I have, and soft-boiled eggs are integral to many of my meals. To justify its presence, I need to give this object a little bit of backstory, shoring up its shortcomings with a fable that'll put it in a better light. So I imagine that it once belonged to an actress who had a man fall in love with her and who, despite his advances, only gave him the cold shoulder. 1 day he plunged his hand into boiling water to prove the ardency of his passion: "A good soft-boiled egg must remain in the water for 3 and a half minutes, madame," he said—"No," the cruel beauty retorted: "4." I relish the story of this fictive egg-holder as much as any auctioneer might.

Cancer Pot Greed Pride

The lowest shelf serves as the receptacle for my 3 gray Teflon-coated pots, nested largest to smallest like Russian dolls. I've had these pots for far too long already. There's no ignoring the white streaks, the signs of wear and tear on their insides. I take care to clean them with the sponge's soft yellow side, definitely not its green scrubber side—a recommendation fallen from the lips and leaflets of prophets, and followed to the letter because, easily swayed as I am, I'm terrified of getting cancer from ingesting worn-away nonstick coating. I should throw these out, buy new 1s, but I'm too proud of what I have to waste money on that. Greed? Maybe. Sloth? Definitely. Shirts, shapkas, and chocolate are all acceptable in my budget. But pots?!

Scandinavian Coffee

In French, the word *café* means both a café and the coffee drunk there, which is what leads me to consider how these 2 coffee cups, with their seductively oblong shapes, bearing Scandinavian flower motifs, ambassadors of excellence from the Nordic countries, underscore how those lands have perfected 1 manner of inner life. If exteriors are continuations of interiors, then drinking from 1 of these cups in my apartment immediately transports me to a crowded Scandinavian café—which makes me all the happier that the café I call my kitchen, and the coffee I drink therein, is cozier and less cold.

Cooking Is an Action

In this kitchen, the apartment's most concretely functional room, the question of the usefulness of art comes to the fore: preparing food calls for so many operations, necessitates such a vast array of commodities and utensils that, unlike my practically empty living room, it's impossible to simply contemplate the kitchen. In a kitchen, things are always happening. A rind sprouts here, the silverware stands sentry there—everywhere fundamental disorder asserts its rule. Proper management of this space necessitates the employment of a range of activities, continually repeated, which I sometimes wearily watch myself enacting over and over, as if daily life were a matter of gliding round and round without any end in sight: pulling plates out of the cabinet, opening the fridge, filling the kettle, putting ground coffee in the coffeepot, running the faucet, pouring water into the pot, etc. Compared with this horrifying battery of acts, as mind-numbing as the stitch-by-stitch tedium of knitting, working in my office, which boils down to typing on a computer all day, seems Jansenistically peaceful—whereas this proliferation of culinary preparations amounts to an outright orgy of uselessness. The hatred certain artists have nurtured toward culinary matters (Zola insisting that his wife cut his meat, Truffaut excoriating the endless little eateries stealing precious minutes away from shooting—and then Sartre on the other hand eating *only* at restaurants so as to avoid dealing with feminism) is proportional to the sheer amount of time they take up. The joy of eating is a meager thing considering the laborious complexity and the innumerable steps required to make even a single dish.

Stovetop

To the right of the sink, slightly lower but still following a visible horizontal continuity, snug in a space circumscribed by the protrusion of the chimney shaft, is my Brandt gas range (4 burners) and oven, as well as a well-stocked nook where I keep my pans, "a little extra" hidden beneath the oven proper— it almost touches the floor. I love how these 2 uses (cooking + storage) are so deeply antithetical that nobody could guess at their combination here, since the nook is hidden behind a piece of white sheet metal that seems entirely functionless. I've jammed tons of pans and molds in there; I let them enjoy the warmth. It's worth mentioning that this appliance (which I've owned since 1989) has 1 small shortcoming: the latch for that little door has come undone, so it would hit the ground if not for an ingenious wedge that I can't take any credit for: it's a cork someone else cut in 2 and glued on.

I try as much as possible to keep the range gleamingly clean, but when it's dirty from recently completed meals, I fold its metal cover down over the extinguished burners: this is doubly advantageous since the gorgeous tilework extending across this part of the wall is thereby freed from the obstruction that hides it all too often. The relationship between the gleam of this white metal surface and the gleam of the tiles is inherently seductive: it's not so hard to draw a little beauty out of 1 simple gesture—in this case, the act of pulling the cover down. Sealing an object, safeguarding its power.

Low Heat

Even though I don't put my culinary skills to much use, I still hold my oven in high esteem. 1 of the clearest signs of low self-esteem is having no oven whatsoever. The French, after all, call vagrants "*sans feu ni lieu*," without fire or home. As for the sham otherwise known as the microwave, which just reheats rather than cooking—at best a sort of food radiator, exuding a gloomy office ambiance, calling to mind dismal lunch breaks in room 315—it doesn't hold a candle to the hearthside ambiance emitted by the word *oven*. 1 of my friends, who could have become a professional declutterer, since that's 1 of his chief talents, took pleasure in showing me the absurdity of the 4-burner stovetop, "since we only ever use 2 of them." A straightforward argument, yes, but altogether too logical for me, and founded upon the flawed assumption that less rather than more heat could somehow lead to a happier home. Abundance isn't necessarily excess. Living with 2 burners would mean a lukewarm life: I'm hardly living like a baron here, and I probably never will, given the career that I've chosen and the kind of literature I'm devoted to, but I'd still like to enjoy a certain level of luxury . . . a level that a 2-burner stove (which stores do carry) would inevitably diminish.

Lifeline

Like bathtubs and sufficient light, gas stoves are 1 of my absolute necessities for habitation. I hate electric hot plates, which are so slow as to be unusable, so thoroughly indistinguishable—whether hot or cold—as to be dangerous, so ugly as to be fit only for mobile homes. Gas, on the other hand, is a sure thing . . . though my gas pipes, good until 2013, are, as of this writing, nearing the end of their warranty. It's rare to come across objects marked with their own expiration dates: 2013, similarly, is when this book will be done. A 10-year-warranty pipe costs €19.99; a lifetime-warranty pipe costs €79.50. Bearing in mind that I'm allotted about 40 more years to live (37, statistically speaking) (unless I commit suicide by gas—a solution I can't envision myself carrying out, considering the grief it would cause others), it's certainly in my best financial interests to go for the longer warranty and so save €0.46: but the idea of a "lifetime pipe" is so ominous to me—it reeks of the clinical—that it practically guarantees misfortune. Anyhow, considering the state of my 10-year pipe, I can't bring myself to believe it'll really be defunct so soon, but then I likewise can't bring myself to believe that such an explicit injunction as its warning label could be wrong. My eyes sweep over the object like a vulture over a carcass, and with a heavy silence I ponder just how long it really has left.

To Build 1 Fire

I love turning on the flame, and I love turning on the gas for the stove more than for the oven: the stovetop flame flickers on immediately, while the oven flame is in its "den" and so doesn't delight the eye. Turning 1 of the knobs and making the pilot spark, I can watch with clear satisfaction as the flame, or rather the flames, since there are several of them on this modern stove, emerge. The yellow "flame of a candle," as rhapsodized by Gaston Bachelard, is proper to a house; but the blue fire of a gas burner, being less holy, better suits an apartment. A simple joy: lighting all 4 pilots at once, setting them ablaze like an air-raid firebombing. A melancholic joy: the single lit burner of the lifelong bachelor.

Projected Ornament

The Brandt range is snug against the anonymous chimney shaft, the 2 of them conjuring up 2 disparate eras of cooking. Sharing the wall with a perfect symmetry, this conduit sticks out about 30 centimeters, giving a shape to the room that I couldn't really call picturesque. I've considered tearing it down in order to get 1 continuous smooth wall that would be more consistent with the visual identity of my living room—and more practical too, since this bulge takes up space and limits movement—and yet I've kept it intact: it adds a kind of projective complexity to this space that mass-produced housing believed it was so wise to eliminate. The shaft's sharp profile breaks the wall's clean line and so enhances the room. The ghosts imprisoned within have projected their thoughts outward. I tap my finger on the hollow wall.

Mixed Use
Wedged right in front of the chimney stack, but set low, is 1 small freestanding structure of 3 white shelves for mixed use (storage/housekeeping), a cabinet open to the air. Everything there is on display, but at shin height; I have to squat down to reach anything.

Supplies Demanded
Food is the most perishable supply in a home, its material in perpetual demand by dint of being ephemeral and putrescible, its transitory nature demonstrated too by its ever-changing inventory—albeit simplified in my case, given that I almost always eat the same things. Even though I don't live in a clan, my relationship to victuals, much like primitive hunter-gatherers', is characterized by the same repetitive cycles of feast and famine. My foodstuffs are classified by location: these low shelves for typical staples, the Frigidaire for everything fresh.

Feedback
My hand-to-mouth life (hardly ugly but certainly grueling) is regimented by a piece of furniture that wasn't intended

for such regimentation. Originally destined for 1 specific occupation—holding bottles—the narrow dimensions of this fully assembled polyhedron (83 cm × 20 cm) naturally suit its intended function, so its builder was astonished when I rotated it from its proposed verticality to set comestibles inside. This astonishment astonished me in turn; the differences in interpretation that crop up between how people think 1 should organize 1's home and what 1 actually does tend to multiply as soon as they question 1's initial decision and 1 feels even more unsure of what 1 actually wants: feedback threatens all shared decisions, each person's doubts redounding upon the others.

Hardly Fortified Camp

A pronounced destitution hovers over my alimentary domain. Or, to put it another way, there's never anything to eat at my place. My camp is so scarcely fortified that it would crumble under a siege: the groaning cabinets of well-stocked houses, their jars of homemade preserves, their spice dishes, have all deserted their posts. I don't live in some domestic fairy tale but rather in a stark universe where every element must sustain itself, drawing its strength from this void of context, just as a white tablecloth would draw color from an orange. Even if I don't disdain those goods of which my home is bereft, I must be clear that they simply have no place in my constrained universe. As I weigh the quality of such goods against the paltry surface area of my apartment, I don't see what a big heap of victuals would get me. Gaining a little space is far more important to me than being able to fortify this bunker I might consider my home, so I've kept my kitchen lean. This enforced frugality isn't depressing, as far as I'm concerned; I simply see it as a different way of living, just like any other, trying to keep my stomach out of the equation as much as possible: it's bad enough that nature already requires me to feed myself an overwhelming 3 times a day (4 if I count my afternoon snack). In such joyless repetition I find a strong argument against the existence of God in this spoilage of the delectable pleasure of eating in its being quadrupled each day rather than simply being doubled. If anything, this would seem to indicate the existence of some false deity unaware of the difference between indulgence and repetition, and who thereby bound humanity to its appetites. It's hard enough to run errand upon errand—a process that always boils down to fits and starts, stratagems and bursts of willpower—but that difficulty is only multiplied by adding on those chores necessitated by the preparation of meals, which themselves call for pulling out dishes and putting them away again, and then all of the above is made possible in the 1st place only by having answered the endlessly recurring question "What should I eat?"!

From this perspective, Raymond Roussel's daily challenge— he took all his meals in 1 go, once each day, and had done with them—rather speaks to me; alas, I don't have his fortitude, and I'd much rather live communally (a prospect I'm certainly drawn to) in a situation where meals would be served at fixed times, prepared by other people, and eaten in a group; I like the idea of degrading the status of food by rationing it out: buying so few groceries is a sort of sardonic rebellion against the purportedly natural order of things. However, I'm far from disdaining food in general; the beauty of all comestibles is in their annihilation.

Narrow Pantry

This shelf for bottles without any bottles stands in for my pantry. Its makeup changes depending on my shopping status: full when it's holding many newly bought products, empty when it's time to go to the store. Its very smallness lends itself to starkness, as if the diminutiveness of the whole must be transmitted to its contents. Small furnishings discourage excess: if I bought too much, it would overflow. Indeed, the goods up front are packed in like sardines in order not to spill over, and even then some of them tend to fall and scatter—a carton of raisins, for example—due to the shelf's modest proportions.

I toy with the idea of putting on a play in which all the action would happen right at the edge of the stage, forcing the actors to perform with the closed curtain right behind them and the orchestra pit right in front: they would barely be able to move their bodies, so we could observe them making the smallest gestures, which would become all the more touching, and so all the more appropriate to the expressive narrowness of humanity.

General Store

In terms of nonperishables, my personal department store is divided into 3 cantons: to the left I have the grocery proper, with its olive oil, canola oil, various spices—including both the classics (pepper, nutmeg, cinnamon) and the occasional fantasia (paprika, cloves, tarragon); in the center, disregarding any overlap due to the lack of intermediate dividers, the "sweets": tea, flour, honey, Thompson raisins; on the right, a bit of a gray area, where various jars mix with orange blossom petals, pasta, white rice, lentils, semolina, and split peas. Nietzsche, writing about himself as a man in his 40s, threatened by cholesterol, showed how the question of food is a philosophical 1—but don't infer from this that the scarcity of my reserves amounts to a similar miserabilism on my part. On the contrary, even if I'm hardly a master chef, I still do happen to like nice things, from Debauve & Gallais chocolate to pear mincemeat, from arugula salad to manchego cheese and 1st-cold-pressed olive oil, which, by the way, beats peanut oil hands down, specifically Lesieur-brand peanut oil, the subpar variety that drowned my childhood. I'm downright fascinated by the way certain ingredients can become irretrievably passé; and while I don't know why peanut oil has become so utterly disreputable, I'm likewise amazed that it ever seemed indispensable.

Alimentary Aesthetics

Now that my friends, who might as well be my unofficial doctors, have converted me to the cult of organic food, I happily welcome semolina, red and green lentils, brown rice, and quinoa into my home—foodstuffs that just a few years ago I would have mocked and scorned. But the time for joking has long passed, and now my health strikes me as no laughing matter. I'm more and more interested (not, I hope, to excess) in nutrition: the original medicine, as everybody knows, rooted in the pleasure of exclusion: banning this or that food from my mouth for all time. Youth, of course, cares not for such details—is unconcerned about what it consumes, barely looking at it, even feeling a 2ndary pleasure at purposely eating 2nd-rate foods; yet there's an inverse sensuality in eliminating comestibles wholly incompatible with the concept of "self-care" from 1's diet: processed food, for example. So, yes, I've said adieu to butter, sugar, salt, eggs, deli meats, and Nutella—just as my aesthetic diet won't allow the consumption of such dubious offerings as the works of Coelho, Chagall, or Katherine Pancol.

Lonely T

The shelf immediately below isn't terribly tall: it holds other, more anecdotal glasses, plastic goblets, green ceramic bottle holders, additional boxes of matches that I'll pass over for fear of overdoing this inventory that I've promised my readers as a coup of sorts (since I do believe that I'm the 1st author to conceive of such a feat). Given the modesty of my needs, there's plenty of stuff here that's surplus to requirements: these goods have accumulated according to no coherent policy, yet it's by no means a contradiction for me to say that I own almost nothing and yet have accumulated plates I never use, as well as 3 terra-cotta dishes still in their original paper wrapping. Clearly I'm just waiting for them to break.

A bachelor's kitchen is like a virgin territory full of riches its prospectors fail to discover. Sometimes I buy myself a few treats as a reminder of how decidedly average my life usually is. And so this humble set of shelves welcomes the occasional black box of Mariage Frères tea, although it's nowhere near as utilitarian as the other foods kept here—this small space suits it nicely. In it are 3 relatively unfamiliar, 1 might even say *misanthropic*, varieties: Alceste black tea, Célimène green tea, and Philinte herbal tea.

The Large Glass
On the top plank of these shelves, visible—quite intentionally— from anywhere in the room, I display my museum of glass. Among the 6 carafes clustered together, the only 1 to bear any words ("*dairy milk*") is a milk bottle like the 1s that used to be delivered everywhere (I don't know if that's still the case) in Anglo-Saxon lands; I swiped this 1 in Ireland as if it were some Celtic spoil of war, and it always reminds me of the song "No Milk Today," which my youngest brother used to listen to and which I still have on a 45 that was reissued in the '80s. This bottle served as a prop for a play, *Virginia*, at the Théâtre national de Chaillot in 1993. I offered up this accessory on the condition that it be returned after the run, and worried each night that the actor who used it in his performance might break it, but in the end, it came home unharmed, though not without fight. The minute the set was struck, when I went to regain possession of my relic, I ran into a small misunderstanding with some stagehands who insisted that making off with a piece of the production's property was a breach of some theatrical

tradition: that 1 ought never to abscond with an item from a performance for personal use. Oh, the recriminations that resulted from just 1 milk bottle!

The carafe to the right of this bottle is also the fruit of a little shameless plunder, a sport I excelled at for many years, as a child; and while it's true that such brazen looting carries far less risk than more Machiavellian forms of theft, its rewards are lesser as well. Not to downplay the little whiff of transgressiveness that still lingers around my crime of preference, but this particular feature of the art of plunder—which follows this declension: nothing ventured, nothing gained; little ventured, little gained; and so on—happens to appeal to my miserly tendencies. Anyway, I stole this small carafe from the terrace of the famous Caffè Florian in Venice in 1983, following a bet (won), putting my braggadocio to the test, in which I was challenged to prove that I really had the courage to dine and dash. Right then and there, I got up and left the table at a brisk walk, in the process upping the stakes by hiding beneath my coat this object that I considered not just lovely but perfectly Venetian. This is now the 3rd object I've mentioned stealing: I'm not, by nature, a thief, but if the opportunity should arise in specific contexts (mainly commercial), I don't think twice. After all, theft is property!

Nestled near the milk bottle and the carafe, the 3rd glass treasure is a bottle that once held mead—not that I had any idea of this when I acquired it. Gorgeously sheathed in brown wicker, it brings to mind a woman tied up with rope for some erotic game. Unfortunately, it's also covered in a layer of dust that's formed into clumps and made it less desirable, since it's now that much less touchable.

The 4th piece in my museum is another carafe, with a heavy base, adorned by the artist Claude Viallat with knucklebones, his trademark, inlaid in the translucent glass. I'd like to invite my readers, in considering this vessel, to ponder too the very idea of an artist having a "trademark," whereby they insist they have every right to wear out a sort of obsessive label or motif ad nauseam for the sake of making their work recognizable. I do want to believe that a crude form can be imprinted as if with an awl upon our belongings ad infinitum, but I certainly wouldn't want to see a writer wear out a given style in the same way, just for the sake of recognizability, and there's no denying the mercenary scent I pick up whenever I see some artist pillaging the latest fads for aesthetic ends—this carafe is indisputable proof of this incessant urge toward branding. There are, of course, artists whose work is driven by legitimate obsessions—Morandi and his own carafes, for example, or Toroni and his circles, or Fontana and his slits—but it can be difficult to distinguish these from those other, vulgar thingummies that merely assert the artist's imprimatur.

The last 2 carafes on this shelf, wholly unlike each other—the 1st being elongated, sort of resembling a pipette, and embellished with a gray plastic cap; the other being squat and wide and evoking a liqueur bottle—make for an odd couple à la Laurel & Hardy. These objects are actors, and since the reverse is also true, I sometimes dream up impossible identification exercises, wherein novice actors would try to embody a fork, or A-list celebrities might play a stewpot.

To the left of the carafes are assorted mass-produced glasses, replicas of Alvar Aalto designs, classical stemmed glasses, Bodum glasses, red glasses shaped like hanaps, and champagne coupes, all of them forming a small glassen symphony. If it were possible, I would invest in even more glass; only my general aversion to owning kitchen items (and clear preference for the conceptual side of things) holds me back.

Mixing Ideas

I've fixated on glass so much, partly in anticipation of pouring an actual drink in 1 of them, and likewise, certainly, because I love the idea of saloons. And, indeed, the half wall that shapes my kitchen is a sort of counterless bar—good enough to lean on, though not wide enough to set down a drink: this was by design, however; the last thing I wanted in my own kitchen was an actual bar counter, which would have had the unwanted effect of making this area seem downright convivial.

The connection between writers and mixologists seems fairly clear to me, not only in a personal sense—many members of my family work in restaurants and regularly patronize drinking establishments—but also for the sentimental reasons espoused by Jean Rhys in her short story "Mixing Cocktails." Tales, concoctions, and ideas in general all mix effortlessly at a bar. Our mouths are the portals to our minds.

Easystrike
All the way to the left of the glass museum lies a double-function receptacle, an ashtray and its matchbox. Set 7 centimeters to the right of the stove, this bowl that holds both matches and their carcasses comes from a selection of Moroccan tableware ordinarily recognizable by its yellow/green pattern, but here covered with soot, all luster lost. Yes, I could wash it, but I don't, out of spite; I consider its sootiness more just. The decline in the quality of French matches—once produced by SEITA, our state-owned tobacco company, which, subsequent to its privatization and merger, has retroactively proven its worth by the very mediocrity of the products that have come to replace theirs—is here made shamelessly clear by way of the Leader Price discount-store logo on the box (in blue/red/white—what a shitty picture of France it paints!), in addition to a brainless illustration showing a skier schussing down an alpine landscape, in total contradiction of even the concept of fire. To avoid sparking the flame of nostalgia (an altogether too facile, if profitable, prospect), I'll say that "I'm not nostalgic, but I do have nostalgias," a declaration Barthes originally

made with the sensitive attention he always gave to matters, as he replaced the past with the memories thereof: in this case, this memory is every French person's, because it's of SEITA's Gypsy emblem, the eponymous Gitane, that smoky woman dancing away on a red-and-yellow match head, as though born from the fire being lit. Aside from being a well-designed logo, the image of an inflammable Gypsy aflame was a thing of graphic and symbolic beauty, so much that it takes every ounce of frosty feminism available to see it as rather sexist. Now, however, instead of this beautiful brunette with her fiery charms, we get a sappy eco-friendly image, even if, in this case, it's been effaced by a tiny blaze that's destroyed its lower-left end, rendering the bar code illegible; fortunately, the customer service number (call toll-free 0 800 35 00 00) is there to answer any questions you might have.

Chef's Whites

The last part of this kitchen corner, which closes off the rectangle, consists of a 119 cm × 60 cm work counter set in both the real wall and the half wall, and is made of the same plastic that surrounds the sink—a slice of the same perpendicular whiteness. The ideal whiteness of l's kitchen is a convention to which I've made my sacrifices, just like everyone else. White walls, white half wall—the same white that has seized control of practically every Western interior, thanks to its absorbent and luminous virtues, and is only extending its dominion. There's no denying a kitchen's aesthetic and moral dimensions; we have to keep it all the more clean, make it all the more exalted, than any bathroom.

I'm attracted to propriety, perhaps because the word is so close to "property," the former being a means of erasing the guilt inherent in the latter, even as it glorifies it. Only in cartoons, where everything is smooth, where immateriality dominates, can you have characters who own nothing—or anyway

own things without putting any effort into keeping them—
and who are thus wholly abstract. As far as literature goes, we
have Balzac to thank for filling the medium with furniture—
not to mention money, dirt, titles and deeds of ownership,
pension funds, plates, and pork filets with sauce. The bleach of
modernity arrived much later, to whitewash the 19th century's
crimes.

Clue
Mrs. White, in the kitchen, with the knife.

A Woman, a Plan, a Locale
The world owes the invention of the kitchen work counter
(which, in French, we call *un plan de travail*), as we now know
it, to an American woman, Catharine Beecher, who might be
said to have invented the concept of home economics. Both a
designer and an educator, C.B. revolutionized the idea of the
kitchen thanks to her functionalist principles, which sought to
maximize the use of space with these *plans*, or counters, and
so minimize the material servitude of women. As a man devoted to his interior, I think of her every time I prepare a dish
on this countertop. And I must note that Catharine Beecher's
initials are the same as Charles Baudelaire's. Making soup can
be learned, but—now I'm thinking of Baudelaire's little prose
poem—what about making clouds?

Culinary Heritage, or a Lack Thereof
My mother doesn't like to cook, my brother eats out every
single day—however *did* I end up tinkering in the kitchen?

Under the Counter
Beneath the left side of the work counter are 2 shelves (and
therefore 3 spaces) meant for storing the rest of my dishes. A

great and frustrating mayhem reigns there, which only a rather
indulgent soul could consider to be as poetic as, for example,
the antique shop in which Raphaël, the hero of Balzac's *La peau
de chagrin*, takes refuge, and in so doing winds up abandoning his plan to kill himself. Isn't it pretty to think that such
a jumble of things might keep a hopeless man alive merely
by liberating and intensifying the appeal of existence? And
yet, emptied of all sentimental value and historical importance,
everything that this cabinet holds is, in my opinion, mediocre,
utilitarian, standardized. Let's have a good look at the least
pleasant part of my domain.

Handmade

I've hidden this territory with a little curtain I'm quite proud
of, since it's 1 of the few things here that I made myself: uniting
2 disparate pieces of cloth—1 white cotton, the other linen—
reminiscent of the curtain mentioned *infra* and *supra*, by means
of staples. Guaranteed handmade, as opposed to this book.

I Love Boringness

It's true that, as I pull this small curtain to the left, my archaeological project has narrowed to an extraordinarily minuscule
scope, but I will not shirk my duty, even as I note that exposing my home amounts to leaving myself vulnerable to ingrati-
tude. On the upper shelf is a heap of plates, a bitter-almond-green
tureen, a plastic salad spinner, an electric hand mixer as real as
the 1 I mentioned back in the bathroom was imaginary, the
heavy base of a stand mixer that I've only ever used once to
make some gazpacho on September 20, 2011, some dish
towels, some plates in boxes, some plastic tablecloths for the
very infrequent parties I hold, some aluminum foil that various
websites now insist can be dangerous to use. If I have to get to
the very back of the cabinet (and sometimes I absolutely have

to), then I bend down and push aside this heap of stuff with a scavenging claw to find a plastic bag filled with the parts of a disassembled apparatus, a gift so old I can't even remember who gave it to me, a stainless-steel food mill for making soup. To keep some semblance of order, I've secreted the foregoing in a huge deep ocher Basque plate that consequently holds more than its 4 adjectives.

The Plastic Measuring Cup

My plastic measuring cup, which I use relatively frequently, is clouded on the inside with a thin sheen of flour that reveals just how negligent I am in caring for it. But I find it altogether proper to allow my flour dust to maintain this evanescent existence, like the breath of nourishment itself, fogged on some glass—its little trademark—rather than washing it away. And, independent of whatever it might contain, this measuring cup, in its humbleness, has managed to follow me all my life, from childhood on: the 1 I have here isn't the same cup, of course, but 1 of its innumerable mass-produced duplicates, found in every household. Its plasticness appeals to me; I prefer it to the glass version: there's something eternal about plastic, even though it's not the same eternity as stone, concrete, or glass: it's a trivial eternity, almost inhuman in the way it's so easily filled.

Disposable and Durable

We thought we'd disposed of all that was disposable, but it accumulates without dispersing, and we wonder what we'll do with all that endures and amasses.

The Boy of Cooking

This pile of stuff also contains my personal notebook of handwritten recipes, which has a cover portraying 1 blond boy, certainly American, licking his lips in front of a chocolate-covered dessert; this collection is now in its dotage; I haven't added a single recipe in at least 10 years, whereas back in the days when its existence was a vigorous 1, I would frequently copy into it instructions for dishes that I found both good and easy to make, like pear gratin, blancmange, meatballs, or *pollo exótico*; this notebook also holds several loose items—*Elle* recipe cards, or recipes my friends gave to me. In addition, hidden deeper within this abode are 2 actual cookbooks, living in semihibernation, 1 devoted entirely to vegetables (which I'm coming to enjoy more and more), and the other, *Cuisine sans souci*, by Rose Montigny, a classic that I've occasionally found myself consulting despite the fact that its age—it was originally published in the '50s and this edition is a reprint—diminishes its usefulness somewhat, since in this realm as in so many others the historicity of taste has closed off certain avenues, forbidding 1 from following those recipes that would be inimical to our modern-day stomachs, not to mention infeasible, such as "Veal Marengo" or "Pineapple Glazed Ham." The 1 truly memorable trick I've pulled off with this book is to have reproduced 1 of its passages from memory during my master's thesis defense as my way of showing the difference between a utilitarian text and a literary text, a rhetorical gambit I'm especially proud of and which may have been what got me highest honors on my diploma.

Down 1 Notch
The shelf below mimics the previous 1. Only the most servile and uninteresting items, all in a row, bearing as little trace of their use as possible: plastic wrap, garbage bags, casserole dish lids—each accessory giving itself over fully to my use, completely devoid of whatever glimmer of narcissism is necessary to make life a bit brighter. As with some men, they also serve who only stand and wait. Yet the dishes draw far more attention

than this Lumpenproletariat does during mealtime conversations, whether between 2 people or only 1 (since I do talk to myself while eating).

Mealtime Conversations
The worst mealtime conversations are conversations about mealtimes.

Even Lower!
On the lowest level, which is the floor itself, we find various cleaning products held in 1 wooden wine case (Miguel Torres, Gran Coronas 1987): this contrast between the container and its contents may be a hackneyed setup, but 1 with enduring effectiveness. I remember the work of an artist who used to put cooking ingredients in the wrong containers, such as oil in a wine bottle, or flour in a saltshaker. Or, for greater contrast, eau-de-vie in a detergent bottle. There's a trickster born every minute.

Cold Chain
The right of the space under the work counter is taken up by the Frigidaire. Faure brand. 85 cm tall, 50 cm wide, 63 cm deep. It's almost always empty, except for the days when I'm receiving visitors. These appliances are usually unnecessarily powerful: I always keep mine on 2, which is already pretty cold; cranking the dial to 6 would have consequences I shiver to contemplate. Modernity boiled down at some point to these sorts of mass-produced things; then was frozen in them, and then it must have been sublimated. And all this time my freezer has stayed an arctic research station. I never open it except to de-ice it.

Standart
The cold goes nicely with empty whiteness. Indeed, the most agreeable thing about these mass-produced machines is their

standard-issue character, which erases all matters of style—
just as supermarkets have the advantage over specialty stores
of feeling nothing like anyone's home.

Fungible Goods

Opening the door to this device—and finding there a few victuals whose vitality hasn't wholly ebbed—I'm struck by how
abandoned it all seems. Right now, there's some sheep's milk
yogurt (which I pronounce "yogour," in honor of a friend who
found this hilarious), 1 wilted bunch of fennel, 1 open package
of Parmesan, some Mexican coffee in a Brazilian container,
some Tropicana grapefruit juice, and 1 opened jar of preserves.
The kitchen in general, and the Frigidaire in particular—
which I've always called Frigidaire, never "refrigerator," as if
brand loyalty had completely usurped the appliance's common
name—have taught me that human beings are equally as fun-
gible as foodstuffs (which, come to think of it, I already knew).

I remove a dead stalk of celery lying next to the vegetable
drawer. And before I slam this chilly coffin shut, I make sure
there's still a bottle of champagne in there, because life is a long
soirée during which it takes endless effort to be even a little
happy.

Mass Customization

There are Faures other than mine—decked out with postcards
and magnets—but mine is unique, its icy beauty marred only
by 1 grease stain.

2nd Service

On top of the Faure, in the tight space (10 cm) still free under
the countertop, I've found a way to slip in 1 red casserole lid,
cracked from the grief of being separated from its better half, as
well as 1 plastic basket holding an additional set of cutlery—
my 2nd service, as it were, and the 2nd mention of those

"doubles" my home is generally lacking, as mentioned *supra*, and which, in their superfluity, inject a little luxury into our otherwise gray days. It's very nice, indeed, to have this 2nd service available: aside from the general impression of quantity, which makes the prospect of dinner parties far less daunting, it establishes a hierarchy between my stainless-steel utensils, hidden here, and the silver 1s mentioned elsewhere. I eat with my silver service every day, not with these substitutes—consider it 1 of those little aristocratic insurrections that add some salt to bourgeois life. Bucking the vulgar notion that silver cutlery should never get pulled out save for "special occasions," I've inverted their role in order to improve my daily life: what a clever owner of stuff I am!

Solving the Riddle

Actually, there are 3 other utensils also living down under the countertop: 1st, a large crustacean with tiny teeth and red plastic handles: an endangered species, since to my mind canned food reeks so utterly of the '60s that I avoid it by any means necessary, but 1 that continues to justify its presence here thanks to the fact that I have to open a few containers of artisanal wild game meat that my relatives in Landes send me each year. This reliable, rock-solid can opener is the antithesis of all the can openers that were inflicted on me previously, each of which were so-called "camping" can openers—basically small sharp knives affixed to metal rectangles that took plenty of shoving and yanking to get any traction and which inevitably led to my receiving cuts generally more psychical than physical, but still intolerable considering that this meant turning every meal into a rather risky ordeal. (If these objects were ranked like pop songs, my red can opener would be number 1 with a bullet on the hit parade, while those dangerous devices beloved by scouting organizations across France would be buried at the very bottom.) The 2nd utensil in this nook is the corkscrew that I use every day (I drink): the sort we call a "De Gaulle," as some kind of national joke, with a spiral screw and winged arms. The 3rd utensil is a pair of kitchen scissors; its points were wrecked in circumstances I no longer remember. (Actually, they're not so much kitchen scissors as fabric scissors repurposed for the kitchen.)

I'd like to be able to piece together a rebus using these 3 objects (the can opener, the De Gaulle, and the scissors), but doing so already feels like more of a riddle than I can handle just now.

Intake

In the recess to the left of my chimney shaft, cheek by jowl with my swing-top trash can, stands my Miele-brand vacuum cleaner. A huge mountain of plastic grocery bags (→BEDROOM) has hidden it from all prying eyes because the machine's plastic body, colored a bright yellow that would be verboten even on a car, easily makes it visible from a mile away. A ruse, on the part of this object, that would be worthy of the great masters of propaganda—brightening up servitude!—if it weren't for its long gray plastic hose, its shiny tube, or its detachable head taking up valuable space as well . . . especially that supple hose, with its aspirations toward independence, which I've been forced to set snug between the vacuum's body and the wall.

The vacuum cleaner is the primary weapon in our miniature housecleaning arsenal; its absence would be quickly felt; unless, like Marcel Duchamp, you've taken up dust breeding, this mighty engine has to be revved up every so often. What a shame that I can't, unlike Jeff Koons, put my vacuum cleaner in a glass case.

Exhaust

Vacuuming is far from being the least exhausting household chore, but its advantage, aside from the guaranteed immediate results of its action, is its monofunctional character: it's 1 of those rare pieces of technology that's truly easy to use. And then, along with the pleasure of making dust disappear, there are ancillary enjoyments to be had in its use: eliminating larvae, for example (a live flea, even, on 1 occasion); or suctioning bits of food off the floor—beans or grains of rice lost forever in the bag-tomb. Vacuuming is exaltation incarnate—uniting power and movement; its modest triumph of life over entropy is well worth the effort involved: namely, encouraging this hefty robot to move from place to place . . . not so different from tugging on a dog's leash to keep it from running amok. (In fact, from time to time, while methodically repositioning its hose, I'll slam this massive yellow conveyance against the wall, not out of any specific sadism, but as if I were walking my master's hound with all the bitterness of a valet.)

In my previous life, when I was able to live in a larger apartment, I was talking to a Sri Lankan cleaner who astonished me with his level of education (a doctorate in sociology). Since then, I've had to swallow my irritation at the idea of cleaning my home myself; whenever I haul this monster out, I think of Queen's music video for "The Show Must Go On," in which Freddie Mercury, done up as a scantily clad woman, pushes a vacuum back and forth. The lesson: take some pleasure in getting down and dirty.

Decorhetorician

Even when admiring my beautiful streamlined yellow vacuum, I refuse to accept the principles of the design world's sleazy creatives, who insist on giving purely utilitarian items a few sexy curves, to help them "cut loose." I admit I might be a bit less resentful when vacuuming with a nicely made machine, but I'm not so naïve or cynical as to presume that an object's silhouette might change the nature of the work it's meant to do. It's ridiculous for my vacuum cleaner or my toothbrush to be "beautiful" when I'm bent double from work.

Reversible Bag

Among my pile of shopping bags there's 1 eco-friendly tote that was meant to do away with all the others, and of which I am ashamed: I've flipped it inside out so visitors won't be able to see where it came from and then accuse me of collaborating with a ridiculous ideology. But it's very easy to see through the thin, cheap material and make out the logo of this brand that believes in Mother Earth. I'm just as exposed as if I were made of a reversible material myself.

Total Trash

My little 20-liter Mr. Bricolage swing-top trash can—said top popping open whenever my foot presses down—is a bit too small; I should have gotten the 30-liter model. I went for the smaller 1 because I didn't want it to take up much space, a sensibility I also apply to minor artworks. The bottom of this trash can, a dangerously thin circle of plastic, cracked after just a few days, giving way under the weight of 1 Bordeaux bottle. I was cheated, conned; I shouldn't have spent my money on this subpar piece of merchandise—and yet it's hard for me to take the notion of buying a fancy trash can seriously. (Of course, I'm thinking about this wrong: between 4-star trash cans and rubbish trash cans, there has to be a happy medium.)

Its cracking underscored how intrinsically fragile every object in the world is, which naturally hadn't come to mind when I 1st bought it at the store: I'm not the sort of person likely to inspect every side of a waste receptacle. (Stendhal's already said that it's not possible to describe every side of an orange.) Now, however, the lesson of my trash can with its cracked base has become clear, as if some tutelary deity were whispering to me to stop trying to get to the bottom of things . . .

Color Counter

I try to set as few things as possible on the countertop, so as to avoid a disorder injurious to the atmosphere of my living room and likewise to respect the implicit charter of all modern kitchens—to stay white, discreet, spare. Out of all the real possibilities open to me, therefore, I've selected only those items that might de-realize that credo: on a vividly colored plate my friend Pascale Bouhénic brought me from Mexico (depicting 1 beautiful brunette astride 1 horse driven by 1 sombreroed man) is a gilded compote dish—*Made in India*—in which you'll find several colorful fruits: confining these fruits in this dish is my own personal version of the historical argument between form and color, wherein a concentration on form, as Poussin's partisans would insist, allows 1 to tame the intemperance of color, whereas Rubens's acolytes would of course champion that very intemperance. Apples, bananas, oranges, or harvest grapes cry out for their shapes to be admired, and so, in the end, it's Matisse who prevails.

The Black Little Toaster

For similar reasons of harmony, my black Philips toaster, which sits a few centimeters away, has been placed up against the white wall. Its plastic success depends on having access to electricity: as such, it has to be set next to the sink, because that's the only place where there's an accessible outlet; its cord is short (a real problem) and when not in use coils into a shapeless latticework; moreover, if I pick up the toaster in question—because I do occasionally use it, not as often as I simply observe it—I can hear, trapped inside, all the stale bits of toast that have fallen into its entrails; and so I do my best to clean them out somehow, shaking the toaster all around in my attempt to extract those little crumbs. There's always a bit left over, however; the stubbornness of this morsel drives me nuts, but now, 40 years later, whenever I face that fascinating sandy sound I remember that distant house in Brittany where my uncle the tinkerer invited me to discover toasters.

Cleaning House
The ideal countertop, after a meal, should become clean and new again, all remnants cleared away. I tidy the counter into a well-groomed landscape, like a child setting out a toy tea set: I make a clean space. A dark-green plastic imitation-glass carafe gleams with Quézac or Evian mineral water and, as in a hotel room, stands always at the ready. Next to it are 2 trivets: 1 of them circular and blue in the Basque style with a cruciform lauburu; the other expandable and adjustable, meaning it can be made the right size for any vessel I use. I pass a dishcloth over the countertop where some walnut kernels left behind by a guest still linger.

The Anthropologist's Dismay at the Nutcracker
This nutcracker was 1 I picked for its simple form: its ridged handle burrows into its hole and splits the nut wedged against its circular inset. Once the oleaginous seed has been crushed, this instrument of torture's handles are pried apart, and all that remains is for some fingers to finish the job and remove the shell. I'm taken by its ingenuity, but the problem is that I don't eat nuts. I couldn't resist buying this tool, but it defeats all my certainties: is the measure of true wealth in being content with next to nothing, while those who hoard find their voluminous possessions essentially worthless? Well, even though I'm ashamed by this redundant accessory, I hide it rather than casting it off, even contemplating the prospect of taking it

apart, which would require the invention of a new tool: a nutcracker-cracker.

A Poor Plate
I carefully and conscientiously wipe clean a dusty plate, its rim lightly ridged: sole surviving castaway from a childhood dish service, bought from a pottery factory in Gien that once made, among other marvels, the tiles for the Paris métro. It struts and frets its hour on display with a color-saturated pattern of flora arrayed around its rim, its lip, and then is heard no more. It is an unused plate, full of renown and history, signifying almost nothing.

Mise en Abyme
In the middle of this decorative abundance that imperils my quest to find the kitchen's raison d'être, affixed to the wall and floating high above, is a framed engraving from my friends Annette and Jean-Loup Bajac depicting a scantily clad young girl watering the flowers on her balcony and bearing a caption indicating that she is the gardener. It's an interior scene: it's easy to make out the details of the young girl's apartment in the background (1 curtain, 1 clothesline, 1 door, some painted paneling); or, more precisely, it's an interior-exterior scene, because the girl is leaning out of her window to water her plants just below the sill—and it's this very action that's resulted in this delicate detail: her bared breast escaping her blouse. It may not be inherently "dangerous to stick your head out the window," as the signs on old trains used to warn us, but it *is* rather exciting, in every home, to cross such borders.

Slow Tea and Fast Coffee
Finally, more or less perpetually on display, as though belonging to this museum's permanent collection, we come to my afternoon teacup and morning coffee cup: the 1 dark green in

a neo-British style, the other a tall cylindrical Bodum glass. As I think on these 2 stimulants, which I take in large quantities, if watered down—Americano for both—I'm not sure which 1 makes more of a contribution to my cozy kitchen. I do know that the teacup's style is more 19th century than the coffee cup's. In any case, tea has to be prepared with exceptional patience, while the jittery effects of coffee seem quite well suited to the swiftness of its concoction. The classicism of tea tempers the "quick and dirty" life to which I aspire.

Postprandial

I love to see immaculate, catalog-ready kitchens ruined by parties. I love to see those rooms ravaged by soirées—love to see how spilled ashes, stained floors, piled-up plates, half-filled tumblers, unfinished flutes of champagne, and partly eaten slices of cake combine in the auroral silence that follows music. A splendid massacre soon dispelled by daybreak.

Beneficiaries

As I leave my kitchen, which is to say the space delineated by my half wall, I want to sing the praises of my scarce home appliances 1 last time, with all the warmth of a homeowner freed from mundane responsibilities. Since they've all gifted me with more spare time for poetry, I've set up trusts for them after my death—for example, should my home be transformed into some sort of terrible writer's museum. My electric hand mixer is entitled to recognition, as are my corkscrew, my salad spinner, and my bottle opener, all of which have at various moments helped assuage various anxieties. I've set down thorough, thoughtful instructions for such a scenario.

Overownership

Whereas for objects, *possession equals ownership*, real estate requires paperwork. The overowner of this apartment, then, must

inscribe each 1 of his possessions in his register. He's working
his fingers to the bone with all these details—but he's only
got himself to blame.

Echo of a Bell

The object that set the rhythm of my childhood meals as a
rich kid was the servant's bell, which I was allowed to ring at
the end of each course, to tell our dear Céleste to bring in the
next, its use producing a "high-pitched, copious" tinkle, para-
phrasing Proust, but a far cry from my doorbell's muted tone,
which now, once again, reaches my ears. This time, I walk
calmly toward my door, hoping against hope for a 2nd ring.

Living Room

(15 m^2)

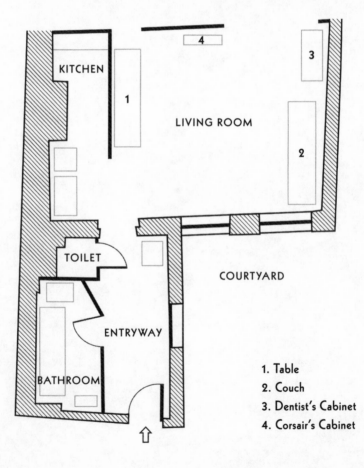

KITCHEN

1

LIVING ROOM

4

3

2

TOILET

COURTYARD

ENTRYWAY

BATHROOM

1. Table
2. Couch
3. Dentist's Cabinet
4. Corsair's Cabinet

Directly on the other side of the kitchen's half wall is the living room, even though, as I've said, the role this half wall plays is more 1 of delineation than of outright separation. Since we've already considered, at the moment we crossed the doorsill, the feeling this room as a whole gives of being the heart of the apartment, we'll focus rather on the living room's 2fold function: the 1st illustrated by the table pushed against this side of the half wall, indicating a "dining area"; the 2nd by the couch placed against the far wall, indicating a zone for "living."

Red Alert

On the table, its dimensions allowing 2 to eat comfortably, 4 agreeably, 6 easily, 8 possibly, and 10 irksomely (it's been done), there's always a tablecloth, which serves to underscore the table's purpose. The tablecloths I have available for admiration number 4: 1 white tablecloth branded with the monogram C, which I use parsimoniously, due not so much to fetishism, per se, as to its undeniable signs of wear and tear, which do, however, give it an aesthetically intriguing nuance of ragged luxury; 1 white tablecloth with dark-red stripes that I haul out for parties along with its 12 matching napkins; and then the 2 most frequently used tablecloths, the red-and-white gingham

1 and the scarlet-streaked 1. (The color red dominates all of my tablecloths.)

Most of all, it's crucial that this table never be uncovered because, despite its excellent design (1 pure 150 cm × 70 cm rectangle with 4 gray cylindrical legs), its white laminate structure is so crude that it absolutely has to be concealed.

A Moment of Domestic Grace

1:45. The coffeepot is on the table. It is full. The tablecloth is red. The hot coffee, bronze. The smell is wonderful. A slat of light slices across the floor.

A Moment of Disgrace

1:52. A sock is on the table. And so forth.

Dining Chairs

Around this table are 3 chairs that confirm that we are in a "dining room": they have to be there (and they're always there) to confer the reassuring, definitive stability to be expected from such a specific space. I own 5 of these mass-produced '50s-style wooden chairs: elongated ovals creased like opened folders, their 4 legs splayed outward, bought at an antique store on the rue de Paradis for the sum of €150.

Write or Eat

Sometimes my desk (→OFFICE) bores me and I sit myself down at the dining table to dream up some other forms of nourishment. I'm not sure if I write any differently here or there, on wood or on cloth, but how dumbfounded I was to learn that, in '68, Patrick Modiano wrote the 1st pages of his 1st book on the patio of a restaurant in Var that my father owned in '82, the brand name printed across his notebook and the grand name of this restaurant embossed across his glass of water consequently uniting with a sort of crystalline joy in the rhythmic syllables of "Claire Fontaine."

Shared Table

For the sake of changing up my workspaces, I'm writing this text on a different, 3rd table, temporary, a card table, which I can put, depending on my plans, in any room, and which I'll describe later, when we reach the rooms in which it tends to be deployed (→ OFFICE, BEDROOM).

Cushiongleton

On 1 of the chairs—the 1 on the long outward-facing side of the dining table—is a blue-tinted cotton cushion, its dimensions exceeding those of the chair's seat. Nobody could accuse me of favoring this cushion—in my mind it's somehow feminine—over all my others, for the simple reason that there are no others. It chose the chair that holds it; I could have sat on so many other symbols of comfort, but I've limited this set, C, to a single element; in modern mathematics we call such a set a singleton. My cushion's nonmultiplication explains my philosophy of furniture more clearly than words could; I appreciate comfort, but I don't cultivate it. This peacock-blue cushion is my 1 concession to the boardinghouse style; all the same, it often falls down, as a sort of mute protest, slipping from its platform too small to accommodate it, only to end up beneath the table, where it eats my dust.

Clue

Mrs. Peacock, in the dining room, with the candlestick.

The Planet on the Table

Describing this table, I've fallen into the trap of presenting an ideal and misleading view, just like travel agencies insisting there's never any rain, or store catalogs showing off their wares as impossibly spic-and-span. This uncluttered table doesn't fool me for a second; it suffers the waste and welter of the everyday. The necessity of living in an orderly world the better to counteract my internal disorder obliges me to present both sides of things at once: a space both tamed and wild. Which version of my table is most truthful? When it's fulfilling its role, bearing some lineament or character, some affluence on its airport-runway of the remains of a hurried lunch, or rather in the rectitude of its immaculate rectangle?

Still Life

As I'm writing these lines, my dining table presents the spectacle that is the battlefield of the quotidian: on the whitish tablecloth, stained here and there with rings, are 1 chipped plate full of strawberry hulls, 1 bunched-up napkin with a gingham pattern recalling those country inns that bored my childhood self to tears, 1 greasy trivet, 1 small pot with scorched handle holding cold coffee dregs, 1 ragged chunk of bread, some cheese rinds, 1 blue plastic bag holding 1 package of jumbo Spanish strawberries, some eggshell shards, 1 crumpled ball of packing paper from the store around the corner, my Scandinavian mug with rim stained brown, and even 1 vase of wilting buttercups . . . The hidden materiality behind plain, austere Dutch still lifes—which I should probably clean up so I can get on with my work.

Tidy

Every day, he has to set the table, clear it, start his various machines, move the chairs and move them again, open the cabinets, plug things in, do the dishes, unplug things again, put away the dishes, shake the tablecloth out the window—time flies when he's cleaning house. Tidying up, at 1st glance, seems a sublimely satisfying task, since it's so easily accomplished; then, however, confronted with the job's repetitiveness, he begins to feel the weight of domestic bondage. Before finally succumbing to the idea of doing a bit of work every day, he dreamed up all sorts of extreme workarounds: giving in to negligence once and for all—taking pride in it!—or living in a hotel. He fantasizes about running a housecleaning company, fixing the unemployment rate by recruiting 3,000,000 servants. Then, faced with the crumbs scattered across his floor, he gets out his broom and takes some pleasure in humiliating himself. Tidying up only drives him moderately crazy.

Untidy
The orderliness I keep with the exactitude of a Swiss guard stands wholly opposed to the domestic savagery in which some of my nearest and dearest live (my father and my partner). Disorderliness can of course produce convincing sculptural results, as in Jeff Wall's photograph *The Destroyed Room*, in which I find myself recognizing the lairs of various people I know, but, for me, I find it antithetical to the superior orderliness of Literature. Yoking the "nobility" of writing to the "petit-bourgeois" tidying of each room, and mixing them with a folk rhythm. I have this inborn inclination for managing a household. Who doesn't? What kind of mental disorder would make me prefer disorderliness?

Death in the Living Room
My living room is where disorder hurts me the most. Moot in the bathroom or toilet, unknown in the entryway, bearable in the bedroom, and welcome in the kitchen, where it's proof that a feast has been prepared, disorder is the death of the living room. This is why I wanted it to be so sparse, empty as some ancient receiving parlor.

Wallpaper or Socialism

Should a living room be emptied out to receive guests, or, rather, filled up? That is, should precedence be given to guests or to set dressing? Wouldn't too much of the latter crush the former? But, then, wouldn't emptiness bother them? And what about intrusive wallpaper? What about a plain white lounge? I try to envision all the possible setups: patterned wallpaper seemingly diminishing the room's dimensions but instigating urbane conversation by immersing the visitor in a convivial space; bareness that focuses attention back onto the guests but offers them no escape; even perversely white wallpaper that tries to resolve the contradiction by a 3rd way. Ideally, complex wallpaper (both understated and effusive) would be best, commingling amiable flowers and little narrative motifs intended to delight and instruct my guests (such as an *Illustrated History of Interior Decoration* or a *Life of Pierre Goldman*). As I await the advent of parlor socialism, I've set my sights upon decorative progress's polar opposite: austerity.

Emptiness and Fullness

The center of the living area is empty; of course, that's usually the case, the layout of such rooms having to allow for free movement. The few pieces of furniture set around this space define it by opposition. The lounge is centrifugal, radiating energy from its center, pushing my furniture back against the walls, flattening their voracious volume. Any other solution—such as grouping the pieces of furniture in the center of the room in order to walk around them—would be impractical. A tangle of furnishings would make them into a sculpture. Their functions forbid it.

Parody of a Château Owner

Making the biggest room the emptiest 1 as well calls for a concerted strategy. As financial constraints have expurgated my superficial desires, I aspire to a bare living room as revenge. (It's only within myself that I can find the consoling poetry of boundlessness.)

Site Comments

"You haven't put anything on the walls . . ."
   "Walls aren't just dead surfaces, you know."

Before Us

The line before us is the edge of the back wall (the largest 1 by surface area, the load-bearing wall of the next-door building), and our eyes land on 2 adjacent elements, my dentist's cabinet and my couch. But it's something else entirely that leaves us speechless.

The Fa—— of the House of Ush——

On the rightmost part of the large bare wall, and even broaching the perpendicular wall that looks out over the courtyard, are enormous paint blisters that bulge across 3 or 4 square meters, like some horrific disease resulting in 20 cm buboes swelling and threatening to burst with gangrenous filth. As a whole, it's not unlike those de-compositions by Michel Blazy, an artist in the medium of organic putrefaction, vegetal rot, and germinal exuberance. It's possible to court disaster and, in a gesture that no gallerist would ever allow, run your finger along this interconnected crazing, these immoderate fungosities, these pimply molderings that warp the wall, flourish like leprosy, even exposing a bit of natural stone beneath the tatters of mural flesh, and find, in the once-damp crevasses, semi-spongy yet dry mounds, lesions, and a putrid sort of eczema, all resulting in the plaster sloughing off the wall. Only a specialist in extreme dermatological disorders, a Huysmans of impetigo, could adequately describe the catastrophe this wall has involuntarily undergone—which insurance companies have baptized with the more sober name of "water damage."

Copro

I have to complete this near-coprophilic story of copropri-
etorship as seen by this apartment building's inhabitants themselves, attesting to the poverty of our imaginations when it
comes to our collective home, thanks to the cult of private
property, which loves to compartmentalize everything, and
loves no less dreaming up all the subsequent legal battles and
litigation. It took 5 years for the property management company supposedly in charge of "my" building to figure out the
cause of this leprosy assaulting my chief room. Though an aco-
lyte of art galleries and their famous white-cube design, I
meekly accepted this mycological ruination of my inner façade,
this moist psoriasis that proliferates in slabs. I neither disdain
my wall's illness nor delight in it, as might those aesthetes who
would call such a formation "beautiful." I simply put up with
it. But I am far less willing to put up with the sluggish machinery of a profession I disdain, property management, which
after so many investigations, missed appointments, shifts of
blame, and discussions, suggested these potential causes in
succession: (1) some leaks in the courtyard drainpipe that, being attached to this part of the wall, seeped into this nook; (2)
the next-door building's gutters overflowing, which resulted
in a lateral leak that landed, by pure chance, precisely on the
3rd floor (my neighbors having mysteriously avoided this fate);
(3) some error in the restoration of the inner courtyard . . . all
these hypotheses calling for years of further observation without action, even as the blisters swell to fantastical proportions.

Heterogeneity

I wanted to inject some heterogeneity into modernism. Well,
voilà.

Dentist's Cabinet

To the left of the cataclysm, adjoining the doorframe leading to
the office, stands 1 metallic cream-colored piece of furniture,
bought at an antique store on the boulevard Germain that's
long since been shuttered. With a height of 130 cm and a width
of 90, this ex–dentist's cabinet is made up of 3 parts: 2 cupboards form its base, while 9 drawers make up its middle portion; the whole is topped by a thick black glass plate, upon
which sits 1 20-cm-deep hutch protected by a sliding glass panel.
Its dual materials—metal and glass—its whiteness from which
11 black Bakelite handles protrude, its '60s neoscientific style,
both functional and elegant, all conspire to give it prominence
in the room. And, moreover, there's a delicate, enduring, yet
barely perceptible odor about it—a touch that speaks of its
former life, hinting at the soft, pink antiseptic aroma of den-
tistry.

Impure Purity

But this Anglo-Swiss object's hermeticism is kept in check by
the many objects that have colonized it, betraying the icy purity of its lines. At the risk of damaging it, I exploit its organizational capacities to the fullest, much as happened with Le
Corbusier's Unités D'habitation, which were refashioned by
their inhabitants to suit their tastes and needs, reappropriating
the too-straight lines, the too-sharp angles, the too-white
whites. Life is theory worn down by practice.

Visible Parts

Literarily speaking, I divide this unit into 2 parts, visible and
invisible. At its summit are 3 piles of "current books," the 1s
I've just bought from stores, borrowed from libraries, or had
lent to me by friends, and which await—sometimes for a long
while—their moment under my eye. These hillocks of books,

being as they are away from their natural place in the apartment, have the disadvantage of obscuring a 25-cm-high and 50-cm-wide stretch of wall and presenting the least interesting parts of their physiognomy, which is to say, the lower edges of their derrières—all in all, an ominous symptom of my home's chronic malady, its invasion by books, a steady encroachment I've failed to curtail, and such an insistent assault that I know I'll succumb to it, someday.

Mah-Jongg

Next to these 3 offending columns, I've set down a dark-red wooden Chinese box as a diversion; it sports 6 drawers and oval side mirrors and is actually an old mah-jongg set brought back from China after a short trip there in October 2010; I bought it in a flea market in Beijing but have never opened it. Indeed, I rue having acquired this curio, which just takes up space, and which accuses me, in Mandarin, of being a traitor, an idealistic petit bourgeois with exaggerated affection for his interior. That said, mah-jongg is 1 of the most beautiful games I know, and I absolutely adore teaching my friends how to play. But there, that's the 1st obstacle: I don't have any friends! Or, to be more truthful (since that last sentence is funny but false), I don't have any friends who would play mah-jongg with me. In any case, now that I'm in my 40s, my days of playing mah-jongg have passed, and I do see how the motives for such an acquisition might be regressive in intent, since I last played mah-jongg many years ago; by buying this set, perhaps I was hoping to regain something lost forever, now a mere specter: the time when I had time (to play mah-jongg).

That means this real object's heft is 2fold, since added to its physical weight (600 grams) is the weight of my past. So it takes all the mental strength I have to disencumber this red wooden structure, to free it of the associations bound to it, such as the memory of all the madcap or poetic possibilities held in the game's logograms, bamboos, and dragons, which delighted me so much at 20 years old that I wrote a short story called "A Game of Mah-Jongg," which ought to be somewhere in my archives and which retold, if I remember right, the star-crossed fates of various players in a Durassian or Morandian tone. Nobody could deny that mah-jongg is a literary game, but the ultimate proof would be that I picked up this game while in the company of . . . Catherine Robbe-Grillet!

Cold Owner

The other method for downplaying the presence of an undesired object consists of changing its orientation. I turn the box to its profile, which makes it seem smaller. Thus do I give it my own cold shoulder.

Oh, My Little Window . . .

Behind the 2 sliding glass panels, I've set up all my notebooks, like a small museum display, private yet accessible. The vitrine plays its double role of intimidation and stimulation quite well, provoking attraction at the same time as presenting an obstruction—"objects under glass" having been the inspiration for so many artists, no matter how wholesome or whoresome. If the eroticism of the showcase is so well established, its inherent charm must be in its capacity to intensify as well as reflect our interest, since it's an *object of objects* that's valuable both in itself and in what it offers up for discovery. These museum or peep-show aspects exude such an undeniable aura that I've seen people put on their own tiny exhibitions under glass: porcelain families, statuettes, knickknacks all somehow worthy of their devotion. I distinctly remember this 1 touching character, a boy who was certainly old for his age, who had set up 1 of these wood-and-glass structures in the heart of his living room and, in order to ennoble his incredible army of alabaster figurines, had even installed a network of tiny spotlights around them: as soon as he activated a little mechanism, light was cast as much upon his miniature museum as onto his peculiar 19th-century eccentricities. But it's certainly possible that I'm cut from the same cloth if I take such wretched pleasure in my own "collections."

Notebooks
My notebooks, set snug together, originally took up only ⅓ of the shelf; to their right was just a big void. In this way I created a spatial image of expectation, implicitly assuming that all the time I would spend writing, all the books to come, would be incarnated by this empty space, like those wild spaces at the edge of civilization waiting for human development. Alas, the persistently unused space wound up irritating me, if not outright infuriating me, and so I watched as this void gradually got filled by other things—1st by a small box of gray candles acting as a notebookend. I only saw the significance of this unintended prop later on: all that paper, filled with my daily notes, leaning against the threat of fire (a strictly symbolic threat, as candles have never burst into flames spontaneously). The idea that my literary apparatus could be set right next to what might destroy it didn't entirely displease me; and then, who's to say that those allegorical candles might not, 1 day, be said to correspond to the flames of genius buried within my notebooks?

As for those notebooks, I can't reveal their contents; not because I have any predilection for keeping secrets (something that couldn't possibly be more alien to me), but because they're the source of several of my ongoing or future projects: in 1 of them is the idea prefiguring the text you're now reading: a jotted-down injunction "to describe my apartment." In order to give some idea of what they're like, however, I can classify them for you: there are spiral notebooks on the left, and bound notebooks on the right. The former hark back to an era now long past (much as in the William Sheller song "Spiral Notebook," a reference that no doubt won't mean very much to my non-French readers . . .). I don't much like those iron spirals, they give me a sense of impending pain—the pain of a leaf being pulled off a tree. The pocket notebooks I've used since my spiral days are most useful for setting down my 1st "inspiration" (I don't like this romantic word), or rather the 1st spurt (I prefer this dynamic word), of an idea to be fully fleshed out. On their covers, white labels bear the year of their vintage, attesting to the care I bestow upon this museum of myself.

Obituary

Some of the notebooks pertain to the obsessions I had in my childhood, such as the mortuary notebook in which I jotted down the names of writers who had died, grouped by age, from 20 years old (Radiguet) to 100 (Fontenelle)—a habit from when I was 25 and was already thinking about myself in historical and posthumous terms. Marking the dead, like a hiker marking the pines he walks past in a forest, was my way of affirming that I was still alive, as a record keeper, and considering myself a potential, if still active, member of the list.

What Do I Know? Everything.

Resting against the Clairefontaine notebooks and the candles is a minuscule portion—39 titles—of the immense *Que sais-je?* collection. This proximity between my notebooks and the volumes of such a famous educational series can be explained by my concept of Literature, which is to express the totality of my world. Encyclopedism excites me. I own such bestsellers as *The Koran* (no. 1245) and *Elementary Particles* (no. 1293), as well as lesser-known works such as *Inertial Navigation* and *Hygiene in Daily Life*, which together contribute to a troubling psychical mosaic . . .

Invisible Glass
The lower part of the cabinet is made up of disappointingly mismatched glass shelves, since 2 of them were broken during my last move. The glazier insisted that it was impossible to reproduce the desired sort of warped glass, akin to the clouded variety found in my bathroom, and it's just this sort of detail that we might use to gauge the shortcomings of any ideology of authenticity that would condemn the fragile steward of such vitreous beauty to eternally lament the impossibility of its reproduction, not to mention the failure of just such fanatics of standardization to insist on uniform tiles in entryways, uniform windowpanes, and so on. Be that as it may, these supporting shelves are at least invisible.

Peekaboo
"Dental" is actually a useful term for any sort of cabinet, implying, as it does, their 2 contrary functions, revealing and concealing. The upper half bares its teeth; the lower half keeps its lips sealed. If I ever open the 2 doors at the bottom of my cabinet, I immediately want to shut them again, because I'm depressed by the complete disorder they reveal: books piled in haphazard clusters, folders shoved any which way, files about to burst apart. To deal with all this, a set of radical solutions comes to mind: elimination (that is, downgrading the status of everything to trash), donation (but who would want the most recent book by X?), relocation (the grand dream of this entire book), or, finally, occlusion (which is always my ultimate decision). All told, I mainly like to meditate on the iron door's sleek elegance, and the hopeless morass groaning behind

it—it's like an inverse skeleton, in which a hard surface of bone conceals the agitation of the organs within. A cabinet is a body near to bursting.

Nonbooks

Whatever could justify such dejection? The fact that my cabinets are filled with books that I don't like at all, and that I don't want to be part of my library. There are more and more things I don't like about them too: the space they take up; the weakness that forces me to keep them; the hesitation that keeps me from throwing them out; the doubts I have about the literary status quo; the irreverence, bordering on contempt, they betray toward Literature; the idea that my own books might, in the hands and homes of similar readers, meet the same fate; their seeming ineradicability, since I don't want to simply throw them out, but I know they're unsellable, by virtue of being both shopworn and uninteresting; the perverse usefulness they still retain, at least some of them, which keeps me from chucking them because I might page through an old issue of *Temps modernes* from April 1965, and find a good article on the Livre de Poche series of paperbacks; the ugliness of their disorganized accumulation; and certainly many other reasons too, not least of which is that the books have generally been given, if not outright written, by people I know, and respect, and sometimes even love, and whom I can't help but think I'm somehow snubbing by ostracizing these gifts that I go on to snub anyway. And now I do understand those old writers who ended their lives surrounded by just a few volumes— the 1s they've decided, at the end of an otherwise more tolerant and welcoming existence, are definitive.

All the contradictions inherent in the way in which I fetishize the book-as-object are here on display: after all, if everybody got rid of their books, there wouldn't be any more writers, because the object that justifies their activity would no longer be supported by anyone. Thus, this shelf of rubbish functions as a hidden counterpoint to my official bookshelves: an underworld of mediocrity, which finds justification as a contrast to my office's bookshelf rows of excellence, just as honest men are proof of humanity's range of possibility.

Cowboy/Chiasmus Showdown

This room ain't big enough for 2 messes, so I've decided to put these 4 shelves in a chiasmus: in positions A (top left) and D (bottom right) are the books, while documents and random papers go in positions B (top right) and C (bottom left); if I take 10 paces back, that'll draw a cross doing its best to make up for a collection that I'm closing shut now. I'm not kicking in the cabinet door like some cowboy would, although I'm using my foot all the same . . .

On Darkness

Coming back to the surface, there's real beauty in the black glass sheet at chest height that forms the cabinet's top surface. More disorder often disgraces this blackness that's so beautiful—so perfectly riveted at both ends—when allowed to remain uncontaminated. Whenever I return to my apartment, this is where I immediately plop down the following things: my métro pass, my current notebook, my cell phone, my watch, some Kleenex, and, in a yellow ashtray—a gesture I particularly enjoyed, back when I didn't carry a wallet—whatever small change I've accumulated. This act of casting off 1's possessions was, apparently, characteristic of François Truffaut, who, upon coming home, felt a physical need to empty his pockets: he even filmed this personal gesture and attributed it to 1 of his fictive doubles in a film the hero of which I, in turn, have come to imitate in his imitation of my imitation.

Ashes and Diamonds

Toss that change in the yellow ashtray. My relationship to money is a scorched 1: I spend it without joy, and the cold ashes of the remaining coins give off no pleasing scent.

The Promontory and the Projector

On this ledge there's also 1 small 10 cm wooden block with a slit in it; I lodge letters, invitations, and other reminders of my exterior life in this crack. Liberated from a Toulouse café where it diligently held menus, it presents me with my present as effectively as a window dresser assiduously updating his display. It's a small promontory, its lighthouse the silver-plated metal lamp 58 cm to its left boasting a swiveling head and a heavy base but providing scant illumination. I aim its paltry beam at the nearest corner: I project a small light so I can admire what I own.

Minimalism & Publicity

The middle part of the dentist's cabinet comprises either 3 columns of 3 drawers or 3 rows of 3 drawers each. Each handle, black and gleaming—finely rendered eyebrows, Nike swooshes, minimalist sculptures—unfurls from ivory bedrock.

1st and Last Numbers

How should these drawers be numbered? It doesn't matter, but I do want to say that numbers 1 and 9 are indisputable: the others change their designations according to the method, whether vertically or horizontally, by column or by row, used to numerate them. Only the 1st and last really count.

Not-So-Secret Compartments

The bottom of each drawer is 1 thick glass plane originally intended to hold the dental practitioner's blunt instruments. These days, they welcome items ranging from mere stationery to the wholly ambiguous: envelopes, notecards, blank notebooks, future munitions in my arsenal. The fullest 1, in fact, serves as a virtual cemetery of information, both official (restaurants, useful addresses, business cards) and unofficial, as in the case of a simple torn-off slip of paper with a phone number hastily scribbled down, along with a 1st name that's usually feminine. Their accumulation proves that life, uh, finds a way. The most Ali-Baban drawers contain various odds and ends, such as ink cartridges, foreign coins in a small bag, rubber bands, perfume samples, Indian lip balm, batteries, etc. (this word, strictly speaking, should be verboten). Every so often I like to pretend I'm playing my old childhood game of rifling through the magic drawers of grown-ups, drawers I used to open with a pleasure mixed with curiosity and fear, hoping to find some treasure within. Now that I'm an adult myself, however, I tend to open these drawers fearing nothing but some wasted time.

Coasters

These depths aren't as deep as they seem: a particular collection of card-stock coasters lingers there. I'd once attempted to assemble a full set, but that collector's impulse has long since gone. Now I touch these white shapes with yellowed brands stamped on them, and feel nothing so much as a faded longing that briefly shines its light and then disappears almost as quickly as did the vague desire that started all this.

Abolished Baubles

39 coupons, which my Chinese dry cleaner foisted upon me, are also scattered here, ultimately redeemable for a massive porcelain vase (maybe even 2) that I'll never claim from him. These small squares of pink paper represent a significant economy of space compared to the ugliness of an earthenware pot made in Zhengdong. I'd never let those baubles—which are

supposed to reward my textile fidelity, but may not actually exist, for all I know—overwhelm my living room: still, I don't want to take my business elsewhere, so if they pester me about this, I'll cash in my chips right before Christmas.

Ash Fire

In number 6 (or 8) I've left a package of cigarettes I bought 11 years ago, and in 5 (or 7) a Bic lighter bought 11 months ago. I could have united these 2 accessories in the same drawer, but I wanted to separate them: thus is tobacco addiction staved off by this distancing of its instruments, as if the 1 might die off without the other—maybe this method of conscious "dissociation" actually succeeds in freeing people from their addiction. (If so, maybe I'll get around to registering the patent someday.) But then why keep this package of Royales, with its coffin-shaped warning message, SMOKING KILLS, when tobacco holds no sway over me? As a souvenir of spring 2002, when, at a loss, I decided to take up smoking for the sake of all the things I'd never done (a wise strategy against melancholy): at the very age when so many people fight to give up this drug, I wanted to try it, and for several days I smoked the few Royales I had at hand, removing them from this package, which now holds just 4 cigarettes. Likewise, along with the idea of smoking itself (which quickly loses its luster), the notion of being able to give a cigarette to fellow smokers intrigued me for its conversational opportunities. This caprice soon passed, without even giving me the least bit of pleasure; all the same, I kept the package of Royales in case someone ever wanted to smoke at my place. The lighter doesn't seem to hail from any particular era, it's red and anonymous and allows me to pull off a performance called "The Poor Man's Serge Gainsbourg," which I could only explain through some medium that isn't paper.

Papers
The 9th drawer, on the bottom and all the way to the right, holds more durable things: 1 Banque populaire checkbook, a payment method that, like so many other of my countrymen, I use less and less. Checkbooks haven't disappeared outright, of course, but they've certainly made themselves scarce, content to sit and wait, like very slow-growing trees still hoping, 1 day, to bear fruit. Once modern, they've become obsolete without even garnering the sympathy due to obsolete things.

The other "important" item here (even though I don't really believe in an item's inherent importance; each 1 is only valuable in terms of my relationship with it) is my gorgeously Bordeaux-red passport. I don't really have a passion for travel, so it can't compete with the papers of devoted world travelers, but, then again, the overwhelming variegation 1 finds in the pages of their passports has never made much of an impression on me. There's only 1 country I've ever visited properly, and that's the apartment I consider my home!

Is the Lounge Passé?
To the right of the dentist's cabinet, not even a hop, skip, and jump from it (1 20 cm channel separates the 2, to let the space "breathe"), my "lounge" finds its function incarnated in a contemporary couch. For some, lounges are on the way out, owing to the 19th-century lifestyle they presuppose, which is made manifest in the couch itself. Did I buy a modernist model to negate this potential obsolescence? Is the lounge passé? It might be, but when it comes to interior decoration, preferences vary: a given client's "request" doesn't mean anything, but rather signals everything and nothing. And, true to that complete nonspecificity, a lounge both implies worldly conversations and can serve to drive people away when they have nothing to say, which is often. But my acquaintances are less like carps than like koi, and I love talking to myself.

1 Couch for 4

My Habitat couch takes up most of the back wall it's set against. As it's 206 cm wide and 65 deep, 4 humans can sit on it. I picked it for its restrained style, reminiscent of the '60s, and I never use it as a bed; in fact, I hate how a portion of the population, overwhelmingly drawn to the prospect of having totally modular homes, considers that prospect a selling point. I want beds to be beds, and couches to be couches. Tautology is the fate of all good furnishings. There's something honest in an object devoting its entire life to a single task; in contrast, the multipurpose style amounts to nothing more than a simpering flattery of its user. Objects with multiple applications are only seductive at 1st, as when we hear some furniture trade-show salesman insisting that the chair of the future will show the time on its armrest, or tell your weight as you sit down . . .

To the best of my knowledge, nobody's slept on my couch save for 1 Italian baby I saw for maybe 10 minutes when I rented out my apartment in the summer of 2006 (€300 for 1 week) while staying at my girlfriend's place in the 6th arrondissement—an experience I won't repeat, not because it went poorly (though it's true that Paris's city council has hunted down several homeowners supplementing their income with this under-the-table subletting), but because the idea of strangers living in my place, even temporarily, for rental purposes, bothers me.

The Awkwardness of Having Friends Stay Over

Better not to have any guest rooms.

On the Couch of an Artist or Snob . . .

This couch's purity of form, thanks to its faux wood structure and the charcoal gray of its cloth, as well as its black metal base, looks good against this white wall. And it doesn't bother me that this couch-cum-bench is only a replica of a more famous model; on the contrary, I'd be reluctant to scorn the inter-twined qualities of comfort and design on such a meager basis. As such, this couch is, if you will, neoclassical, or neo-modern, both of which are absolutely intolerable in literature or in art; when it comes to furniture, though, I'm much less interested in "classification," in "labels," than I might be in those other spheres. There was no museum here before I de-cided to assemble this 1. And in the same vein, the couch of a snob has to assert its values upon its uncaring surroundings, whereas an artist's couch is self-sufficient—for better or for worse. (And the artist shouldn't be confused with the aesthete. Their respective apartments are proof thereof.)

Brief Dialogue Between These 2 on the Couch

"Real artists care about their art, not about their apartments."

"Real artists inject their artistry into everything, even their homes."

"No, because to have art in everything would mean the end of art. Nothing could be differentiated."

"My painting isn't negated by being hung on a painted or wallpapered wall!"

"It's diminished, though."

"Pass me a Coke."

"In a Lalique glass?"

Purity Furnished

The couch's perfect lines suit its immaculately dark cover, which has never—knock on wood, as they say, and specifically the wood of this armrest—suffered any stain or blemish. And on that front I recognize a concrete component of my person-ality: conscientiousness, being far more respectful of posses-sions than are many members of the human population. It's the antique collector's fantasy to keep an object intact indefinitely.

My couch will certainly survive its owner. Its purity is, all the same, tainted by the presence of the magazines I've heaped in piles on its left side (where I never sit), and likewise by the television, which is situated more or less in front of them. These peripheral couch-zones offer up moments of fleeting distraction: casual skimming, inattentive listening. I do indulge from time to time.

The Guests Haven't Arrived

I invited Walter Benjamin and Paul Scheerbart for aperitifs, but they never came. I also invited Ernst Bloch, but I made a mistake and called his homonym who, even so, didn't get the invitation. I ended up all alone, like a fool, on the couch sipping from my champagne flute. I thought back on all the parties I'd hosted, and I shut my eyes.

List of Famous People Who Have Visited My Apartment

N.W., J.C.M., J.P.A., D.W., V.M., Q.B., L.G.T., A.O., F.A.-T., E.S., O.S., J.M., P.B., J.B., B.S., T.S., J.P., S.R., E.R., S.B., S.B., A.B., A.B., E.L., B.C., J.C., J.P., J.P., T.C., T.C., M.C., M.C., J.M.C., V.A., J.M., B.C., S.D., J.C.-F., M.F., G.D., J.M.F., L.F., M.-E.F., B.G., L.G., S.G., S.G., C.G., M.G., P.G., N.H., F.C., V.L., L.J., S.M., J.L.J., F.L., F.H., G.L., M.T., F.M., A.L.-R., P.B., A.D., A.T., F.F., S.R., M.B., M.K.

Marxist Illumination

On the floor, a huge, luminous white plastic ball is both decoration and illumination. A cord connects it to an outlet behind the couch, but the light switch on the right when 1 enters the room turns it on and off. The distance between the lamp and its controller is about 3 meters, and they're not even at the same height: a banal sort of magic that suffices to unite mind and matter. In fact, the ball's position on the floor corresponds to my preferred approach to illumination, from the bottom up (and, as per my diatribes against ceiling lights, not from the top down). As far as illumination, as in so many other domains, I believe the lowermost things define the uppermost. Marxist illumination is far more effective and noble than aristocratic illumination with its sad hanging chandeliers scattering lifeless light over yellowed rooms on late Sunday afternoons. I love it when light, like joy, rises.

Ball of Nerves
Touching this ball, even when the light is off, is soothing: spherical forms, globes, round objects all create an atmosphere of warmth. Still, nobody would ever want to live in a housesphere. Circles on a grand scale are unnerving.

Gender Inequality
As I contemplate this ball, it reveals a luminous truth. Interior decoration is design made mundane. Design exists for its own sake, but as decoration establishes its dominion it still can't erase that unnerving, uncontrollable trace of its triviality. Decoration barely hides the crime of its nature. And as if the gender embedded in these French words were playing out on a human scale, the femininity of *la décoration* has a seductive hold over its masculine rival, *le design*: an unwonted, almost sexist, certainly French lust keeps pulling me toward those objects that, in my language, are always feminine—*la lampe*, *la radio*, *la carafe*—to hug them close.

Spatiovoracious
Right in front of the couch's left side, set on a black plastic Tam Tam stool, is my television, a gift my friends Quentin and Emma Bajac gave me after they purchased a flat-screen. The block jutting out behind these older models is considerable; old technology simply devours space. Sony-branded, gray-

colored, square-framed, pockmarked with holes for emitting sound, its screen has, even when turned off, an indefinable pond-bottom color in which are reflected the occasional magazines on the couch 10 centimeters away: thus is the written press reflected in television's dead screen, a perfect allegory of journalism today.

The years of my childhood were bathed in anti-television iconoclasm, but I switched ideological channels for a time, only to return to the 1 of my youth, when the images I devoured were (as they now are again) of wholly other kinds; it's unthinkable that I would sit in front of this box, which I barely watch except for sports (soccer/tennis) and TV news (like the fastest-aging part of the population), less to inform myself and more to feed on leftovers: no dish offers such an immediate array of flavors, ranging from horrid to divine, revolting and delighting the palate.

Remote

The TV is now inseparable from the Freebox-brand router and cable box on its right, which is controlled by 1 of the 2 remotes I keep on the TV's housing, the other being the remote for the TV itself. Remote controls count among those modern objects practically devoid of any special aura, having by now been produced in such large numbers by the industry that their magic is all but gone. When remote controls 1st appeared during my childhood, I remember being mystified by the "magician" who, having hidden his remote, turned his television on and off by snapping his fingers in front of my stupefied eyes.

An Inquiry Concerning Propinquity

What can I do without moving? What is the full range of actions available to me without changing position? On the couch, it's switching channels while flipping through a magazine; in bed, it's grabbing a book from the mantel, picking up a pencil behind the lamp, aiming that lamp, drinking from the bottle at the foot of the bed, pulling out the tissue hidden in my pillow-case, tapping on my cell phone; in my bathtub, it's using some soap or shampoo, adjusting the water with my foot; sitting at my desk, it's surfing the Internet, with a glass in my hand. Moving around bits and pieces of my home.

Telefairy

From the beginning, television was something out of a fairy tale: for almost all children of my generation, a primordial wonderment radiated from the set. Now it's been supplanted by the Internet, its presumably unique empire having been proved unexceptional, and I suppose its relative decline con-tributes to the particular sympathy I feel for this old plastic dinosaur with all its pathetic vainglory, turned off more than on. The television is like an outdated future—obsolete as only a truly backward machine can be—whose posthuman, maybe even postapocalyptic character can be seen in the dust that's settled on the screen (I almost never "clean" my television). Even its blocky form—modernity was never so angular again— is undeniably dated. So it's safe to say I've foreseen the fate of this idol with feet of clay set upon the round plinth of my light-weight Tam Tam stool (far lighter than the TV itself).

Support

The Freebox cable box rests, physically and consonantly, upon a cardboard box that acts as a low table. This box's 6 faces are covered with a trompe l'oeil design of piled-up books: this little piece of nonfurniture was a gift from my brother and sister-in-law, and echoes the very real books that furnish my apartment—an ironic allusion to my bibliomania. I accept such things only grudgingly, if they're an imposition—"beware

Greeks bearing gifts," and all that—but the affection I feel for the aforementioned people made it easier to break with convention on this point (I guess my conventions aren't very serious). It goes without saying that the place 1 lives in is always going to be shaped to some degree by others, which is why I'm taking the time to point out the provenance of any objects I've received as gifts, as well as naming their givers, both out of a partiality for precision and because, after all, intimacy is also extimacy.

The bookish cardboard base and the cable box on top of it serve to connect the 2 dominant medias of our time, literary and audiovisual, which I've never dreamed of pitting against each other, unlike certain literary hacks who, at this point, are hardly worth mentioning.

Fetterbox

Honestly, I don't have any respect for this Freebox device (or for the eponymous company), for the simple reason behind all my primary objections to technology—it's not straightforward. If I want to watch TV, I now have to perform 3 actions, in stark contrast to the simplicity of old: 1st, I have to wait 10 seconds—during which the time showing on the box's little screen, in ugly greenish letters, is followed by equally useless, redundant words I never asked to see, like *rock-n-roll*, *video*, *television*, and even *network*—for the Freebox to start relaying the channels; 2nd, I have to turn on the set; and, for my 3rd gesture, I finally press the button for the desired channel. More than 30 seconds to achieve a result that once took as little time as the miracle of electricity itself . . . Which is how I've missed, thanks to slight miscalculations, various crucial moments: soccer-game kickoffs, for example, or the faces of people in politics or in the end credits—all thanks to a crew for whom the term "sons of bitches" is wholly inadequate, leaving me to nominate the term "computer scientists" as our insult of preference. Because this doesn't even take into account the numerous times the whole system has completely crashed, whereupon my best-laid plans for a measly night in, watching TV, filling a prime-time slot in my equally measly existence, have gone awry.

Strings Attached

This highfalutin box that purports to be free is actually chained by a quagmire of wires leading to a power strip, itself connected to another power strip plugged into a wall outlet that somehow still works despite the rampant humidity in this corner of the room. I almost never venture over there. I do like prowling around my apartment, but I steer clear of danger zones like this, where the cords are clearly a trap.

Networks

And here is where I happen upon my 1st spiderweb, a real 1 woven among the electrical twists and turns. I leave it alone, with its small 8-legged occupant untouched.

Making Some Noise

Standing right behind the television is the 60-cm-wide span of the wall separating the 2 living room windows. Bathing the room in strong light despite taking up only a small part of the wall, both face the inner courtyard, just like the 1 in the hallway-entryway, which makes it possible, when there are 2 people here, to talk from 1 window to the other without occupying the same room, thanks to the properties of all right angles. Conversations held in this manner are playful but short-lived: the fact is that the entire courtyard is open not only to light but to sound, whether at 4th-floor-Chinese-neighbor volumes—the 2 of them speaking at such a different acoustic level from myself that they always seem to be yelling at each other—or at the virtually ultrasonic volumes utilized by the mysterious character on the 2nd floor whose hysterical outbursts regularly erupt and must surely overwhelm the poor management consultant on the other end of the telephone line with screeching about how such and such a business's profits aren't even coming close to meeting expectations.

The Bad Glazier

These ancient 6-pane windows with espagnolettes—which the man installing my double panes, using the old-fashioned argument that things should be kept new-fashioned, tried in vain to convince me to replace—boast blemishes in each pane. When I pointed this fact out to him, hinting that this might be a problem he'd have to fix, he put a stop to his spiel straightaway, suddenly realizing just how a life with these flaws in the glass was actually a more beautiful 1 for these imperfections; and as I felt the stirrings of regret at having allowed him inside, I hurried him out.

Waiting Area

Both the windows have curtains made of the same white cotton as the 1 in the entryway, and both have an inner sill that serves as a shelf. On the farther-back window, by the couch, I've set a 45-cm-high Altuglas lamp with a white lampshade; it gives out a gentle light, and next to it are a diverse collection of catalogs, programs, booklets, brochures, and photo albums that anybody at the left end of the couch could just reach out and take to read in the natural light of the window or the artificial light of the lamp. In short, it's a "waiting area" that has aspirations toward being a saloon, despite not having most of the requisite trappings: a piano, a cactus, a few little chickadees, and some brandy.

OCD

I lean toward the lamp and twirl its shade so that its seam can't be seen anymore.

The 2nd Window (or the 1st)

Leaving the couch, and wending my exaggeratedly slow way like a performer making his entrance, I walk past the 2nd window—unless it's the 1st. This unquestionably pointless distinction isn't actually all that pointless, since the rearmost window is the 1st for anyone exiting the room, but the 2nd for those entering: to write this book, I take inspiration from Bruce Nauman's artistic method, which consists of exploring 1's own space, not in toto, but room by room.

Window Box with Flowers of Evil

This particular window is the 1 the burglar came through to get into the apartment. As such, it's accursed. Most of the time, its curtains are drawn. An ever-growing number of books practically prevent it from being opened anyway, so it stays closed and generally untouched. In addition to this ridiculous double protection of the books and the locked-shut window, there's also the window's exterior wrought-iron bar, to which the burglar, limber as a monkey, secured his rope, and which allowed him to climb up from the 2nd floor, break the lower-left pane of my window, pop open the espagnolette, and enter my apartment. This black bar now holds a box full of flowers that have lost all their innocence (to get rid of the bar entirely would cost €150 [off the books])—after all, it's demonstrated to me the unlimited ingenuity of evil. Whether we're arrogant owners or all-terrain thieves, we all take advantage of every possible opening.

Courtyard Spying

The 2nd window doesn't show exactly the same part of the courtyard as the 1st: it offers a direct view into a bathroom belonging not to a buxom neighbor but to a sexagenarian. At the risk of belaboring truisms, I find myself abstractly philosophizing that the view offered by a given window can't, of course, anticipate the viewer's position (much less that of the viewed), and that the various perspectives that can be observed therefrom depend wholly on the viewer's exact placement. In this concrete instance, the most diagonal of his possible perspectives goes all the way into my bedroom, such that when I'm lying in bed I can spy on 1 transom on the 4th floor, from which I myself, in turn, surely must be the object of a corresponding surveillance.

Telephone 1
The main function of this waiting area is the "telephone function." On this sill, which I'd prefer to be cleaner, I've draped 2 small lengths of linen and velvet, leftover cloth from hemming the doorway curtain, as sill covers akin to tablecloths. Corded phone number 1 (the 2nd being in my → OFFICE) rests atop this further demonstration of my textile fetishism—an admittedly "grandmotherly" touch meant to . . . muffle conversations? This bottom-of-the-barrel Doro-brand phone and handset is just as touching and repulsive as its own coiled cord writhing in empty space, but I use it so often that I've just accepted that I have to keep its long wire plugged into the phone jack (← ENTRYWAY). It's a bit too long for the width of the sill, so whenever I use this phone, I have to hold the base in place with my fingertips as I talk, to keep it from falling, especially when things get animated. If the conversation drags on, I usually sit down in the armchair; generally, though, I stay on my feet, there by the window, where it's more common for me to be seen talking on the phone than looking out at the courtyard myself: I go blind, so to speak, when the voice on the other end of the line takes me far away . . . as befits the very word *telephone*.

This device is on my France Telecom line, and I use it to *receive* calls: I could make them too, but that would cost me €0.58, whereas my Free device, as its determinedly un-French name suggests, grants me all forms of communication free of additional charge. It's a sign of the times that so few people use landlines anymore; maybe it's a sign of my age, as well, that so few people call me now at all. I'm a good ways past my child-hood, when I spent hours on the phone with my girlfriends or best friends. All this phone really does is magnify a not-entirely-unwarranted loneliness: a slightly sticky dust evinces how little I use this line that costs me €30 each month. Manager/administrators everywhere tell themselves that it's useless to keep a landline when the dominion of mobile phones is abso-lute, a fortiori when a 2nd line is installed. Yet this small fee isn't wholly futile considering the sense of security this landline gives me, not to mention the beautiful, classical, easily memo-rized 10-digit number indicating exactly where in France I'm located, which sits so nicely in my mind beside the numbers my hyperthymesia links to the people I love—so much more ap-pealing than the monotonous and uninformative Free phone prefix that's so hideous it actually discourages me from calling anyone who has it.

Such Numbers, Such Letters, Such Drawings

To the left of the phone, almost in a ministerial role, 1 *note-book* + *pencil* stand guard, ready for teleprinting, for preempting those little dramas of "Wait! Let me find a pen! A pencil!" A mini-exhibition of phone-call doodles on Post-its interlaced with information jotted down haphazardly (numbers, addresses, digicodes), which cumulatively comprise a paradoxical archive of forgetfulness, especially when the name connected to a given number has been lost. To exorcise my errors, I've also set a blue candle here, bought from a Guyanese witch doctor's dispensary (which, for anyone who cares, is described on page 79 of another of my books, namely *Paris, Museum of the 21st Century*).

Checking My Box

A phone call: I'll pick up (it's so rare). A muffled voice asks me if I live in a military bunker, a 2-star hotel, a show home, a bourgeois pied-à-terre, a medieval castle, a company apartment, a luxury mansion, or a concierge's quarters. I don't know which box I should check off because usually, on a Saturday morning, the only calls I get are either from prospective tax consultants or someone trying to sell me new windows.

Decorating or Working?

That's enough of using the phone as a phone. Now I'm playing with the handset, testing its sturdiness, and then I decide to arrange everything on this sill in a para-artistic way, starting by bisecting the space using the hardy telephone as a divider. Decoration is in my genes: Do I have to remind my inattentive readers that my great-grandfather was a painter of religious objects at Place Sulpice? On this piece of teal cloth, I've put together 1 of those little decorative embellishments I happen to adore, in this case a colorful row of small ceramic fruits and vegetables bought at the market in La Garde-Freinet, a town dear to my heart: kitschy but endearing markers of Provence in the form of a lemon, a clove of garlic, an onion, etc., in which all the South of France's schmaltzy childishness and sensuality is on full display. These tchotchkes, swapped in and out based on the seasons, call to mind Matisse and Dufy and Marquet, those great decorators, bringing an additional sun-kissed touch to an apartment that many people already tend to insist calls to mind both the countryside and the south. So I don't get tired of receiving the same compliments over and over, I switch out the trinkets for new decorations as often as I can.

Paris Salon

Farther to the left, the eye lands on a gray wire sculpture depicting 2 birds, the material for this having come from the
hangers given to me by the dry cleaner to whom I entrust my
dirty clothes. The overabundance of these hangers in my armoire (→ BEDROOM) led to these birds' spontaneous creation,
following 1 of those eureka moments common to all the great
innovators—as if I were a Brancusi of the 10th arrondissement, or a Giacometti of the interior, or a Tony Cragg of the
living room: the path forward was suddenly illuminated, and
I was driven to recycle them.

Intending to throw away 1 of these hangers, but struggling to fit it 1st into my wastepaper basket and then into my
all-purpose trash can, I started twisting it, infuriated that this
piece of trash refused to fit in either container, but marveling
nonetheless at the malleability of its metal alloy: the object
quickly took shape under my hands, I fashioned it into the
base and central column of a mini-sculpture, flattening and
bending the hanger's hook to make the head of a metal duck. I
repeated these actions with a 2nd hanger, which I wove through
the previous 1, and set the 2 ducks on the sill, 1 within the
other, curled together doggy-style. I'm no sort of artist, in
any literal sense of the term—I don't know how to make or
manufacture anything—but thanks to this *serendipity* (← EN-
TRYWAY), I was proud to have channeled my rage at 1 object
into making an object of another sort, never mind the aesthetic value it might or might not have: considered from an art
critic's point of view, after all, my ducks could even be as lowly
a creation as 1 of those artisanal-decorative artifacts found at
every stall in folk markets, or at the feet of street peddlers in
every major city. But I don't care, my wire-hanger doggy-style
ducks bring me a simple, pure joy more than worthy of their
(temporary) display. Every time I look at them, so nicely put

together, I debate whether I've merely decorated my home or whether I can say I've now done some serious artistic work. As I've been unable to decide on an answer, I pick up the phone and pretend to punch in a random string of numbers in order to ask the opinion of the 1st person I reach.

Colonel Mustard's Armchair

If, worn out by our slow, meticulous progress, the reader of this book wanted to take a brief pause, he or she could find repose in the armchair placed in front of the window farther from the couch and closer to the entryway, almost jammed up against the radiator; on its right, the corner of the Freebox device also serves as a short coffee table. This low-slung armchair, its 2 back feet curved and its 2 front feet straight but twisted, exudes an impression of comfort and stability thanks to its heavy volume, its depth, and its plush armrests curving around the seat. Covered with mustard-yellow velvet, it evokes the identically named character in that game whose board reproduces the layout of a house . . .

Clue

Colonel Mustard, in the lounge, with the revolver.

Furniture Sculpture

Living room furniture is the only kind that might explicitly serve as sculpture; whereas most other furniture is stuck along the wainscoting, there's some space for play behind these, between their backs and the wall with the windows. Indeed, the contrast between the solidity of these objects and the openness of all that could be done with and around them invalidates some of the stasis implicit in the very concept of "furnishing." Consequently, whenever I walk around 1 of these pieces of furniture, I move it a few centimeters this way or that, much as the Renaissance-era owners of trunks and chests (*cassoni*) hid the erotic scenes painted on their backs by pushing them against the walls, hoodwinking their visitors.

Labiche Communism

I asked for this stereotypically bourgeois armchair as a present for my 20th birthday, a detail that still embarrasses me. I'm ashamed even to set it down in writing, since the idea of associating "the best time of life" with a squat armchair seems somewhat sinister, despite the chair's quirkiness, and somewhat overbearing, despite the chair's coziness, as if I were preparing for a future as a Labiche character. And would you believe me if I told you that the person who did lob precisely this same caustic remark at me 25 years ago was himself the descendant of Eugène Labiche? Probably not, but you'd be wrong. (Céline's already denounced "Labiche communism," which is to say a standard-issue attachment to standard-issue household comforts, to the ownership of identical mass-produced goods, populating all French interiors.) Anyway, whether or not this admission impugns my character, it's true that I appreciate my armchair with all the amiability of a petit-bourgeois gentleman pondering some brilliant crime while sipping a very nice whiskey. The fact that it's survived so many years, in contrast to nearly all my other furniture, is quite moving to me, especially considering that not even its seller has had such good fortune: an antiques dealer in Le Marais back in the '80s who no longer himself surveys the decrepit rue Vieille-du-Temple where his store still stands. I do like to repose in this armchair from time to time; when I've "got company," though, I leave it for some distinguished guest. As I settle myself comfortably into Mustard, a tagline from the series *Alfred Hitchcock Presents* pops into my head, something like: "Sitting back in a nice armchair? Got the footrest up? Now get ready to enjoy . . ."

Romany Art

Sometimes I use this armchair as a temporary coatrack. And
in winter I use its back, facing the radiator, to dry my clothes
faster; having thus turned my living room into a wilderness, I
then turn myself into a stereotypical Gypsy, and in my fantasy
I'm renting a luxury vacation home so that I can ruin it completely: do some barbecuing in the bedroom, clean and dirty
clothes flung everywhere, tools lying haphazardly, food in
heaps, all the TVs turned on, car parked dangling off the edge
of the swimming pool, and so on. What a delight to wreck a
house like this, a hotel room, a *villa triste* . . .

Meat on the Balcony

Sitting comfortably in the armchair and reading, in a position
where ¾ of my back is facing the window, my mind carried
away by fiction, my body stuck in fact, I suddenly sense, behind
me—enough to distract me from this swashbuckling adven-
ture novel—the presence of something that shouldn't be there.
I turn my head and, stunned, jump up at once. The top of the
window has been engulfed by . . . meat!

Before running up to the 4th floor for some explanation,
I examine these long strips of dark-red flesh hanging in the air
from a plastic hanger. Chinese pork or poultry held in place by
tiny clothespins. A nightmare from above.

Inalienable Object No. 7

Just behind this armchair, anchored beneath the right-hand
window, is the 1st of 3 electric wall-mounted radiators that I
"own": the largest 1 (60 cm × 44 cm), commensurate with the
room's size. This kind of device is a blemish on the reputation
of any good bourgeois apartment dweller, for whom heating,
as a criterion, is paramount, and therefore most legitimately
incarnated in the form of heating known as central. A warm

home is a good home: as I was 1st about to start arranging all my furniture, an architect friend of mine reminded me of this aphorism—1 that tends, if such work is begun in spring or summer, to be forgotten. The wisdom pronounced by men whose areas of expertise we know nothing about becomes like poetry. But it wasn't due to a lack of foresight that I opted for electric radiators.

Charmless, Aimless

My electric radiator is disappointingly charmless. I look at it frequently, giving it another chance; on its best days it seems like a sort of infrasculpture, on its worst it's simply itself, not even offering the pleasure afforded by a 3-dimensional wood-burning stove or a portable radiator on wheels, which can at least be observed from every side. Because of its relative efficiency, I simply judge it in terms of its function. If, feeling cold, I look to it for the heat I don't have, I have to concede that it works: that, as with any heating device, immediate results are their most reassuring quality, but in this case, its sphere of influence doesn't extend past a few meters. In winter, or "Novembapril," I often spend stretches of time standing right in front of it, feeling the heat permeating my clothes from back to front, rubbing my hands, or dreamily drinking a cup of tea. There, I am observed by a chilly impersonality, calm, its gaze empty and aimless as its warmth radiates into my idle form, and soon I'm nothing but a mindless body, made torpid by the heat—a robot that has become 1 with this living room. Then the convection galvanizes me, and having been fortified with a healthy dose of heat, I can go.

Light Show

On the most dreadful winter nights, to better engage the enemy, I've come up with a thorough plan for mobilizing all the forces at my disposal: activating every heater switch in the entryway, and while their power builds, turning on my oven as well as its 4 stovetop burners, plugging in the teakettle, lighting my candle (→ *infra*), and flipping both living room light switches at once, so that its every inch is alight. A light show, an absolute spectacle, in which everything comes together to make the place blaze with luminous heat!

Getting Up from the Armchair . . .

Getting up from the armchair, where I've lingered for too long, I take several steps over the floorboards, which I've varnished attentively. This honeyed plain stretches through every room in my apartment—flowing into my bedroom as well as my office as a contrast to the white walls. The ensemble confers a perhaps uncritical but nonetheless profound sense of belonging to the austere fellowship of Parisians who prefer to strip away all deception. I see my communal condition reflected in the gleaming varnish of this glorious, persuasive parquet. I congratulate myself on having freed it from the immoral prison of linoleum imposed by its previous owner—a man of a very different social position from myself, who apparently lived in a hovel!

Image Found in the Lino

Pulling up the linoleum revealed a treasure: a color photo showing a man in swimming trunks, posed on a platform, during a summer performance at some '70s-era Club Med in front of an audience of cheering women dressed in long tunics, among whom I immediately recognized, beyond a shadow of a doubt, my landlady, only 20 years younger—the photo an exact contemporary of the linoleum.

Banalities

If, as Poe insists, "a carpet is the soul of the apartment," then my apartment has 0 soul. I'm well satisfied by the bare planarity of my floor, and I don't want to add a 2nd layer to it with a carpet that would subsequently accumulate enough dust to constitute a 3rd. If I had to put in a carpet, I'd choose 1 with a design resembling dust . . . But whereas my white walls positively revel in their blankness and require no art to glorify them—notwithstanding the plaudits this wordsmith is now providing for you—my floorboards are so basic and banal that they welcome every possible banality by way of description: "home sweet home," "tonal harmony," "cheap bourgeois junk" . . .

The Corsair's Cabinet

Now I'm nearing the wall 3 meters in front of the-armchair-from-my-20th, close to touching what is without question the most beautiful piece of furniture I own, so beautiful it surely must have caught my visitor's eye upon pushing aside the linen curtain on the page he or she entered the living room. In fact, set in the middle of the wall separating the 2 entrances—to my bedroom on the left and to my office on the right—it's front and center, intentionally set in a place of honor. This dark-brown wood piece of furniture on 4 sturdy legs, 160 cm high and 77 cm wide, is from the 16th century. It belonged to my father, who gave it to me. Person-size, it serves as a cabinet and as a set of shelves—in short, a repository standing a few centimeters off the ground. The upper half houses a vault sealed by 1 latched door; below are 2 23-cm-deep shelves; last comes the empty space between the 2 supports forming its base, revealing the floor between and beneath its feet. Its rough-hewn look defies my living room's arbitrary modernity, offering a determined antithesis. Its murky, veined wood calls to mind a ship; I call this my "corsair's" cabinet; I've been around it all my life, as it was a part of the apartment I lived in during my childhood in Auteuil—a place I've never seen again, in contrast to Lars von Trier, who, as you may know, bought his childhood

home (an endeavor that in my case would be both difficult—
considering that prices per square meter have multiplied by
200 since 1965—and psychologically reckless). Carrying its
past life along with it, the "Corsair" imbued this space with a
new splendor. I'd happily recount the complete history of all
its owners from the 16th century onward, but since I don't
know all the facts, I guess the only way I could call the history
"complete" would be if I filled things out with quite a bit of
fiction . . .

It charms me to think that my cabinet existed alongside
Rabelais or Jean Bart; a stranger to more refined eras, such as
that of Louis XVI, whose style leaves me cold, it harks back to
epochs that better suit my own idea of culture, vibrant 1s such
as the Renaissance, which it celebrates in full measure. This
piece of furniture is a metonym for my father, and I associate
it with him not only because it stood in his office when I was
a child but also because it emanates the same sort of compactness, of virile charm. Even though there's no question that the
cabinet is the centerpiece of my apartment, its aesthetic qualities
have hardly condemned it to a merely decorative function: its
uppermost section, shut, safeguarded by a small hatch reminiscent of a lip-height confessional, serves to hold my various
liquors and liqueurs, just as it did (or so I'm told) for its previous owners. A warm woody scent, as if the cabinet were per-
spiring alcohol, seeps out every time I undo the latch that
protects its contents. Next to some bottles of rum or Ricard
or wine, my eye lands on a cocktail shaker, some napkins, some
herbal teas, or some candy reinforcing the "secret stash" aspect
of this unit that I imagine a priest or a pirate might have used
to hide a ciborium, or some money, or a firearm. As for my
father, he used it to hide away the Browning gun that so fascinated me when I was a child and, being both accursed and
esteemed, anointed him with an aura of holiness, his life with

an overtone of intensity—and what could be more important than the intensity of life?

Some years later, a woman I was in love with came to my place. She was as struck by the cabinet's mysterious beauty as I was by her own, and she asked me what was behind its door, whereupon I let her see. Opening Pandora's box, revealing Pulcinella's secret, namely the secret that there is no secret (as in Henry James's novels, in which characters wait entire lifetimes for revelations too irrelevant to ever come to light), I immediately regretted having obeyed her wishes, as if in doing so I had shattered the very image of desire, symbolized so well by the image of a box being opened that Titian himself depicted it in the middle ground of his *Venus of Urbino*, now at Florence—I never saw the woman again.

Its 2 Shelves

The cabinet's 2 shelves hold books that, because they aren't on any coffee table, I wouldn't consider coffee table books. It's rather difficult to fit them in there, especially the biggest 1s; I have to do it like those movers able to angle furniture so carefully they can maneuver it through narrow porticoes or into an elevator cage—namely, in my case, pulling out X volumes in order to add in just 1. As such, I very rarely touch these cloistered possessions that enjoy such extraterritoriality in their distance from my official bookshelves that they don't blink twice at the sound of language far saltier than a librarian's stern "Shush!" Open to all onlookers, instantly accessible, these exhibit catalogs, magazine issues, curiosa, and other colorful printed matter (whose numbers I keep to an absolute minimum) have been brought together here in a wooden structure that surrounds them absolutely, completely, superbly. Which is not to say that there aren't several actual books here that are quite dear to me, mostly on the upper shelf, though these sit alongside other books that inspire utter indifference, all in a disordered order whose chaos adds some spice to my pirate library, in accordance with its coarse and barbaric container: François Truffaut's complete correspondence, a present for my 19th birthday, the same year he died; the catalog of Le Grand Jeu, Surrealism's little-known rival group, the book that sparked my triple attachment to avant-garde movements, serious games, and 2nd-stringers; a collection of American objectivist poetry, which completely put me off of the French neolyricism of René Char and Saint-John Perse; various issues of *Trafic*, *L'Infini*, *Trouble*, *Lignes*, *Poétique*, and *La Revue littéraire*; and an orphaned middle volume of *Le Robert historique* (F–PR), as lonely as a blank alexandrine. The 2nd shelf parallels its sister: 8 issues (out of 12) of *Perpendiculaire* magazine appear alongside 2 issues of the *Revue de littérature générale*. Other scattered copies of *Poétique*, the *NRF*, and *Fig* complete this incompleteness peculiar to magazines, in which we must resign ourselves to browse at random, content to find, I don't know, an article telling us that the boatloads of cataphoric pronouns in *La Duchesse de Langeais* are matched only by something wholly unconnected, like the number of Peruvian pop stars. Then there are the aforementioned exhibit catalogs, which I hardly ever touch: some on the American artist Shirley Jaffe, whose work is vivid and colorful; 1 titled *72* that offers up some "artists' projects" even as the climacteric number "72" exerts a particular effect on me; it harks back to the year when I attained "the age of reason," the year of my father's downfall and my parents' separation (I love when an event completely extrinsic to a book's contents deepens 1's interest in it retroactively); 1 collection of uncaptioned black-and-white photos by Hans-Peter Feldmann, drawn from various earlier books of his, making up a sort of massive tracking shot across his life; 1 biography of Dominique de Roux, whose fascist proclivities seem not to have hampered his decisive flair; 1 *Polyphonix* catalog celebrating the festival's fusion of oral poetry and performance; and 1 *Guide de Paris mystérieux*, revised edition, given to me by my friend Bruno Gibert—which is odd, because my father kept an identical copy of this book in this same bookcase circa 1975. My own book collection was assembled partly out of a desire to refute my father's, but there are still some points of convergence. If this bookshelf were a parking garage, and so each shelf a different concrete level, it would take a long, long, long time for all the old cars to drive away and be replaced with brand-new imports.

The Glass Chimes, the Candle Burns, the Aesthete Dies

Occasionally, at the top of this beloved cabinet, a long candle will burn in a glass tube adorned with a cross, which complements several other glass tubes kept down below with pseudo–Louis XIII elegance. The set is overshadowed by a terra-cotta vase decorated with white seahorses in ceramic medallions. Oh, the aesthete in me could just go to heaven!

Built out of Pliz

I clean this masterpiece with our version of Pledge, Pliz. Alas, my can of this concoction must have lost some of its strength, because a small brown mound has built up, nonetheless, by the spines of these books, as if some ghost were eating away at all this from within. Not termites—just the Corsair's very slow decomposition, forcing me to come to terms with the ephemerality of all things. I've always lived in a dream of eternity, a denial of death, which means I like to believe that buildings, houses, furnishings, and artworks are all unchangeable. And so I keep dwelling anxiously on Paul Chemetov's line: "By the time they've paid off their mortgages, their houses won't be worth anything because they were so shoddily built . . ."

Lamp at the Foot of the Edifice Feet

By its left foot (which is to say my right) stands 1 60-cm-tall lamp with a round base crowned by an opaque white glass bowl which turns on with the pull of a little cord wired to a low switch. The juxtaposition of a unique piece of furniture with a workaday object is a proven decorative strategy, making for a wonderful effect that shows off each piece at its best. An apartment filled with nothing but unique furnishings would come off as rather loud in its over-refinement, whereas an apartment completely furnished with mass-produced objects would wind up rather eerie. I reject those homogeneous interiors set forward as models by "deco" magazines, which love to lavish their attention on wholly Milanese living rooms or homes filled with strictly '50s-style furniture; setups that, as fashions change, will seem only trite and tired, while, for my part, it'll still be the mongrel or faux Charles III articles, the future-folkloristic ornaments that go on catching my attention.

The Clue Game Board

I make my way through my apartment like a piece through a game of Clue, in which the value of each piece (and room/square) can only be deduced from the others. I don't have any preference between regional pieces of furniture and anonymous pieces of furniture, or between the toilet and the bedroom. The game only progresses through the successive positions I take up. But, nevertheless, the murderer is always with us, peering out from every nook, ready to slash your throat.

Noble Rot

This lamp's base is wobbly; it sways. The Corsair's door is cracked down the middle; I can hear *la phalle* dripping. All my belongings are slowly decaying. I can't be bothered to care, and in fact there's some pleasure to be gained from this. A

certain insistent tendency toward entropy in indoor life that I
might call "noble rot."

Switch Up

10 centimeters above it, the harsh light the lamp aims upward
outlines in sharp relief the light switch that controls the office
lamp. It illuminates its principle, in homage to what outshines
it. On the edge of the square switch plate, I've attached a clothing label that hangs in uncertain balance. This bit of black cloth
crowns the switch with a significance that escapes me.

Architectural Rhetoric

Walking along the boundary between the living room and the
office, it's impossible to miss the huge square arch that signals
this transition: metallic I-beams that support the floor above,
put in because of the Dantean consequences of the renovations
I had done between October 2001 and January 2002. There
used to be a dividing wall here, instead of this opening, closing off a room that its former owner used for storing hairdress-
ing equipment. In order to make myself an office that wouldn't
be separated from my living room, I had this dividing wall
torn down, but not before checking with the building's architect, who went by the name of Tartaglia, and who assured
me that I could do so without worry. And yet, as they broke
through this dividing wall, the workers I hired realized that
the ceiling was about to cave in. I frantically phoned the aforementioned Tartaglia, who called me back 5 days later and suggested that I put up supports right away. Since the damage
had already been done, I was then fortunate enough to be
graced with 1 of the most extraordinary feats of architectural
rhetoric ever delivered by an architect, in this case from the
lips of the forenamed Tartaglia, who in his attempt not to lose
face after this proof of his incompetence cooked up the ad hoc
concept of "half-load-bearing walls," thereby extricating him-

self from any liability related to the removal of the obstruction that just 1 week earlier he had declared was irrelevant. In these sorts of buildings, he announced with expert poise, *every wall is in fact more or less load-bearing*. The endless work delays and accumulating costs were just the price of living here. My square arch hides the evidence of this misadventure in a "temple-entrance" style—and is, indeed, something of a miracle, all in all.

Looking at the floor, you can still see where the wall used to be. It was covered with a combination of slaked lime and gravel that streaked the parquet in spots. In such modest lodgings as these, the inhabitants tend to prefer not 1 large room but its division into smaller spaces that allow their things to be stored away out of sight: my broker told me that in the '80s, 5 people lived here, which seems unbelievable. The concrete conditions of life have always fascinated me, and I wouldn't have undertaken to draw up a thorough representation of my interior if there wasn't, deep within me, the intimate belief that the fact of *having* is always punished by the mere fact of *being*.

Lighting Out for the Territory

Now we're back by the left side of the dentist's cabinet, which is separated by a narrow 22-cm-wide valley from the right side of the square arch. I haven't wedged this cabinet firmly against the artificial pillar, in order to avoid the impression of overcrowding. On the floor, an electrical outlet powers the spherical ambiance lamp described previously. I'm practically at the territory between the living room and the office.

Continuum

An apartment is a series of walls with doors and a floor that leads to rooms with windows reflecting back the cabinets and cupboards that contain your things.

Swordsticks

Between the pillar and the left side of the dentist's cabinet, a black cane leans on the diagonal. This Moroccan cane with sculpted handle has a band that unscrews to reveal its sword, which is pointy but not especially sharp, and the use of which is forbidden in French cities per the law of April 18, 1939, regarding knives and bladed weapons. For this reason I almost never carry this blade, save in mitigating circumstances, such as on March 24, 2012, at the Centre Pompidou, when I stood in front of an attentive audience and sliced apart books written by various enemies of mine.

The Doorbell Rings!

The doorbell rings again, but in vain, I'm not going to answer, I can't let myself become a valet who answers every time the bell is rung. My hands distract me by toying with 2 objects lying on the dentist's cabinet's shelf—my watch and my cell phone.

Space-Time Watch

My watch can be counted among these free-range objects that have no definitive, assigned location; it floats around, here and there, resisting every prospect of taking root. This chromed silver Bulova came from the Ouen flea market and, before that, Switzerland, where it was made in the '60s. I realize that "in the '60s" is imprecise, but the fact is that I bought this used watch 3 years ago, to have it repaired by a specialist in my neighborhood; it doesn't bother me at all not to know the exact assembly date for an object acquired to replace my alarmingly precise '68 Pierre Balmain, which was stolen during the break-in.

No doubt the fact that I was born 3 years before the anti-establishment '68 protests shaped my sensibility and spurred me to set my watch 3 minutes ahead.

Used

Refusing to buy used items because they might be haunted by their former owners is just as ridiculous as shoving a phoenix back into its ashes.

It's Not Ringing Anymore

As if simply paying attention to my watch had managed to deactivate the doorbell, I suddenly notice that it's not ringing anymore. Feeling superstitious, I leave my cell phone alone, which, of course, is also bound to no particular space; I put my faithful Bulova on my wrist, and, taking a few steps back toward the center of the living room, I turn and face my office.

Office

(9 m^2)

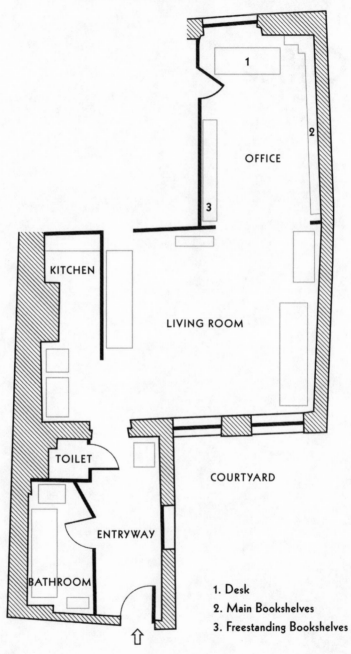

RUE DU FAUBOURG-SAINT-MARTIN

1

2

OFFICE

3

KITCHEN

LIVING ROOM

TOILET

COURTYARD

ENTRYWAY

BATHROOM

1. Desk
2. Main Bookshelves
3. Freestanding Bookshelves

Boundary of the Establishment

Reinforcing the boundary between the living room and the office, a chair identical to the dining table chairs has been—intentionally—positioned with 2 of its legs on the living room side and 2 on the office side: this literalization of "sitting on the fence" is an homage to every awkward situation in human existence. This boundary-chair's act of straddling is also a wink to this text's vacillations between fiction and document; it keeps wavering, keeps refusing to be just an inert chair.

Brinkmanship

We're on the brink of the office, but still haven't entered. We contemplate this room facing off against the living room. We admire the view it offers thanks to the window at its far end, which, 3 meters away, overlooking the street, seems far bigger than it actually is. Because of this open border with the living room, the office may be seen as a wing of the latter, a draft of fresh air, of added space. The lack of a door is a positive boon. On the floor, between the boundary-chair's legs, runs the mark of the erstwhile dividing wall. I could have hidden this scar on the floorboards by replacing it with a slat, but I prefer leaving it visible, like a rift, a dangerous precipice.

Conquest of Space

This office didn't exist before (my predecessor was a hair-dresser). In bringing down the dividing wall, I ran the risk not only of turning what had been sold to me as an authentic Parisian "3-room" apartment into a questionably "2-/3-room" apartment, but also of destroying the prospect of seclusion that a workspace offers or even necessitates. But the benefits of this opening were immeasurable; in adding to the living room's surface area by connecting that of the office, I brought together 2 spaces already connected by their parquetries' solidarity. And bringing down this wall was, above all, what allowed the light pouring in both from the street and from the courtyard to flood the entire space. This doubled source of light hits my office wonderfully from both ends. Thanks to a little demolition work, I was able to make this space wholly my own.

Threshold Threshold Threshold

Despite opening directly onto the living room, the office is set back enough that it's a distinct space. As I'm not the same man when I'm eating and when I'm writing, I have to maintain a separate space in which eating is wholly forbidden: this distinction—in addition to my leaving the traces of the fallen wall in the floor, and building the squared-off portico with its 2 pillars recalling nothing so much as the entrance to a temple—is yet another way of marking out the otherwise intangible boundary between the 2 rooms. Because of this, and even though it's right there, the office seems to be behind an invisible wall, so much so that I've even had people ask my permission to enter this open sanctuary, to cross a threshold that may not exist materially but certainly does symbolically. It's also notable that, when I'm having guests over, they keep their distance from this sacred space, as if they sense that they would be entering a territory that isn't meant for them. All the more reason for me to make that clear.

4th Chair

Now we have a better idea of the 4th chair's role—its 4th dimension, if you will—which is essentially that of demarcation. At a remove from those in the living room—except when I'm having guests, at which point it returns to its original status—it usually holds files and papers that need to be dealt with. Today it's colonized by a folder full of essays to be graded; tomorrow it'll be covered with unruly piles of random papers. Seeing it so ill-used, as an extra flat surface that can't be sat on, is a torment to me; I just really want to free my chair, to unburden it of these papers, to restore it to its original purity of function.

Suspended Motion

But then I stop: Where else could I put this stack of essays? Moving objects from 1 place to another presupposes open spaces that I simply don't have, except in my daydreams, where I hang each chair by cables from the ceiling . . . And while I do sometimes make a few middling attempts to rearrange my apartment in hopes of suffering a little less in this 50 m² space that so constrains my dreams, I always end up having to concede that I don't have the know-how to turn those fantasies of spatial comfort into reality. I'll just have to leave such sorcery to those gifted with the requisite ability.

When reality is measured in square meters, the writer in his room must take his revenge with an infinitude of intangible constructions.

Musical Charms

I don't take any particular interest in this exact chair, which is identical to all the others. On my way past, I decide to replace

it with 1 of its clones: it's no good for this space to always be occupied by the same chair. The game of musical chairs is a perfect
metaphor for this egalitarian vision of interchangeable roles—
a game I've only played once, as a child, though the memory
is still clear in my mind: I'd been invited to eat at the home
of 2 girls, and ended up musically lost because I'd fallen in love
with both at the same time, suddenly unable to decide between
Delphine and Léa, between 1 seat and the other.

Erotic Chair

As I walk up to the chair to grab it, I notice that my gut is at
the exact height of the large circular opening in its back: this
horizontal gap calls out to me, and I find myself with an erec-
tion. I simulate sex with the chair, gripping it with my 2 hands
as I thrust into it, looking over the chair's 4 legs, its alluring
aperture, its warmth, its fleshy hue that transcends the wood
out of which it was carved. I could pick it up, put it in various
positions: even considering that *chair* is the French word for
flesh, this chair's eroticism still catches me by surprise; I plop
my ass squarely upon it. Didn't Saverio Lucariello, in an extraordinary video, once try to seduce a chair by shimmying
around it to disco tunes?

Effaceable Trace

Just above the folder on the chair, along the pillar of the
temple arch, are some brownish traces of friction. I've taken
great pains never to lean the chair against this support, but
to no avail, the furniture's traces seep into the space all the
same. Modernity's white interiors are always being contested
by life—filthy, sweaty life. Whiteness, that vast beautiful deception, practically begs to be blemished. My 1st, housekeeperly
instinct is to cringe at the sight of this blemish and then get to
work erasing the trace as best as I can—which only ends up

making things worse. I'm still torn between the purity of modernity and the crimes it inevitably invites: stains and cracks, scratches and marks. Who wouldn't love never to leave a trace? Even the glass house Paul Scheerbart dreamed up as an antidote to the bourgeois home leaves traces behind. I can't hide what I am: my interior is an autobiography in glass that's been dirtied by an entire archive's worth of particles, signs, and lines, each 1 betraying my hopes of purity. It would take a true criminal to efface the traces a bourgeois-artist, a decorator-writer, had carved into this space.

Where to Begin?

Which should I introduce 1st, the flat-topped piece of furniture that gives this room its function or the enormous fortification full of books that fills our view and turns this office into more of a library? The product or the process? That which furnishes or that which is furnished? To sidestep my neurotic hesitations, I might instead sing the praises of the white frieze hiding the electrical wires up above, or maybe a paper clip or some bit of grit stuck in the crevices between the floorboards, but no, the aforementioned masses still dominate this space: directly ahead, my desk calls to me like the Homeric Sirens; while to my right, my bookshelves unfurl their tendrils to ensnare me and draw me into their world.

I'm disoriented enough that I can't take a step in any direction. The sheer scope of my task has stopped me dead. In front of the threshold where I set down the 79 cm × 79 cm portable card table that currently holds my computer, I am overwhelmed by vertigo. The mind reels.

Rolling Dice

To solve this dilemma, I decide to roll dice to pick the 1st object I'll describe: the desk if I roll 1, 2, or 3; the bookshelves if

4, 5, or 6. But where can I find a die? I know there's 1 around
here, a gift from Julien Prévieux, an artist who loves playing
tricks of all sorts: it's a perfect sphere! But I'm positive I've got
a normal 6-sided die somewhere too; I vaguely remember playing a game of 421 here at some point, maybe I left the die in
some forgotten corner of the kitchen? The wine case full of
cleaning products, yes, maybe . . .

He Gives Up, But . . .

He keeps rummaging around but can't find the die in question because he's mixed up this kitchen with another 1 in 1 of
his former homes. Then he realizes that every room in his
apartment that he had presumed to be autonomous and solidly
separated by walls is in fact always already haunted by its
brethren of earlier days, that this kitchen blurs with all other
kitchens, this bedroom with all other bedrooms, and this living room with now-dead living rooms—that his apartment
contains all the apartments he's ever known, that the entryways he's entered have only served to multiply the times and
spaces he had always presumed to be divided by his seclusion.
Behind these white walls he sees other white walls in succession,
covered with burlap or wallpaper from his childhood; his nicely
waxed floors lead him to even more nicely waxed floors, which
lead him like a surveyor to all the houses he's ever known. How
many apartments are hidden behind this 1?

Voices in Both Ears

He spent his 1st months at 1 rue de Lille: he remembers being
a baby and hearing those thin walls exhaling the complaints
of Jacques Lacan's analysands, as well as the master's replies,
since his practice was at number 5.

From then until he was 15, he was able to walk the halls of
a 14-room apartment on rue Mirabeau—a spatial experience

never to be repeated—then, from 16 to 23, he resided at 5 rue de Quatrefages, where Georges Perec once resided, and where his voice still echoed. Then, after a stint in a cave on the rue de Paradis, he came back to the rue de Quatrefages, albeit to number 10, where he nonetheless heard again the voice of the author of *Things*. He then moved to rue Saint-Maur, next to the former women's prison at La Petite Roquette, where his great-grandmother was briefly imprisoned; then, on September 11, 2001, as the 21st century was so rudely ushered in, he landed where we are now.

Parisian Numerology

So, in order: Paris arrondissements 7, 16, 5, 10, 5, 11, and 10, which adds up to 64, divided by 7 = 9, the next arrondissement I'll live in? And maybe, since the French word for new, *neuf*, is also the way to spell out the number 9, my new arrondissement will be a clean break from all the old 1s.

Literal

But enough of these mathematical flights of fancy. I'll be literal now: the piece of furniture that gives this room its purpose comes 1st. Solid like a bull, the weight of his desk drags an artist down to the level of an employee, a bureaucrat, a paper pusher . . . And yet, how could anyone try to jettison the very thing that gets a writer writing? A desk jockey is nothing without his desk; players play, assassins assassinate, writers write. The Romantic poets never needed any desks; I, on the other hand, have made this the site of production.

Bureaucracy

I work at a massive and mass-produced desk made out of oak, the kind that used to be de rigueur for provincial government offices. This piece of furniture—which isn't in Louis XIII style or Empire style or Art Deco, but simply "Bureaucratic" style—has such a vast work area (137 cm × 77 cm) that I could lie down on it, stands at a height of 77 cm, has 4 drawers on each side and 1 center drawer at torso level, and can be fully disassembled. A deep cavity where I can stretch out my legs and set them against the desk's back panel. This desk, both brutish and warm, beautiful and practical, has an entirely un-pretentious presence; it commands me to work (nothing is more childish than a small desk). I bought it eons ago for ₣1,500 at a long-since-forgotten furniture store on the street my maternal grandmother lived on. However, though I count it among my most indispensable pieces of furniture, in the sense that it en-ables the primary activity of my existence, I'm not as attached to it as some might think, and I've occasionally considered sell-ing it in order to get a more modern version, the only problem being that I still haven't found the ideal replacement. I'd love to betray my desk—and it doesn't suspect a thing. On top of this faithful friend many equally faithful pieces of paper keep it an-chored in my office.

By My Green Candle

To the right is 1 green glass lamp, shaped like a mushroom and shining a weak, bifocal light (25 watts), with 1 bulb in its shade and the other ensconced in its translucent base: when it's turned on, all the green glass gleams. It's fragile, and I worry that I'll never manage to break it, because the only objects that I tend to shatter are the 1s that I worry I'll shatter, thanks to a sort of logic that amounts to a blindly self-fulfilling proph-ecy. This 40-cm-tall lamp did once suffer some damage due to my complete imp(r)udence, but I managed to find a replace-ment for the original cone-shaped base; if the same thing happened today, however, I'd be completely out of luck. The green light the lamp gives me is more agreeable in principle than in reality, a discrepancy that annoys me by reminding me of Théophile Gautier's horrid theories. But when I acquired it more than 20 years ago, my decoraïveté was precisely what drew me toward this cloven object.

A 2nd green glass object echoes this lamp, a translucent square paperweight that was bequeathed to me by my friend Laurent Goumarre, and I take heart in its luminous density as well as in its weight; I think of it as a lucky charm, just like everything else my friends give me. I keep this object around less for practical use and more for its mere presence, but I do now grab a sheet of white A4 paper and slide it underneath. Bringing together this white and this green is enough to make me happy, and I stop worrying about specifics, about whether the paper is *under* the weight or the weight *on* the paper.

Just a Bit Farther to the Left . . .
About 10 centimeters to the left, a metal cup holds a dense thicket of pens, scissors, pencils, markers, and other points, including a thin silvery letter opener reminiscent of a Shakespearean dagger, which I use to open my mail (except when I'm in a rage and tear up every piece of junk mail with my hands). If it's a bill, I aim the letter opener at my heart and declaim 2 or 3 choice lines from the Bard: "On, lusty gentlemen . . ." As for the writing implements, I ask nothing of them save that they work. And I can think of nothing more delightful than grabbing a thoroughly used-up pen and throwing it right in the trash.

3 Black Fountains
My preferred pen is a simple Parker fountain pen, the Jotter model (€12), 12 cm long, divided into 2 equal and evenly balanced sections and thereby lending itself to an equally equilibrated sort of writing. The downward-pointing arrow clip on

its cap lets me keep it in the inner pocket of my jacket. I hate having to hunt for my implement and I'm terrified of losing it, and so I have 3 versions at hand (red, black, silver): all the same, I spend quite a bit of time misplacing and hunting for them. The Jotter has been discontinued; I stop into every stationery store I see in hopes of finding the last 1s still in circulation.

Modified Pen (Courtesy of Anne Bonnin)

The blue ballpoint with a red cap.

Sinistral Lamp

I'm hemmed in by a 2nd lamp on my left, the counterpart to the lamp on the right: besieged on both sides. This heavy Fase lamp from the '50s, pleasingly ocher, has a metal base that supports a huge curved piece of wood (which serves as a counterweight) that unfurls 3 parallel chrome stems at the end of which blossoms the single, overhanging hexagonal head. This lamp, which inclines toward the horizontal, and which produces a tight yet respectable circle of light, is connected to the outlet by a thick white cord; it's lit with a push button embedded in its base. This push-button switch is a beautifully simple design decision: there's no ambiguity at all between on and off.

Resistant Reality

I trip over this cord that likes to coil up and get in my way; I crouch down to pull—actually, *yank*—its firm male head out of the socket: there's no safe way to open the door to the bedroom, otherwise, because the cord gets wedged in the groove . . . and yet there's no other way to arrange things: I have to work with reality, pure and simple.

Telephone 2

My 2nd landline is within reach of both my left (princely) and right (pauperly) hands. In contrast to the 1 in the living room,

this Alcatel is useful for *making* calls. Part and parcel of a Free
telecom package, its sound quality is average. Like millions of
my fellow citizens, I surrendered in the face of all the purported savings Free offered, being able to call a certain number of numbers (but not all) for "free" as part of the monthly
€35 rate that's turned telecom CEOs into multimillionaires
by a diabolic extension of the principle of property applied to
time: every second, in the world we live in, is now accounted
for—which is why I now compose far fewer Dial-A-Poems than
I used to.

Assistive Device

I picked out a phone with oversize buttons in a store for the
blind because nothing used to bug me more than those old
rotary dials made for fairies' or children's fingers and which
only multiplied the likelihood of my misdialing. Why should
skinny fingers be a prerequisite for accuracy? Why should im-
patience impede our pianistic virtuosity? My phone's 9 buttons are 3 cm wide, and the only patience required in using
them is during the time it takes to move my fingers from 1
immense button to the next. The safety and quality of various
devices has become increasingly the prerogative of the infirm;
able-bodied people have the right only to junk: as such, I think,
it's a case where society has given all the more consideration
to the downtrodden so as to be better able to forgive itself for
its total indifference to the well-being of the majority. Take
my advice: buy your appliances at stores for the elderly and
disabled.

Regal Apple

The king of my office, upon which I'm writing these lines, is
my Apple iBook G4 notebook computer, bought on credit
for €1,500 (3 installments). While I have no great passion for
computers, and care even less for those who build their careers

around the sale and repair of these devices, it is nonetheless necessary—with regard to the instrument upon which I do my daily work—to temper my technophobic temperament. When I acquired this 32 cm × 23 cm apparatus in November 2005 (which is to say, in the language of computer technicians, prehistory), it was the ne plus ultra. I've always been faithful to Apple, just like the majority of "intellectuals," and I do take some pleasure in the fact that its share of the worldwide computer market is distinctly in the minority. While the PC signifies the world of alienated labor, Apple, with its flat form and its white lacquered-plastic housing, is the apple of every nonconformist's eye—the global icon of a bitten apple signposts the sort of home office where inventiveness is truly possible. Actually, I reject this notion of "inventiveness," since it's so ludicrously contemporary and refuted by every real artist, but the fact is that the computer, that antiromantic appliance, puts a new spin on the myth of a perfect tool, of a divine creator. Steve Jobs's death left me wholly cold; my desire for technology is that it be authorless, that it negate all biography. My ideal would be for men of science to disappear behind their own inventions.

Curved Angle

Sympathetic forms
Have rounded corners.
Authoritative forms, right.

Center

However portable and transportable my computer may be, it still spends the vast majority of its time at home. I only export it on (working) vacations. Contrary to its design, I treat this object as an immobile piece of furniture: it holds court over the office. I've come to realize that writing happens only at the center: it's a centered, central activity that necessitates 2 equally sized spaces on each side. All the rest falls into place around it.

Stolen Soul

The 1 other place in my apartment suitable for my computer is the sanctuary where I store it when I'm away. This spot has to remain secret, so I won't say anything more about it; I don't care how many real-life apples thieves make off with, but if 1 of them were to filch my Apple, that would be like stealing my soul—really, I ought to praise my burglar for having been more interested in my watch than in a machine that clearly struck him as beneath his notice . . . Or maybe he just didn't see it because it was sitting in plain sight on my desk?

Suprematist Composition: White on White

Pressing a sheet of A4 paper onto the screen.

Parent Company

"Home is the most important place in the world," declared IKEA; but Apple retorted that, these days, people live online. With a distinct advantage over libraries and other such enclosed spaces, computers lead to a hyperspace. The object itself is perfectly solid if I open its lid; but within its few inches is contained an entire, intangible universe (which isn't for public display). Computers hold so much in so little space that they almost seem boundless. The computer overflows with realms; maybe it's everything an animal isn't.

Wireless

My computer is, alas, wired. 1st to the printer, which in turn binds it to paper; then, on its right side, to the power outlet, which keeps this beast well nourished. Its battery barely lasts

2 hours, so it has to be fed, like an elderly shut-in, through a plug with an oblong end (which resembles, in miniature, the entryway's ceiling light), which draws energy from 1 white square block, often quite hot, that connects to the computer via 1 long cord. I know that the newest computer models do away with nearly all wires, and I'm delighted because I hate those things. Wi-Fi has already weaned us off the main yellow cable. When, at last, every cord is cut, the future really will be now. And as if it could hear me, my power cord, drawn by a fundamental force, slips across the desk and lands on the floor like a dead snake.

Tumbles

Thus does my mute apartment succumb every so often to a fleeting animism; a tumult over which I have 0 control wrecks every object. A bulb will simply pop, who knows why (though, when I was a child, I myself was why: I once poured water over a bulb I worried was overheating: the glass's abrupt shattering terrified me, and that image of bodies maimed and ruined by my mistakes turned me away from medical practice altogether). The mysterious tumble of a book, a bag, or a bit of food creates some magic in the heart of the everyday. There's no rhyme or reason to such occurrences. And yet, if I listen carefully, I can hear my belongings' political demands: they protest the close quarters I keep them in, want to reclaim a bare minimum of space in this city where there's practically none. The uncooked spaghetti on the floor becomes a giant game of pick-up sticks.

Sacred Left

The desk comprises 4 drawers on each side for a total of 8, in perfect symmetry, though I'd hoped to reserve the left side for what I consider sacred, and the right for what I consider profane, thereby establishing a sort of monument to opposition.

The left side is the empire of the archive. The uppermost drawer, the most accessible 1, since I can open it without my left hand (the 1 I write with) exerting any effort, is for work currently under way. (The presence of my "more present" hand and the "currency" of my current work have a relationship I couldn't necessarily explain, but which I simply know must be the case; clearly 1's body is always in the present tense.) I also keep my cell phone charger in this drawer. 1 could be forgiven for considering this dainty black appendix to be so purely an accessory in our era that it's just about worthless, seeing as they're given away for free with every new phone. And while it might call to mind the age-old tradition of knotting a string around your finger to help remind you of something, the many knots that keep cropping up in my charger's cord only serve to draw attention to how thin and shoddy it is, its reach being reduced with each successive use—if my cell phone rings while it's charging, the cord isn't long enough for me to maneuver, and I have to adopt an awkward, almost painful pose that amounts to me slumping toward the ground and twisting my neck toward the phone, stuck in that position so I don't yank the cord out of its socket. It would be better to kneel, I think, although that would make such conversations still more bizarre, even if I, being opposed to videophones, were the only 1 to know it, so the best solution is to set the charging phone on a low shelf and to let the cord hang slack.

In his poetry, Francis Ponge liked to give such mundane objects a voice; sometimes, though, I think he might have done better to let them keep their mouths shut.

USB

I also keep my 2 USB thumb drives here, although "keep" might not be the right word: they're so small that they always and immediately get lost in the depths of the drawer (45 cm deep, 12 cm high); the moment I want to grab 1, I'm forced to pick up various folders and rummage blindly through the undergrowth. I don't know what USB stands for (although I have a feeling the *S* is for "security"); Fear and Prudence drive me to always keep duplicates of such items—objects whose loss would be felt far more keenly than those of greater proportions: alongside the small 6 cm Emtec with its transparent cap revealing its metal connector, I have a 2nd drive that's 8 cm, brand name PNY, in gray aluminum with a translucent pink window that displays the beautiful French word *attaché*, befitting this thing that keeps our lives on a leash. These 2 drives contain all the texts I'm currently working on, about 100 of them total. They are as small as their potential is grand!

Technology: Gender-Neutral

As I focus my attention on these drives, I find myself mentally associating them with both clitorises and penises. Their size, their smallness, their power all remind me of the combined delicacy and strength of female and male genitalia, and so I wonder if technology's gender isn't perhaps simply Neutral, making it equally desirable to our entire species.

Genesis of *1 Apartment*

In the 2nd left-hand drawer, which I can still reach without moving, is another set of colorful folders containing multiple texts, organized by genre and title, such as *1 Apartment*, the 1st draft of the book you're currently reading, which constitutes its genesis, and which I will preserve for future researchers. Although I have a particular aversion to the genetic criticism that literary theory, completely overwhelmed by the formalism of the '70s, saw fit to make the foundation of a new religion, exhuming masses of ur-texts and alternate drafts, I can't in good conscience rebuff the gravedigger's impulse, and I'll even facilitate their task by saying here that the flat, preliminary title above was quickly replaced by the 1 that wound up being final. After all, *Voyage Around My Room* was already taken, and moreover wouldn't be accurate in terms of the surface area covered by my book; as for *My Big Apartment*, well, I'm not too keen on the ironic approach.

Past Clercs

Opening the 3rd drawer calls for 1 sideways shift and 1 slight hunch downward: as we tend to distance ourselves spatially from what's become distant temporally, so this drawer contains older folders, already gone a bit yellow, that I barely ever look at: aborted or abandoned or abrogated projects that feel as though they hail from another era and only make me shudder in this 1. Then, in the final drawer, at the bottom of the desk, you'll find the various notebooks comprising my diary from the distant epoch ('85–'90) when I wrote by hand. Although I've typed up the majority of those texts on my computer, I still keep these artifacts, not so much out of fetishism as out of a simple conviction that paper is at less risk of destruction than the contents of a screen: there's no such thing as a paper virus, after all. Down here I've planted the seeds of a literary genre that draws its paradoxical prestige from being situated below most human beings: minor, infra-aesthetic, insignificant, bordering on the pathetic, in which the sublime is confounded with the trivial, in which literature gets into bed with daily life, and whose sole concern ought really to be the question of how best to verbalize a mass of facts that only the act of writing could ever dignify. I'm unlikely to publish my diary: Cocteau believed that publishing a diary during 1's life ran the risk of revealing all the diarist's inadvertent falsehoods, which is why I'm convinced that doing so would be an error in the eyes of truth, and as much as I might admire those who do go public with their private records, I know I don't have such courage—which is exactly why I admire them. And on top of that, there are no great revelations to be found in my diary;

the life that I've set down there could be of interest only to those who consider life to be a great revelation in itself.

Profane Right

The left hemisphere of my desk contains manufactured items, the right hemisphere the tools for such manufacture. And this very nicely satisfies my penchant for keeping realms distinct, hewing to the beautiful, symmetrical classifications of the classical era, as well as to my own propensity for militant inversion: as I'm left-handed, the sinister is my proper domain, and thus, contrary to society's natural assumption as to which side is sacred, the domain of creation, in this case it's—rightfully—*gauche*. Literature isn't innately up-right: it's imperfect, fragile, sometimes even a failure, and it finds success only in its own clumsiness and deception. The right side of this piece of furniture, therefore, is the 1 I've chosen to devote to the material and blameless domain of the secretary.

Paper Tiger

The 1st drawer from the top, the identical twin of that on the right, is devoted to paper of all sorts: sheets, cards, envelopes, etc. The 3rd drawer contains about 100 worksheets, 21 × 29.7 cm sheets folded in half, crosswise, on which I typically summarize the many books I'd have liked to write. The particular fold of these homely sheets allows me, by imitating the form of a book, to have a 4-sided sheet and not merely a 2-sided 1: what I lose in length I gain in depth, and this little paper ruse spares me from any confusion with the other, unfolded 21 × 29.7 sheets as I stack them and grab them without looking.

Price per Square Sheet

I pick up 1 blank sheet. I turn it in different directions. I could put some black on this white, to give it some value, but I can also fetch a decent sum just by setting it on the floor: if we measure its worth according to the cost of 1 Parisian square meter (€8,000), we get its price: €498.96. Its virtual cost is in 2 dimensions, whereas real wealth, of course, is in 3. What if the decrease in intellectual value were a direct function of the exorbitant price of surfaces? Then who would be able to hold a salon these days?

Otherworld Order

Any harried reader certainly will have overlooked how, in the terrible succession of descriptions I've inflicted upon her or him, I've jumbled the order of the drawers, going without any warning from the 1st to the 3rd, when it would have been more correct to list the contents of the 2nd drawer in between—but textual order and real order are 2 different things. My reason isn't strictly a literary 1 (even though, notwithstanding how it may appear, this book isn't meant to be a simple snapshot of my apartment, but really my apartment in written form), but rather lies in the violation of the principle I stated further up, when I decreed the division of prerogatives between the creative left and the performative right. As if this binary scission of space hadn't done justice to these objects, I haven't entirely succeeded at avoiding any confusion between the sacred and the profane.

Performance Drawer

The accordion folder that resides in this 2nd drawer is pudgy; its flaps break free of its black straps and its bulk hampers my attempts to get the drawer open; I yank anyway, denting the corner of the sleeve titled *Performances*, which I've willfully destroyed. When life annoys, irritates, or outright hurts me (I do have a delicate sensibility), I start in on this compensatory tic: opening and shutting the drawer several times, quicker and quicker, in order to make the damage even worse. By carrying out this conscious cruelty, I project my frustration onto the 1 expanding folder dedicated to my performances, an activity to which I devote a good portion of my writing time, and have done since 2007. The word *performance* suits this willfully repetitive gesture, which subjects my folder to exactly the same sort of activity that it serves to archive. And I'd like to end this digression with a theoretical problem that's always bothered me: Does a performance require an audience? If I apply my definition of "performance" to this act of repeatedly opening and shutting a drawer, in order to execute the (minor) depredation of an object, is this really a performance, or is it so to only my eyes? X claims that brushing his teeth alone in his bathroom can be called a performance; for him, I guess, it certainly can, but to the degree that there's no audience there to witness it or appreciate it, I would say that it only becomes a performance at the moment when it's addressed to someone else, via some form of mediation. As such, my own performance—"The 2nd Drawer"—finds its raison d'être in its being recorded here, on pages 201–202 of *Interior*.

Profaner Still

In the most profane and profound drawer, the last, I've stuffed all my digital debris: computer manuals, ISP phone numbers, plugs, cords, external hard drives, and other accessories. I try to minimize to the maximum [*sic*] the problem of opening it, like so many other problems I'd rather keep thoroughly buried: and so this choice of the bottommost drawer is propitiatory, because I dread those "technical issues" a lack of proper education has left me perpetually unprepared to deal with.

Cleaning

The only item in this reserve that I attach any value to is the universal screen cleaner, 1 small spray bottle protected by 1

small cap, which I use to get rid of dust, bits of grime, finger-
prints, and other signs of general wear and tear that assault
the creamy purity of the iBook G4 that Stéphane Mallarmé,
way ahead of his time, called "the white disquiet of our canvas."
I have 0 idea whether this cleaner is right for my Mac's chassis,
but I use it anyway, on the assumption that I can't go far wrong
simply spraying a product made in Germany on the surface of
another from Japan. To finish up the operation, I use a former
table napkin. Reusing and repurposing objects fills so many
chapters in the history of art; this particular repurposing might
be modest, even a bit degrading, but that's the fate of cloth,
this material made from next to nothing, born in splendor but
ending in misery, and touching us with its similarity to our own
destiny. In this same vein, to wax my shoes, I use old T-shirts or
old mismatched socks, and to clean the apartment I put on old
jogging pants that are as inelegant as the pantaloons that ven-
erable dukes who had fallen on hard times and become pen-
sioners wore with illusory opulence before accepting the rags
of Welfare. The fantasy of pushing snobbery to the point of
wearing brand-name clothes or expensive fabrics for menial
housecleaning work gives me a peculiar delight in which I can
still recognize my bent for subservience, humiliation, degenera-
tion. (And to think that these base lips of mine once touched
the napkin now consecrated to dusting off my sacred screen!)

Center Drawer

I open the center drawer, which is large and deep as a pensive
belly. Among various articles for schooltime use (1 ruler;
some tape; scissors; a pocket calculator that the Banque populaire gave me in hopes, I suppose, of becoming even more
popular; 1 pencil sharpener; some thumbtacks and staples;
etc.), all of them in a box that formerly held Turkish delights
bought in Istanbul, the drawer holds 3 additional objects, tal-
ismanic in nature: my planner, my address book, and my map

of Paris. My planner will take its place, at the year's end, alongside the other black planners in the freestanding bookshelves
(→ *infra*); other people may use iPhones, but I've stayed faithful to paper, which has never failed me. My address book isn't,
like my cell phone, errant; rather, it gathers all the people I
know together into 1 space, along with their mailing addresses
(how quaint!). As for my Paris map, it crushes Google by giving
me an overview that isn't so much local as global: I've never
had to help so many tourists on the street as when the good
old paper map was supplanted by electronics (and it's quite clear
they'd all rather have recourse to some random photocopy
than be forced to interact with the likes of me!).

In any case, GPS, the death knell of spatial memory, is
something I've managed to keep in abeyance with my map,
with my love for my territory. For my part, I'll leave my reader
with a small floor plan of my home—though if our species'
memories of the spaces we inhabit go on blurring into nothing-
ness, then maybe, 1 day, I'll also include an appendix featuring
numerous photos of this apartment (for a small additional fee).

Wastepaper Basket & Co.

At the foot of the desk, my wastepaper basket alternates between 2 possible positions: either, as at this particular moment, with its back against the window, or else perpendicular
to it. It's always set on the right side of my desk, suggesting its
dependence, and always gets full very quickly. I empty it regularly into a provisional paper bag, so its contents can be trans-
ported swiftly to the yellow bin in the building courtyard, which
itself has its contents sent to a recycling center.

Dangerous Beauty

This gray iron-mesh wastepaper basket is shaped like an
upside-down lampshade. It's openwork all around, its rim and
base crenellated with merlons in a ring of occasionally sharp

points. If these rings weren't made of wire, they would be absolutely perfect: whenever I grab the basket to empty it, however, I have to remind myself not to cut my fingers, as if the
dangers of this workaday object were completely disguised by
its fine structure. The theme of the prospectively benign but
dangerous object was masterfully explored in 1 of my favorite
films, Éric Rohmer's *La collectionneuse* (1967), in which 1
of the main characters, an artist—Daniel Pommereulle, essentially playing himself—has a sculpture consisting of a paint
can with razor blades affixed to it, so that it can't be picked up
without getting 1's fingers cut. This untouchable object has
since remained embedded in my memory as an exemplar of art
as fortress: protecting and defending itself.

My wastepaper basket's thin wire points hint at the dangers embedded in its delicate, metallic, airy façade, much like
that of the Eiffel Tower. But, in contrast to the monument,
nobody's petitioned for my basket to be torn down, and it was
in the area around Elle Décoration (a store on rue Saint-Sulpice
that's now gone) that I acquired it in a fit of frivolity. It claims
its prestige from being the sole place in my apartment in which
I allow myself to deposit unwanted paper, although it's occasionally seasoned by empty ink cartridges or pencil-sharpener
shavings as well, and so certainly outclasses the mere trash can.
To keep it from getting ideas above its station, I also use it as
a playground.

Shot

1 of my favorite sports when I'm letting my thoughts wander
is a game that all bureaucrats play well: launching wads of paper into the wastepaper basket. It soothes the nerves, whether
we're talking about the occasional off-the-cuff throw (when I
come home in the evening, I tear up any envelopes from that
day's mail, wad them up into balls, and shoot them into the
receptacle), or else the slightly more involved game I've invented

in order to keep myself occupied: it not being uncommon for me to make a wish 1st—such as for the success of this book, or of the woman I love, or of my close friends—and then, if I pull the shot off, to raise my fist with a triumphant cheer, just like the child I've never really stopped being. If I miss, though, I just give myself a 2nd try—this game of apartment basketball jolting an afternoon out of its doldrums. Even if I fail, I still manage to win, because I cheat ever so slightly, by shooting over and over until I finally get a basket, or else by wishing for things that it's okay not to get, such as Stade Rennais's winning a soccer game against Paris Saint-Germain, or a particular secretary of state being forced to resign.

Halftime
The austere labor of writing calls for endless subterfuges. The Internet does provide some distraction, but it only redoubles the problem of our dependence on that same old screen. The Frigidaire makes for a more delectable ally, although it can easily become a trap. Tea calms me. Naps tempt me. The phone distracts me. The window soothes me. The television diverts me. Sex drains me. The street roars at me. The toilet . . . does what it does. Nothing is as good as a leisurely stroll around my home.

Clue
Professor Plum, in the library, with the lead pipe.

The Immovable Object
In terms of volume, the primary piece of furniture in my apartment would be the bookshelves (which we might consider immovable). They are in 2 bodies: the main bookshelves that fill the full length of the right wall, transforming that flat plane into a dramatic bas-relief; and the small wing on the left that extends the former shelves perpendicularly along the wall

behind my desk, to the right of the window—architecture that could be considered both structural and mural, that catches every eye peering in from the living room. What a thorough disappointment this literary monument must have caused my thief when he realized just what kind of person he was dealing with!

The Book of Books

Upon crossing the border into the heart of the Bookshelf-lands, a doubt assails me, or maybe a sense of vertigo, about the overall soundness of this project, which I'll only be able to finish if I stick to the purely surficial method I described much earlier, although it now carries a measurable risk of overwhelming my discursive zeal, since the fact is that I own 700 books. It's not their description so much as the relationship I have with each of them that could send this text spiraling into a Borgesian infinity: a volume that would collect dust in his famous Library of Babel under the title of *The Book of Books and Grains of Sand*. If his or her bookshelves are a writer's true homeland, then their delineation really should constitute a full volume of their own, and that's why I've decided for the moment to postpone setting down the series of descriptions that they necessitate, amounting to a row of Russian dolls containing not dolls within dolls but dreams within dreams . . . And I can already hear the objection that my devil's advocates will make, to wit, that I always seem to shy away from the sheer scale of my project by avoiding this or that particular aspect (as I've already done with my archives), and, as such, that it would appear this voyage into the heart of my apartment is more than my meager talents can manage. (Indeed, my last book was devoted to annotating every street in Paris's 10th arrondissement, and there's no denying that I still have 19 other arrondissements to survey.)

What can I do but save this readerly documentation for
my golden years, whereupon my work will have come full circle: I predict that my final book will be entitled *A Personal
History of My Books* (to be published in 50 years).

Prominent Room, Missing Room

The extension to my main bookshelves has wedded itself to
my desk, and this coupling, I'm all too aware, was completely
foreseeable. Such obligatory pairs (armoire–mirror, table–chair,
curtain–window, etc.) are thoroughly unavoidable. Making
his way into this office, a nonreader would feel practically as-
saulted by all these orderly troops standing at attention, ready
to launch into a battle for which he's entirely unprepared. That's
why I would have preferred to give my bookshelves a room
all to themselves—a more private, more personal room that
wouldn't just scare away ordinary folks . . . and I don't mean
to make myself sound grand: such intimidation inevitably does
occur. But look, I'm always wishing for 10 more rooms; I might
just as well dream of having a hacienda . . .

Shelves

In the meantime, however, I have to keep some order in this
perpetually disordered interior I call my apartment, and face
up to the impossible task of keeping my obsessions in check.
The abovementioned number of books in my library, 700, is
already null and void: glutting my shelves and overflowing onto
any other available flat surface (the corsair's and dentist's cabinets, and the mantel of the fireplace in my bedroom), my library is an army teeming with new recruits who rarely ever
die. My devotion to books is expressed through acquiring them,
an act so indispensable to me that I feel, almost every single
day, the same brute desire, comparable perhaps to an erotic
impulse, to buy new volumes. Nothing seems more revealing

to me than their glaring absence, which I've found as often in
the most disadvantaged strata of society as in homes of the
representatives of our contemporary neo-bourgeoisie. Whereas
intellectuals proudly pose in front of their shelves, the businessman simply floats in his frigid space, and the poor man in
his shack doesn't bother at all . . .

Alpine Summits

While my shelves don't go all the way to the ceiling, the air is
certainly thin up there. The void above them makes the highest shelves float in a practically alpine isolation. I'm not sure
that this was the right choice—maybe 1 more row of shelves
should have been put up, so the tops of those volumes could
have brushed the ceiling, making that the "natural" top of the
bookcase; but, on 2nd thought, the already dizzying height
of this little mountain library dissuades me from retrieving the
uppermost titles—which is why some people tend to keep only
their less respectable, generally lower-status books on their top
shelves, in short, the books they'd consider 2ndary. It's really
not right, after all, to sacrifice authors from A to B (especially
B) to those hinterlands. But as alphabetical classification is a
system I am incapable of abandoning, I've adopted a solution
that explains the presence, along the shelves, of my Tam Tam
stool.

Mont Thabor

This fire-truck-red plastic Tam Tam stool counts among the
various accessories in my apartment that I've rechristened.
Since, in French, stools are called *tabouret*, I've given this 1 the
nickname *Mont Thabor* or *Montabour* to differentiate it from
the black *tabouret* that holds my TV in the living room; I never
sit on this stool, but rather use it exclusively to give me a leg up
when reaching for books.

Horizontal Solution

A disdain for compromise drove Le Corbusier to make radical choices in terms of interior layout, especially where it came to ceiling heights, which he decided had to be relatively low, certainly lower in any case than the previous standards that we (we, the people who live in these buildings that Le Corbusier devoutly wished would be destroyed) are used to enduring. And it's true that shelves that flowed from 1 end of a room to the other at human height would seem to be the ideal solution to avoid climbing up or stooping down to retrieve a given book: it's a solid idea, but it overlooks the fact that such a reduced capacity would never be able to accommodate the ceaseless flood of new arrivals. Better to have more shelf space than books to fill it all; at worst, you wind up with immense empty shelves bathed in sunlight, akin to the stunningly pure, unencumbered planes of the Villa Noailles in Hyères, where space itself becomes exquisite.

Crack

My endless indecision about the height of my shelves found a concrete justification in the fissure on my ceiling that threatens the upper right corner of this room. It's a result of my upstairs neighbors' contempt for their floors, but I don't know the exact cause: there's a child running around up there, loudly enough that I sometimes have to go up to the 4th floor and ask the Chinese family there to tone down his playtime fun; I'd prefer that it were a stockroom full of boxes (they work in textiles) of unnerving weight. Still, whether it's a result of a clandestine warehouse or that interminable stomping, this threat of this fault line growing larger is rather worrisome. Proust, irritated by a similar pounding of children's feet above his head at 102 boulevard Haussmann, had felt shoes made for the kids so they would be less noisy. I'm of a less delicate constitution, so I'm just waiting for this family to move out—which will surely be after I do.

Neighborship

My theory of neighborliness: neighbors always cause us more frustration than we do them. Application thereof: in terms of water damage, my neighbors have clinched a 3–1 victory; as for myself, I don't think I make too much noise, but then again I take off my shoes far less often than I should; I do listen to loud music, but only the popular kind; I do walk around shamelessly nude, even though there's the inevitable risk of causing my neighbors shame, since my curtains aren't shut nearly as often as they ought to be; I avoid conversations on the landing; I absolutely forbid the display of meat outside my window. If this crack in my ceiling is the death knell of co-habitation, it's still a far cry from the Argentine film *The Man Next Door*, in which a crude neighbor comes and upsets the quiet peace in which his young, high-powered neighbors live by hacking through the wall that separates them.

Library of Exactitude

Obsessed by establishing order and conquering space, the author and the architect both create volume(s): the 1st conceives, constructs, plans; the 2nd plans, constructs, conceives. The former builds monuments out of a few scribbles; the latter builds his scribblings into another kind of monument. I've had these bookshelves built out of a material called "medium-density fiberboard," a composite of wood fibers with a density certainly above medium and a chestnut-purée color; then I tailored my Library of Alexandria to exacting personal requirements. 1st, that every row be perfectly straight and solid: since nothing is worse than planks sagging under too much weight. Next, that there be very little space in front of my volumes, meaning that the edge of each shelf should coincide with the spines of my books, creating the illusion of fusion between container and its contents: in practical terms, a result fairly difficult to obtain, as not all books come in the same format. Similarly, the desire to display certain small curios here (which come with their own specific problems, elaborated *infra*) forces me to grant them a space of about 4 centimeters from the shelves' edge.

Cover Price

Nobody would dispute that books make for an essential decorative element—aside perhaps from those idealists who think that decoration is irrelevant, or else those philistines who don't even think about the existence of such things—but it's not the book qua object that I care about. I'm not insensitive to that aspect of book collecting, but I do refuse that suspect relationship inherent in bibliophilia (which I tore to shreds in my 1st book, about Maurice Sachs). To be fair, the few beautiful books, or rather rare books, that I own are 1s that I keep less because of their market value than because of their rarity, pure and simple: a rarity that would make their disappearance quite definitive, in contrast to losing, say, my Garnier Frères edition of *The Red and the Black*, which would only deprive me of Gérard Philipe's likeness on the cover. I couldn't even guess what this or that book in my collection is now worth, as I have 0 idea what the market for them would be. The sole and somewhat sulfurous volume of value I can point to here is Céline's screed *Les beaux draps*, which would probably fetch something like €100, but which no doubt will lose its value once it's thrown off the shackles of censorship and been reprinted. I have several weathered out-of-print books from Gallimard, some early Minuit titles, and some books inscribed by their authors to me personally (including a few compromising instances with lines consequently blacked out), but ultimately nothing sensational. All the same, if I consider €20 to be the average price for a volume, multiplying that by the number of books here, well . . .

Multiformity

Taking into account the formal diversity of books, the idea of organizing them by publisher—as if I lived in a bookstore or the home of 1 of those French professors proudly putting their Pléiade editions on display to be noticed even at a distance—makes my heart sink. The varied hues displayed by my shelves, all the irregular sizes and shapes, the oldness or newness of those rectangles, all contribute to a tapestry as multiform and multicolored as Literature itself. Uniformity tends to transform bookshelves into wheatfields of Gallimard editions or snowscapes of P.O.L tomes, cotton plantations of Minuit volumes, or prairies of egg-yolk (practically canary-yellow) Garniers. A 'pataphysical solution would be to make personalized book covers for each and every 1 to give them a particular cachet; I have to confess, however, that I don't have the courage to do so. I leave such eye-catching practices to the likes of Rodney Graham. Alphabetical classification, in the meantime, gives enough of an aleatoric aspect to this monument.

Habitation

The main part of the shelves is a block of compartments arrayed in 5 columns of equal width (78 cm, except for the last column on the right, which is narrower and just 27 cm, striking a very successful contrast with the rest) holding 9 shelves each. Each shelf has a uniform 16 cm depth. Only the leftmost column breaks this horizontal alignment, because it only has 4 shelves of books while its central space serves as a music center. So, in all, there are 42 units in this block, 40 of which are for books, resulting in a 90% occupancy rate.

Brief Note on the Art and Craft of Sorting Books

The problem of classifying books is classic, and Georges Perec discussed it with absolute class. With equal scrupulousness, I decided at the very start of my career as a sorter to order them alphabetically, which sorted out the question once and for all. By virtue of an exhaustion that all obsessives know intimately, the act of "sorting out a question once and for all" engenders a sort of inner peace. Clarity is the advantage of using the alphabet; its indirect charm is that of setting authors who have nothing to do with each other cheek by jowl: Homer immediately preceding Houellebecq imbues these shelves with a touch of the unexpected, elevating the whole above methods of organization driven by strictly personal considerations.

That said, some problems remain: anonymous authors, for example—I shelve them under ANON rather than before A and at the head of the entire library, as so many advocates for Barthes's theory of the death of the author would no doubt prefer. They dream of literature escaping overly nominal frames of reference, but this is my library and author names remain the name of my game. Still, that doesn't save me from the problem of reference works such as dictionaries or grammars, where I hesitate and waver between falling back on author names (of which these volumes sometimes have several) and the equally nonintuitive but generically useful term "Dictionary": the *Dictionnaire des œuvres*, for example, is under the letter *D*, whereas I've shelved the *Dictionnaire du cinéma* under the letter *L*, for the name of its author, Jacques Lourcelles, for the simple reason that Jacques Lourcelles is the only credited author. Collective works present their own sorting difficulties, such as this psychoanalytic opus titled *Le désir et la perversion*, which has 5 authors, and which I've ended up filing under "perversion" rather than "désir" because it's certainly a perverse book. Critical texts on particular writers are the iffiest 1s: 1 must choose between following strict alphabetical order, removing the object of the critic's attention from the equation, or else forgetting that steadfast rule and shelving the book under the name of the author being discussed: should I put Gilles Deleuze's *Proust and Signs* under the letter *D*, or the letter *P*? Wisest would be to put all critical texts alongside the books by the author being studied; but if I'm looking for Deleuze's work and I don't happen across *Proust and S.*, will I remember to check the Proust section? Well, probably. (This example is theoretical, since I don't own the book in question.) When the scholarly—or rather, I should say, extracurricular—volume doesn't register in my mental files as an author's own book, it would be better to shelve it alongside the subject's own works; but this dispute will never end, because real books will always and inevitably get hidden among these false friends. I go back and forth: I've shelved my own book on Maurice Sachs under both *C* and *S*. And so my double role as writer and critic is evinced by a classification system that entails, appropriately enough, keeping duplicates of various titles.

Alphabetical Start Delayed by 1 Queer Consideration
The small left wing of my shelves contains, up high, the 1st volumes: the very 1st 1 ought to be the letters of Abélard and Héloïse, who would only have the phallocentric ordering of their names to thank for not having their book shelved under the letter *H*. To express my political dissatisfaction, then, I've moved this book to the latter letter, and so another book has been left with the burden of being "the beginning." And so we've already found proof that every premise rests on principles

that are immediately called into question, that have to be reass-
essed on a case-by-case basis. As so often happens for clerks
and Clercs and other, generally clerical folks (except perhaps
for those devotees of the Swiss preacher Zwingli), it's a book
by Stefan Zweig—which I've never read, actually—that closes
out my shelves. Indeed, my shelves are occupied by a nonnegli-
gible percentage of books that are still unread, and while I'd
happily think up a shelving system that depended on this 1
operating distinction, I'd rather find a subtler way to indicate
which books I've merely leafed through. The danger, in effect,
would be of giving myself away: I might adopt such a system of
organization only to find out that I haven't read practically any
of my books!

Alphabetical Start

I own 64 *A*s, which take up all the 1st shelf, a fact that doesn't
displease me, because here the perfect relationship between
container and contents offers an eye-pleasing harmony. As for
the letter *B*, which contains a plethora of 1st-rate authors, including several favorites, they lead from Balzac to Brautigan
by way of Baudelaire—and I wouldn't dream of passing over
the complete works of Barthes in silence, considering that I'm a
specialist in his work. The 1st *B*, all the same, is Bachelard,
whereas the last *A* is Aymé, which enables a French pun based
on *aimé* being the word for "loved" and so gives all due respect to the eminently sympathetic author of *The Poetics of
Space*. As for *C*, there are 106 inhabitants: the 1st is Cadiot,
the last Croce. The letter *D*, which starts with a book featuring
the Dada writers, contains an extraordinarily striking case of
neighboring authors, thanks to Dustan (Guillaume): it was so
that he'd come right after Duras (Marguerite) in bookstores and
libraries that he chose his pseudonym—a literary and spatial
homage of which I know no equivalent. The *D/E* switch hinges

on Duvert/Eisenzweig, a pedophile novelist and a theoretician
of literary terrorism; *E/F* collides Exbrayat (who, if we're to
believe the cover bearing B.B.'s face, must be *a ravishing idiot*) with Fallada's *Every Man Dies Alone*, whose French title is
"Alone in Berlin," and which I bought when I was, myself, in
that same city and same situation. The last *F* is, inevitably,
Fromentin's *Dominique* and the 1st *G* is Galbraith's *Money*.
We pivot poetically from Guyotat to *Haiku* (an anthology). In
H, the *Odyssey* of Homer, the 2nd book in the world, glitters
with undeniable beauty, whereas the *Iliad*, which would be
the 1st chronologically, merely leaves me amazed. After *The
Cattle Car* by Hyvernaud (Georges), Iacub (Marcela) asks *What
Have You Done to Sexual Freedom?* The letter *I* is typically
underpopulated, so I've slipped in a *Quick Method for Learn-
ing Italian* to bolster the ranks. If my mother had offered me
a copy of the *I Ching* in English, it'd be here, but as we're both
French to the core, I've shelved the *Yi Jing* in *Y*, while it's
Itard who rounds out the section, before Max Jacob, who's
rather difficult to dethrone from his spot at the head of *J*. Juve-
nal/Kafka make strange bedfellows practically begging for a
punch line. With Kundera/Labarthe, then Luzi/McCullers,
we're in the belly of the beast. The most dissonant volume, its
green spine sticking out like a sore thumb, is *Langelot et les
espions*, by Lieutenant X, the only survivor of my old green
and pink shelves, sparking vivid memories of my early, indeed
earliest, childhood readings: Enid Blyton or Georges Chaulet
greeted me long before Flaubert or Molière ever did, so I've
retained here 1 master of children's literature, whose motto
"*solitaire mais solidaire*"—solitary yet in solidarity—seems to
me the most apropos statement regarding 1's existence as a social organism. The 1st *N* is Nabe, and nipping at his heels is
Nabokov, an especially invidious collision, while Novalis/Ollier
is, on the contrary, a very "literary" conjunction. The letter *O*,

always unaccented, closes on Ovid. *P*, with its hordes of warriors, ultimately sets Proust (but of course) snugly next to Quincey (Thomas De), while opening with Pagès (Yves), and then, in turn, Quintane prepares the way for Rabelais, who counts Racine as his antipode. *R*'s heel also counts as the end of the built-in bookshelves, and their turn to the freestanding shelf to be described farther down. I encourage the reader to hurry there (→ *infra*).

Kult

As my hands glide over the dregs of my little library, I can't deny the stamp of intellectualism everybody insists on imprinting upon my person—or, worse, that of "a writer's writer." How could I dispute it? There's 0 sense in talking about my "literary side" because I don't draw any distinctions between 1 side or the other; rather, literature plays such a large role in my life that to conceal it would be a betrayal not only of my being but also of my very conception of art. If I wanted to sum up in 1 phrase the role that Literature plays in my life, I would say that my readings have been far more decisive than my experiences. Even in the tenderest years of my childhood I saw the world through books and found a kinship with all the other clerks and Clercs and generally clerical folks (sometimes dead, usually living) out there who attached the same value to the experience of reading; I found my original sentiments, which were already deeply rooted, multiplied almost to infinity by the inexhaustible feast of books I devoured, discovering in reading and then in writing an infallible way of intensifying, of amplifying my life. I was never much taken with those drugs and distractions that so many people succumbed to out of a sheer need to escape the conditions imposed upon them, and pledged myself instead to the cult of Words, the singular divinity with 2 faces (reading/writing). From the beginning (which itself was a kind of ending), I felt that there was a distinct difference between myself and other men, those for whom reality, in and of itself, sufficed to provide a satisfaction that I myself could enjoy only on the basis of some fundamental misunderstanding. Of course, to write, 1 must desecrate literature, but to become a writer 1 has to have thoroughly consecrated it 1st! And intellectual as I might seem to some, I'm by no means unquestionably so in the eyes of these same intellectuals: they're convinced that something vigorously resists my aspirations thereto.

Musical Interlude

To my left, as I face the bookcases, my music center clearly juts out beyond the shelves: it protrudes. Deeper than the other shelves, because an LP is bigger than a book, this 1-m-tall, 60-cm-wide nook has 3 compartments: the 1st 1 holds my turntable as well as the LPs I've kept despite the industry-wide shift of the '80s that brought about the advent of the CD. After a very long period of disuse, I recently had the machine repaired at long last (€30) so I could take some pleasure in the clicks and pops of my childhood. Rediscovering and restoring to use an object by rescuing it from the purgatory technological advances had consigned it to is my small way of playing the hero. All that this Technics-brand device is missing is its original protective cover, which I lost; however, the black plastic circle meant to play 45s is still in its place.

It's Still Rock and Roll to Me

Organized as they have to be—vertically—my LPs are among the most ambiguous of my objects of affection: the undeniable affective charge they give me, drawn from the memories that my life in the '80s carved just as deeply into me as these songs have been carved in the records' grooves, is at odds with a general indifference I haven't shaken off, for a couple of reasons: for 1, I just don't have the same mania for rock and roll now that I used to have between '78 and '85, and then I've already parted with a number of my records as much for financial reasons as out of incipient disinterest. I do regret this absurd act that's altered my record collection, and which I've repeated several times—the act of declaring that a given period of my life has come to its end, thereby manufacturing for myself a reason to rid myself of whatever seemed to have embodied it. In much the same way I've dispensed with the 1st novels I wrote, my complete collections of pink and green children's books, my G.I. Joe figures, my Yamaha organ, my working-class cap, etc. I wonder what the next things I'll abandon will be.

Counterhistory of New Wave

The vast majority of my 70 records belong to the rock genre, and more specifically to the subgenre called New Wave, which was my favorite during the '80s, the decade in which this style gained currency. I was the perfect age for this musical style that was born at 1 specific moment, the very moment of my childhood—which has to be the reason for the "affective charge" that I just mentioned and that draws its profound significance solely from the intersection of its creation and my childhood. Here we can find the leading figures of this movement: Elvis Costello, Joe Jackson, the Cure, the Jam, the Clash, the Ramones, or the ska bands that made my whole body vibrate, like Madness, the Specials, or the Selecter. Next to some records by David Bowie, whose *Lodger* is the best representation of this whole era, I have some favorite records, like Blondie's *Parallel Lines* or Kraftwerk's single "The Robots," and although I've had the foresight to keep several albums by the Boomtown Rats and Stiff Little Fingers, I still rue the impulse that drove me to sell off the B-52s' very 1st album, along with Siouxsie and the Banshees' debut, and then had me loan the Sex Pistols' *Never Mind the Bollocks* to some idiot. The ranks of this faltering army will only swell once more if I summon up the courage to undertake the short *Counterhistory of the New Wave* that I'm sure is hidden somewhere in my future.

Amplification

Under the turntable shelf is, at desk height, the shelf for the Tectronic-brand amplifier that used to belong to my brother Jérôme—in 1 sense it still belongs to him, but as the saying goes, possession is 9/10 of the law—and it's worked without even the least hint of any trouble since the '70s, as if the metallic simplicity of this heavy rectangle (silvery on its front side, black on its top and side faces) betokened this amplifier's uncomplicated nature, its range of functions thankfully kept to a minimum (1 on/off button indicated by 1 red light, 2 slider knobs for adjusting intensity, 2 buttons for sound and balance between the speakers) demonstrating the excellence of particular smaller brands despite the blatant yet, alas, commonplace injustice that sees their better-known counterparts so frequently applauded merely for having more features than their shadowy competitors, despite none of these bells and whistles being well implemented. All in all my preference is for a modestly outfitted device that does its job so well that it turns austerity, paradoxically, into an amplification.

Amplifiction

I set down the tone arm, the turntable starts whirring, the blinking orange light turns on, the speed is set to 33 rpm, I watch the record spin, I set my cell phone on the platter, the rotation is gentle and silent, contact has been established between Nokia and Technics, I watch the 2 devices turn like a merry-go-round; distant eras collide, and a new 1 emerges.

HP, I Hate You Profoundly

To the right of the amplifier, practically within reach when I'm sitting at the desk, yawns the paper-stuffed maw of a gray Hewlett-Packard printer. I can accept its aesthetic nullity, but even so, I hate using it. It's muscled its way into a subcategory of objects that are indispensable to me, and yet this infuriatingly slow bitch of a machine makes me livid every single time I use it, mainly because I have no way to stop it from printing a test page every single time it's turned on. After trying in vain to call customer service (because this business won't provide a physical address, undoubtedly because it wants to forestall its customers from murdering its employees), only to find my call redirected to a country in the Maghreb where an operator unable to understand my questions answered me in an HP French that was equally incomprehensible, I assigned 2 local specialists to the case who smirked at my idiocy but frowned when, after more than a half hour of coming at the problem from every direction, they themselves couldn't make any headway in deactivating this function clearly devised to drain half-used ink cartridges empty. A TV broadcast revealed that French factory sites were closing. Secrecy must be the byword for all these companies; every honest autobiography is the enemy of society itself.

Crushed Sound

My 2 huge speakers (60 cm × 32 cm) fill their allotted space so thoroughly that they've practically merged with it. They hark back to a distant era when the size of acoustic devices was seen as amplifying their quality. They've been hamstrung, however, thanks to an odd spatial arrangement, hemmed in 7 cm in front by the desk's right flank, which dampens their sound to the point of practically crushing it: an aficionado of musique concrète would certainly appreciate the effect of hearing a big deep bass sound horribly compromised and compressed by the narrow channel it has to push through. If nothing else, 1 could look at it as a small revenge against music itself, an art form that fills the public sphere these days so aggravatingly that it brings a smile to my lips to see the wind taken out of its sails.

Brown Noise

Over time, these hefty brown speakers protected by their microscopically woven fabric—also brown, but closer to a chestnut hue—have taken on an incredible aesthetic superiority. The artlessness that undergirded their manufacture has, paradoxically, become an unintentional style of its own, which places them somewhere between objet d'art and stark furniture.

Fragile Freebox

On my Freebox—the Internet box, since the television box has already been accounted for (← LIVING ROOM), sitting atop 1 of the speakers, I want only to see the 4 glowing numbers indicating the time, which means that "it's working"; if I see anything else, I risk seriously losing my cool. It's enough to consider the sheer cost of these devices, as well as their less-than-absolute reliability, not to mention all the hours inevitably wasted dealing with the repairs, fine-tuning, setups, and resets they constantly necessitate, and the various hiccups they constantly experience: the sudden death of applications that I find have "shut down unexpectedly," disruptions, failed connections that wreak havoc on my well-being and my day with a simple *click* . . . Seeing the fragility of these devices, it would appear that power and strength are not at all the same thing.

Twilight Zone

Snug between the desk and the bookshelves, overlooked in
the apartment floor plan, is 1 of those bleak spaces that escape
the control of every resident. This 8-cm-wide, 80-cm-deep
stretch is like a narrow, dark ravine, and contains a horrifying
morass of cords and wires: those of the green lamp, the computer, the scanner-and-copier, the speakers, and the amplifier,
as well as the Freebox and the phone. I hate having so many
crucial functions buried in a single zone that's cramped and
almost completely inaccessible, dark and dusty, like the RER
tunnel to some clogged suburb. I do everything I can not to
go spelunking in this space, but I really do need to go in there
with a headlamp soon, because my 5-outlet power strip, for
some unfathomable reason, isn't working anymore.

Site Comments

"It's hard to see in here."

"No, it's hard to see *everywhere*."

Façadism

I get back up and, positioning myself in front of the main wall
of shelves, I take 1 step back, as might a couturier proud of
the dress he's designed, the better to assess the woman wearing it. I become absorbed in contemplating a world, an analysis of form. Setting aside the 7th shelf on the bottom, with its
lesser height (19 cm high), the entire façade is unanimous in
accommodating books.

68 45s

To the left of this atypical shelf, right up against the recessed
music center it mimics, is a set of 45s that suffice to confirm
what some might call the atrocity, and what others might call
the eclectic nature, of my taste, because there are classic rec-

ords here, such as Gainsbourg's "La Javanaise" or the Rolling Stones' "Paint It Black," alongside far less accomplished platters such as Afric Simone's "Hafanana." I think it's safe to say that rock takes up the lion's share of this part of my collection too, in contrast to the limited array of French music here; testing this hypothesis, I grab the whole stack with both hands. My love for classification confirms the score: Anglo-Saxon pop 44, French singers 24, making for a total of 68 45s bracketed by my hands. The set has been bounded.

(Though, thus bounded, both ear and turntable are out of bounds—and so, quickly, I unbind them again.)

CD? More Like Cee-*Die*

Just as my vinyl collection summons up memories as intense as the beauty of these objects derived from black gold, so do the few CDs in my possession leave me indifferent. The smallness of this assortment shows how little I've invested in that medium—which should also be clear from the absence of a CD player here, not to mention the absence of any of those aesthetically intolerable "CD towers"—tempted though I was by them when they 1st appeared on the market, their small square shapes promising to save me who knew how much space: O economy, where is thy victory? As for the argument about which medium has better sound quality, I'm sure I'll never give CDs their due, since I have trouble ever believing that tomorrow's technologies will be better than today's. The CD will die before I ever cede that point.

Farther Right

Farther right is a red forest of books enumerating legal codes (Penal Code, Civil Code, Forestry Code, etc.) that I pulled out of my apartment building's trash, where they had been abandoned in a bag by a neighbor for whoever found them—

which was me. Recent but already outdated, these volumes pander to my punctilious side. Reading utilitarian texts is an efficient way for me to relax: laws, as Stendhal once declared, shed a truthful light upon the world, while also repudiating lazy prose. Compared to the uprightness of the Law, Literature might as well have 2 left feet; the latter is an affront to the former.

Primitive Hut

An African object from my father reminds me of him—but isn't that the intent of all gifts, to animate matter by evoking their donors? It's a small terra-cotta hut, white and brown, from the Bassari country (Mali). I like African art and if I had the means I'd fill my living room with masks and perhaps get a few good scares out of new visitors, but in the meantime I just go to the Musée du quai Branly to satisfy these longings. Further to that point, Douglas Huebler's line comes to mind: "The world is full of objects, more or less interesting; I do not wish to add any more." This fragile, primitive hut, leaning against my legal codes, is 1 of many physical counterparts to this text in which it is described. I wish it a long life, which I suppose isn't really the most successful of performative utterances.

Take a Picture, It'll Last Longer

As it's practically inaccessible to anyone who might want to poke their nose into my library, I have to get down on my knees if I want to pull out my collection of postcards. Their vertical organization collapses together reproductions of artworks from various parts of the world (the only rule: they have to be of the 1s actually on display in the place that was visited) and near-forgotten full-color views of inane places, such as the Dourdan swimming pool or the Uruguay-France high school

in Avon (*département* number: 77), where I wasted so much
time. I've told some of my girlfriends about my love for these
absurd scenes in which comedy clashes with pathos, where
buildings have been immortalized without any clear reason,
as if they were grandiose monuments, by a pathetic sort of
proof of existence that's forced upon them a continued reality
for which they never asked. I do realize how this book is as
much a trace or a replacement as these postcards are, but I
could never simply dwell on the colors and wish-you-were-heres!
that a Breton named Perec, deploying 243 such mementos in
his book *Species of Spaces*, revealed to be dead ends; like Sol
LeWitt before me, with the photo book he called *Autobiography*, I feel the need to set out and breathe life into all my
belongings. Notwithstanding my predilection for ownership,
I can't really call myself a collector: I don't have the perseverance that's integral to the life and passion of true collecting. My
pursuits tend to peter out quickly, either out of sheer indifference to the object in question, or out of my hostility toward
having to expand my domain, or even out of a dilettantism that
unwittingly belittles my own flights of fancy. I generally do
nothing to increase my stock, but then I also won't refrain from
the occasional acquisition of whatever might bring a smile to
my face. And so I've recently bought (without even the remot-
est thought of kitsch, which, by stripping things of their innocence, also deprives them of any interest they hold) 3 postcards
already written on by various strangers.

Recent Acquisitions
An apartment blurs with all its comings and goings. As such,
I've set down an untenable tenet for myself: while writing this
book, I must neither acquire nor discard anything at all (even
when this latter decision might actually have had a positive
effect), and thus make sure that my apartment stays more or less

the way it was when I began. 2.5 years of inertia at the cost of a few recent acquisitions.

Doodads

Several objects "decorate my bookshelves (a closing quotation mark would only increase my ambivalence about that particular verb, so I'll use just an opening quotation mark here—it's not every day that I get to invent a new form of punctuation). In effect, even though the few doodads I've set among my books do add variety to these otherwise uniform shelves, part of me still shies away from the idea of decoration, especially when I think of how it's done in other people's homes. Still, whether I like it or not, I do have to concede the appeal of having particular objects to underscore my belongings and particular belongings to highlight my objects.

Mangled Nativity

Here there's a mini–crèche scene assembled with 3 plaster Bedouins, 1 of them standing up, the other 2 hunched over, bowing down as if praying. These painted figurines, remnants of a mangled Christmas nativity scene, grace with their soothing presence a world now so at odds with the Muslim sphere. A slightly less irenic interpretation would accuse me of not being able to bear the Arab world unless it's contained within a Christian context, and such an accusation would underscore the fact that I'm already committing the horribly Occidental sin of Orientalism; in any case, I've isolated these Arabs from a context that I would never dream of reconstituting in full. It's possible that these 3 figures are just my way of showing how much I prefer 2ndary characters, forgotten or scorned by History, like these old-world Palestinians completely erased by Catholic representations, an erasure for which we've paid such a horrifying price, as Jean Rolin so thoroughly outlined in his book bearing the frank title *Christians in Palestine*.

Double Museum

My bookshelves function as 2 museums in parallel, and this text is where I can share some pictures from (both) these institutions. In my eyes, the distinction between the worlds of literature and the fine arts is nonexistent, and nothing better emblematizes my double love than this William Wegman postcard that shows him seated and reading 2 books at the same time; he seems to have the same sort of strabismus that I myself experienced in childhood.

Napoleon Meets His Hullabaloo

My authoritarian tendencies are made visible (but also neutralized) by the presence of a small 6.5-cm-tall sculpture of Napoleon in lead, which was given to me by my maternal grandmother, and which depicts the man standing in a characteristically Napoleonic pose. To downplay its stance of triumphant virility, I've set this imperialistic figurine next to the works of André Gide. Since the very idea of Napoleon contains both the shaggy Bonaparte and the tyrant with his close-cropped coiffure, this little narrative device nicely fuses together the 2 extremes of masculinity. Such more or less accidental museum displays convey a nicely straightforward sense of existential desolation, I think, by transforming my home into a personal, multifaceted gallery space. If I had no philosophy of interior layout, I'm not sure what point there would be to having an interior in the 1st place.

Mod

More discreetly, I've also put a modish badge on display here that I wore during the brief period of my existence (1981) when I was a card-carrying member of the mod subculture. Blazoned with the U.K.'s tricolor, this plastic emblem reading MADE IN U.K. reminds me, again, of my teenage love for rock music, and especially the band the Jam, as well as my old

Anglophilia, which has more or less dissipated completely now because of that country's selfish economic liberalism. I recently found in Susan Sontag's journals another slang use of the word "jam"—not meaning "sperm," which is the most obvious interpretation here in France, but a lesser-known application, referring, in fact, to the sexual preferences of the majority of the global population.

Nonanonymous

Among the pieces in my permanent collection that I rotate in and out of storage, there is currently on display an oval photograph of 1 middle-aged man, dressed in a 3-piece suit, sitting in an armchair with his legs crossed and posing with his right hand on his thigh. Turning over the card to identify the man in question, the mystery only grows—there's no caption. For years I had no idea who this man could possibly be, much less where I might have found this image in the 1st place. I told myself that it had to be a stranger—after all, my attraction to anonymity in all its forms is hardly incompatible with my love for proper names—and so was always caught off guard when various liars, looking at this portrait, claimed to know who he was. Alas, the postcard's mute strangeness dissipated completely when I finally discovered, unwillingly, the answer to my question. During a short stay in Brussels, at the gift shop located in Victor Horta's house-turned-museum, I came across the image's exact double, and realized that I'd even bought the card there: at that stele erected in honor of a most admirable architect of the interior.

Household Muse

The decorative proliferation to which I've devoted myself is my way of thwarting the overly metaphysical nature of Literature; clutter reminds me of my status as a man-object. I have

the same feeling walking through my little cave as I do visiting the overfull Sir John Soane's Museum in London, or the
museum-house of August Strindberg in Stockholm. These are
places where the Absolute of literature may be chipped away
by the Relative—just as some torturers will dog-ear the pages
of books. I won't rule out, once this journey is complete, the
possibility of opening my apartment up to public viewing, of
adding it to the list of Parisian museums that welcome visitors
for a handful of hours each week. Entry: €3.50. Please call
ahead for school-group visits.

Temporary Exhibits

My apartment's exhibits have to be rotated—the paucity of
space here necessitates it. So that I don't become habituated
and forget that wonderful injunction to "look with all your
eyes, look," I regularly modify the iconographic displays on
my shelves, which, at the moment, display the following: 2
black & white '70s-era collectors' photos of cars from that
same period, 4 Diptyque perfume packages exuding the tran-
quil fragrance of their original contents, and 1 invitation to an
exhibition, its words surrounding the image of a prestigious
residence as seen through the fence of its conscientious owner.
Thus do various small optical diversions glitter among my
arrays of books, the better to please those who follow the instructions given by Verne and put on display as an epigraph for
Perec.

Zoom Out

A young man bathed in an orange light with his left hand in
the pocket of his white pants, which are neatly tucked into his
boots. He's wearing a black redingote and a black hat. He's
looking off to the side, his right knee bent and thrust forward.
In front of him is a huge draft horse with a silky black coat

rearing back in deference (its back left hoof is raised slightly). The beast is harnessed to a tiny, elegant Duc carriage with unevenly sized wheels. But, zooming out, the young man, the horse, and its harness seem to be perched on a long horizontal plank beneath which hangs a small ring in profile clasping a larger ring facing outward in turn containing the letter *H*. And this entire scene is set within an even larger disc, or medallion. And, as I step back farther still, I find, emblazoned across an even greater portion of this luxury shopping bag (found in a trash can), the word *Hermès*.

The Formerly Bare Wall

But I can't back too far away from my book-lined wall, because only 2 or 3 full steps would make me collide, backward, with the other (freestanding) bookshelves along the facing wall. I turn 180°, pausing momentarily to look at the wall shared with my bedroom, which includes 1 door and ends at a window. This part of the wall stayed bare for a long time, its vast emptiness a contrast to the grandiloquence of the wall of shelves. I fought to keep it unsullied; I lost. An early symptom of the slow and deadly encroachment upon my person and personal space by books, books, and more books. I stagger back to my desk.

Blue Chair

My chair turns its back on me: its curved blond-wood frame suits the desk, the bookshelves, and the hardwood floor, even though its seat and backrest are upholstered in bright blue. As I pull the chair toward me, it glides noiselessly over the parquet thanks to pads affixed to its feet, and, greeted by its wholly blue face, I really don't know what to think of this alliance between white ash and flashy moleskin that's accompanied me since 1991—its austere modernist form adulterated by royal-blue padding. Oddly enough, I don't have the same affection for it that I do for its more humdrum cousins (← *infra*, LIVING ROOM). It's just a piece of equipment. I admit that it's comfortable, but its blue quietude has no effect on me, just like a piece of furniture in a catalog or on display, with a history that has 0 connection to my own. Once we've been convinced they will serve us faithfully we don't waste any energy fretting over our furnishings. Ownership makes us go soft.

Rearranging the Seating Chart

The blue chair, elevated above the other seats in my apartment by the place of honor it occupies, plays its leading role with pride. It's superior to a Ron Arad chair, but less beautiful than a chair dreamed up by Donald Judd: it sits somewhere between being a chair for an artist to work at and a chair for a fence to offload. I bring it over to the center of the office, where it has no reason to be, simply to place it in a situation new to the both of us: by detaching it from my desk, I've liberated it, given it back to itself, restored its painful freedom. To force upon my apartment an asymmetric or even antisymmetric arrangement of furniture is a power I exercise with the stubborn obstinacy of a man determined to decorate and redecorate and re-redecorate his home ad infinitum.

Voluntary Discomfort

Instead of sinking into my chair, as I usually do, I deliberately only perch on its edge; I don't sit squarely on the seat, pretending to be 1 of those men who only half-sit when they sit at all, ready to get up and move at the drop of a hat. I sample a taste of the discomfort of the provisional—a voluntary discomfort, in this case.

Jesus' Place

This irritating position ushers me into a strange dream: Mussolini has been invited to dinner at Jesus' place. He arrives at the street Jesus lives on, but can't find the right house. Pacing authoritatively, he knocks on the doors at numbers 22, 24, and 26, calls out, but doesn't get any answer. Then he realizes that Jesus doesn't have a house, that he's been tricked. Mussolini doesn't want to lose face, so he turns on his heel and stomps down the street, all the while loudly imprecating the Lord as he repeats his famous curse: "Fascism is the enemy of domestic comfort!"

Incomplete Position

Awake again, I'm back in my office's gaping center. Sitting suits me. Hunching over suits me too. Even slouching with my butt glued to the seat suits me; and yet, this isn't the whole story—it glosses over some complications that I'll reveal *infra*, once I'm standing again and walking.

Scores of Shelves

Obliquely to my right is the small section of bookshelf that forms an angle with the main shelves. It doesn't take up its entire section of the wall with its 8 rows, the 2 on the bottom being blocked by the desk. In Paris, as you may know, building numbers are calculated vis-à-vis the Seine; in my office, I number my 8 shelves vis-à-vis the floor, the number 1 by the parquet, number 8 by the ceiling. Numbers 8 through 6 hold nothing but books, so they're just more of the same, whereas numbers 5 to 0 are a little more equivocal.

Objective Crime

On the outer edge of the 5th shelf, 80 cm from my face and 40 from my outstretched arm, I've pinned up an illustration that breaks up the sober beige: I lean forward and decide to yank it cleanly off; the fact is that I tend to prefer to see a given material nude than gussy up its fundamental emptiness; the medium is sufficient unto itself. Between my living fingers the image protests, citing as evidence my teenage love for covering my bedroom walls with personal icons, household relics, stupid photos, newspaper clippings, and record covers. Jean Genet, whenever he moved into a new hotel, took possession of his room by pinning a photo of the murderer Weidmann to the wall. But Genet lived at no fixed address, and when it comes to decoration, I follow the school of Adolf Loos, which declares: ornament is a crime. Which must make me . . . a criminal?

Oranj Jaz

Part of the 5th shelf is taken up by a square Jaz clock (20 cm × 20 cm) with rounded corners. It affirms its '70s style with its orange plastic and its embossed numbers protected by a glass pane. It brings to mind the start of a well-known novel: "Anton Vowl turns on a light. According to his Jaz it's only 12.20 . . . ," the mention of this particular brand—neither Kelton nor Patek Philippe nor Rolex—giving the reader a clue to the compositional process of the novel in question.

Down with Unity of Time!

Its ostensible provenance from a bygone age could be seen as a concession to my usual nostalgia; but the stylistic coherence-through-incoherence of my furnishings, resistant to all unities, repudiates this facile explanation. A genuinely antique clock, as superfluous as the idea of time it represents—like 1 of those grand old models found in aristocratic French homes— would drive me up the wall. I need a semirecent clock to defy time's diktat. An hour produced by a clock from 1975 still seems to belong to the year it was made, steering me back toward the time when I was a happy, unpunctual child.

Temporal Lapses

As for this clock, which I've now nearly made my way all around (and I do insist it's part of this project to make my way around each object around me—a quixotic aspiration that will no doubt wear me out completely), I'm the only 1 who knows there's a crack in 1 of its sides, since I knocked it to the floor in circumstances I no longer remember, a sin that has engendered everlasting guilt. Pondering the integrity of the clock's casing, forever lost, I draw my fingers along a seam of hardened glue.

Got the Time?

No matter where I am in my apartment, it's always easy for me to see what time it is. Having the hour perpetually on display ought to make me panicky, but it actually calms me down. A truly fastidious devotee of time might have clocks in every room, but, making a careful count, it turns out there are only 4 ways to tell the time from my current position, at this precise second: the panoramic clock, my nomadic wristwatch and cell phone, and also, I guess, my computer screen, which displays the time in its upper right corner, and is actually the most reliable timepiece here, since it's synchronized with "universal time," a phrase that I'm admittedly skeptical about, as it feels like an affront to those many domains, Literature included, where I defy the universal.

4 Times, 5 Brands

In fact, the 4 slightly different readouts provided by each of the aforementioned chronometers don't quite align with each other, and so give a clearer, more asynchronous image of time. And comparing these sources on the spot, I notice that

Bulova gainsays Jaz, which corrects Nokia, which is itself disputed by Apple. The latter is corroborated only by the Braun (→BEDROOM).

References

Shelf number 4 displays my reference books. I've reserved a place of honor for the 2 Roberts. Their symmetrical format (Vol. 1: *Langue française* / Vol. 2: *Noms propres*) is a deliberate artifice meant to give credence to the naïvely ironic idea of a harmony between words and things. Next to them stands a Bible, inscribed by my parents, who gave it to me for my 1st communion in 1977, the year of punk. Here, the most famous book in the world sits next to the Roberts, but, to me, the dictionary is the definitive book, the holy book that contains all others (I have a project in mind that would involve rewriting the dictionary . . .), while there's a phenomenal number of words and things missing from the Bible—"Kafka," for example, or "cogwheel." The false totality of religious books is due to their inviolable character, written as they are during 1 era for all eras; only the totality of the dictionary is true and beautiful, rewritten, as it is, for every era.

High Books

Meant to hold oversize volumes, the 3rd shelf has more height than the others, but wasn't well thought out, as I don't actually own any books 40 cm tall; even art books aren't that tall, and although there may be some publishers out there who do produce books in such a gimmicky format, I'm not what you'd call their ideal market. The idea of "books as objects" is disagreeable to me, the sole exception being those false, hollow books, holding a flask of rum or a Colt 45 or a tapered deck of cards, as are so often found in the homes of self-described pranksters or other such cultural provincials.

In any event, there's a 13-cm-tall empty space floating high above the tallest literary peaks of my collection, the record for height being held by *Hitchcock/Truffaut*, which is 30 cm tall, head and shoulders above my thesis (which isn't a book at all, just a bound sheaf of A4 pages) and other tomes of lesser importance. In this array, from the left, are the 1st 5 volumes of the *Grand dictionnaire encyclopédique Larousse* in 10 volumes (1963 edition), recognizable for its black hide stamped with gilded letters. Volumes 1 through 9 were a familiar part of my childhood; I was so fascinated by that array of massive dark cakes that I can still remember and recite the letters on their spines, like so many other incantations I find myself mumbling, now and again, like some Cro-Magnon: "DESF–FILAO! FILAR–HYDRA! ORM–RALS!"

Hard to Reach

The most noticeable detail about this shelf is that it intersects perpendicularly with my stereo system, which, projecting forward beyond the shelf, makes for a partial obstruction. As a result of which, in order to reach the books obscured in this fashion, I 1st have to pull out the 1s hemming them in on the left—the fat dictionaries that are hardest to shift around. This unintended niche very nicely conceals those works I might prefer to keep away from prying eyes: a casual glance isn't enough to tell what's back there, though, since I can make out only the top edges of the tallest volumes . . . So I get up to make sure that what I'm keeping there really deserves to be hidden away—I have to pull out *Hitchcock/Truffaut* to relieve the suspense and see just how disparate the contents stowed here really are: next to the (dated) *Vocabulaire de la psychanalyse* is the *Petite fabrique de littéerature*, which I absolutely fell in love with when I 1st discovered the Oulipo, then the *Dictionnaire des excentriques du cinéma français*, which unfortunately contains no entry for myself, and then an issue of the magazine *Actes sur la recherche en sciences sociales* dedicated to sexuality, against which 2 pornographic magazines bought in Antwerp are leaning.

Porn Data

Will I reshelve these volumes before going on with my narrative, or will I flesh out my remarks while I'm holding and paging through these? You'll never know. In any case, the fact that a sociological investigation into sexuality should find itself neighbor to hard-core porn serves to confirm for me that every obsessive is thoroughly obsessed—a banal and practically tautological remark whose accuracy is nevertheless demonstrated by this hideaway secreting its theoretical and practical assemblage. As I quickly flick through these periodicals of Dutch flesh, I notice that they no longer have any effect on me: Internet pornography has thoroughly destroyed this subgenre, and it's only out of documentary interest that I keep these magazines . . . though, saying that, I can't help but smile, since this is exactly the kind of argument that hypocrites like to spout to justify their pleasures.

Very Hard to Reach

The 2nd shelf, almost completely hemmed in by the desk, positioned down low, welcomes the rest of my encyclopedic dictionary, volumes 6 to 10, augmented by 2 supplements published to keep this edition—very popular in French households of the time—up-to-date. These supplements were a failure, by contrast, as the desire to stay up-to-date beyond 1960—with inventions that seemed to be at the cutting edge of progress quickly becoming anodyne, political leaders losing status, actors coming and going, countries shifting their borders, writers' fame rising and falling—soon foundered, as if bewitched, under the steadily encroaching curse of obsolete knowledge.

STRIA–ZYTH

My childhood collection was missing STRIA–ZYTH, the last of the 10 volumes. This absence actually saved me: I had a space to fill; I had to make *myself* number 10 (in soccer, growing up, that was what we called the position now known, quite respectably, as the playmaker).

And what would I have become if we had owned only 1 single volume? A decorator? An interior designer?

Hidey-Hole

The end of this shelf plunges so far down behind the desk that, as opposed to my merely inaccessible books, it's practically impossible to reach anything that might be back there—it's such a perfect hidey-hole, in fact, that I have no idea what it's hiding. I hesitate to rummage around what might be buried here—out of sheer laziness, really, not out of any particular desire for secrecy. However, since I've set out on this journey, I've had to remove obstacles at every step that would otherwise have compromised my forward progress, and so even as I talk the talk, I go ahead and—in contrast to the viscount Xavier de Maistre, who could depend on his good servant Joanetti to do the heavy lifting—walk the walk. Moving objects alongside words: if this is an archaeological dig, it's being run by a topographer in tandem with an archivist. So I get up, I push the heavy desk to the side, speaking the magic words "Oh, my back!" in order to open up a passage into the forbidden zone just mentioned, whereupon I have to kneel down—taking care not to knock over the green lamp—cough a few times in all the dust I've stirred up, untangle the inextricable tangle of cords, making sure not to accidentally pull any of them out of their sockets, and press onward between my desk and my speakers—under constant threat of muscle strain—taking care not to hit my back or my head against anything, crawling on all 4s in a ridiculous, humiliating, painful position. Only then am I finally able to get close to the shelf/hidey-hole, out of which I carefully pull the remaining Larousse volumes 1 by 1, and take all the other tenants too, only to verify that there's not much back here, as I had feared, aside from a few more catalogs of contemporary art—or, rather, not-very-contemporary art, since I haven't thought about them for ages. The only notable exception gleams in the shadows, *Russian Folktales*, a book I've never bothered to read because of the instant boredom induced by its title but which will reveal its riches upon being rescued from this oubliette, its cover—coated with a thick layer of dust—illustrated in the mannered style of formerly Soviet republics.

Photo of Musset

And, indeed, stuck between the 3rd and 4th pages of the *Folktales*, I find 2 documents that, not content to merely substantiate my prediction, give this otherwise insignificant book its true evocative power: 1 vignette of Paris's public schools, crowned by the national motto of the French Republic, and, down below, the note *Distribution des prix*, which shows that I received 3rd place in 1975. Underneath it I find a rectangular black-and-white photograph, 17 cm by 10 cm, showing the CM2 B class in the courtyard of the school on the rue de Musset (Paris, 16th arrondissement). Beneath the courtyard horse chestnut tree, 1 row of 11 students is standing behind 1 row of 11 others squatting down in a perfect symmetry that neatly denotes the strict order with which my school was run. As I was part of the *shorter row*, I'm on the far right of the photo, the last of those squatting down. I'm wearing a pair of bell-bottoms, a dark pullover with a long-point narrow-spread shirt collar sticking out over it, and some Kickers. I'm smiling. My hair is long and blond. As I look at this photo, I run through all the names of my buddies, which come to me practically without any effort even 35 years later. And so this photograph at last makes its way to the light of day out of the dark pages in which it had been imprisoned.

Unreachable

Finally, the last shelf, which doesn't even deserve to be called a shelf, because it's just a kind of storage space delimited by the floor: a nearly unreachable gap. My bookshelves' invisible subproletariat—the books I almost never touch. Just like those supermarkets that stock their lowest shelves with the least attractive or least useful or least pricey products, or particular bookstores that cynically shelve poetry or art criticism in the spots that require the greatest lumbar effort, I've chosen this spot for the books whose claims on my sympathies have waned the most over time—comics. To identify them takes a bit of light, or anyway a bit of memory jogging: *Tintin*, *Lucky Luke*, *Astérix*, some of which formerly belonged to my older brothers, their covers worn down by multiple generations, their corners folded or sometimes even torn, and occasionally reaffixed with shiny Scotch tape over the red, blue, and green spines. These primary colors are vivid even in this darkness.

High Culture, Low Culture

The position of my comic books at the lowest depths of the abyss isn't a complete accident. A sociological analysis of my 1-man culture could easily demonstrate that I've reserved my lowest shelves for those cultural products I consider the weakest aesthetically. And there's enough truth to that assessment that I don't see any point in protesting—even though, that said, I do like comics, and the mere fact of their being on my shelves (I count 65 of them here) proves it. Still, comics are, historically, a minor, newfangled art when compared to the other literary forms. I can't accord them a status comparable to the other works I keep, even if I do consider a few graphic novelists to be true masters and hold them in greater esteem than some authors included under the rubric of "official" literature. My tastes on that front are classical—I would give up all the works of John Perse for a single volume of Hergé, and all Heidegger's flights of fancy for a single *Blueberry* collection.

3 Connected Actions

I stand up straight, I push the desk back against my shelves, my left buttock brushes against the radiator.

Radiator 2

This radiator, the 2nd of its kind, is positioned between the window and the door to the bedroom, and is a perfect storm of shortcomings: it barely works and wasn't cheap. Even so, I want to set aside its functional shortcomings for now and breathe some life into this ugly little object, which is smaller than its homologue in the living room, but is made out of the same cold, grayish metal. The apparatus's body, emblazoned with a red WELCOME stamp, is topped by a horizontal board containing 6 gill-like openings to let out its heat. Visually, its best aspect is this series of alveoli that look exactly like 9 small basement windows.

On the Bone

Carving up the radiator like a Christmas-dinner capon, I find a charm in it that the machine's totality can't provide. My gaze is like a carving knife—it's better, even, since it can't actually stab anyone or slice them up. Once it's anatomized, the object almost becomes poignant; vivisected, it radiates.

Existential Gradation

Beneath the flat board topping this appliance, sloping almost imperceptibly, is its temperature dial, made out of serrated plastic, going from 0 to MAX. I rarely use the full range of temperatures: if I'm trying to warm the entire room, I set it to 5, 6, or even 7, but never MAX. Am I scared of overdoing it? Or of breaking this thing? I'm always suspicious about pushing an object or machine or tool to its maximum, as if it were dangerous to use anything completely: my oven never has all its burners turned on, I don't open my faucets all the way, I never turn my stereo up to a scream. When I was a child sitting in the family car, I watched the speedometer on the dashboard and noticed that it could go all the way to 240 even though we only ever hit 120, and even then had the feeling that life was best lived well short of the full range of possibilities.

Cold at Home

1 of the meager benefits of living in a small space is that it heats up more quickly. Sometimes, though, I'm determined to do without basic comforts, and so I test my ability to survive the cold all by myself, preferring to put on an extra sweater rather than deal with all those switches on the fuse box (← ENTRYWAY). This little game doesn't really work in the opposite direction—nobody is stupid enough to intentionally heat their apartment in the summer—so I would deduce that wintertime just makes people Nietzschean. Saunas are so oppressively sweltering that I can't bring myself to replicate 1 here, not even for the irony of wearing a T-shirt during the

winter. But that at least would let me have a laugh or 2, whereas being wrapped in sweaters and pullovers in an icy apartment is merely depressing. Between the rigor of 1 kind of asceticism and the debauchery of 1 kind of luxury, I don't want to have to choose—or get stuck in between.

Prop Art

The bulging backside of this heater is firmly anchored to the wall and (in the summer) doubles as a display stand for records. The beauty of record covers has contributed to the foundation of an authentic form of pop art, their 21 × 33 format allowing for a broad visual component that rounds out the acoustic essence of a given LP (and makes a fool of CDs). And I could never get tired of Kraftwerk's gorgeous *Autobahn* record cover, which I've co-opted to make into a piece of art on display here, supported by the radiator. Every week I tell myself I should swap it out with something else, to make this area into yet another rotating exhibit.

Door-Bridge

I step right in front of the door to my bedroom, which connects the 2 rooms. I'll open it only when we're there, farther down (→BEDROOM), to bridge the gap.

Window on the Street

As we prepare for that great and emotional moment, we find ourselves in front of the window overlooking the rue du Faubourg-Martin, right by numbers 37 and 39. I've filled this huge illuminated gap in my wall (and its twin sister in my bedroom) with a double-paned window in plastic moldings, which replaced the previous antiquated wood moldings that betoken the lodgings of the poor on the façades of their humble abodes . . .

Site Comments

"But aren't you ashamed to have used PVC?"

"You're 1 to talk!"

"But it's so ugly!"

"And expensive too—€300 for the pair . . ."

"Has it done the trick, at least?"

"Go see for yourself, in the bedroom."

Double Exposure

Looking out onto the street is crucial for me. I like my domiciles to retain some degree of sovereignty, bounded though they must be by the outside world, allowing me to enjoy the spectacle of life on the street while still having the freedom to step back and sample the calm of a courtyard. From this point of view, the apartment I currently occupy suits me perfectly, as it overlooks both street and courtyard, and I wonder, now that I've reached maturity, whether this principle of "both at once" isn't precisely the principle, if not of happiness, then at least of general balance. The desire to unite opposites, which I would have considered vulgar in my youth, and sneered at as though it were a moral shortcoming, seems to me, now that some of my passions have subsided, eminently advisable; and, as my mind's eye peers through a window from my past at some landscape I remember hating, I have to admit that wanting things that are incompatible is, on the contrary, the hallmark of someone happily drunk on life.

No Exit

As inwardly focused as I tend to be, as keen as I am for the "courtyard side," I need the infinite theater of the street to distract myself and feed my daydreams with dense, rich reality. I've even positioned my desk in such a way that when I raise my head, I'm face-to-face with 2 contradictory continents: the bookshelf wall and the ever-bustling outdoors. Plenty of desk-ologists would differ on this point of interior design, since the spectacle of the street could well distract me from my screen. I do understand that argument, but the prospect of working while facing a wall seems far too ascetic for me. Which is why, by turning my desk to be perpendicular to the window or even facing the window, I've landed, I think, on a solution that serves as a good compromise, allowing me to concentrate while still being conscious of the pulsating street. My 2 screens fight to occupy my field of vision—and as I type I synthesize them.

Flip and Tuck

It's very rare that I change apartments, because I tend to de-fend my way of life as if it were a kingdom: so, in order to get a small taste of moving, I sometimes rearrange my furniture—pushing my desk against the window or turning it around to face the opposite direction (as if this were a real office in which I had to receive visitors), orienting the couch differently to clear space by the back wall, etc. The room immediately feels rejuvenated.

Rail

Beyond the window it bars horizontally, a wrought-iron rail asserts its thoroughly Parisian arabesques. 4 circles adorned with leaves and plumes hark back to an age when Art was put in everything to renew life. These ornate decorations appear in 1,000 variations—such as, on the windows of the building fac-ing mine, those elongated crosses curving to make an oval me-dallion. Embellishing the inside as much as the outside, they reestablish the equivalency between 2 wrongfully separated worlds. Who knows whether these patterns have some occult significance? Maybe they speak to each other in a code that became indecipherable when the group of conspirators who imposed this fate upon every building cast this spell upon our society? The kind of poetry they exude is both esoteric and bourgeois, industrial and mannered (and filthy).

A Worldly Man Never Looks out the Window

Will the view I have of the street free me from myself? "The spectacle of the world" gives me, itself, a joy far greater than anything I might see within it. Some person steps out of my field of vision, someone else walks into sight, a 3rd goes out, and so on without end: a wholesaler opens the door to the textile store; the garbage man collects green bags of trash and throws them into the back of his truck; the 47 bus goes by; traffic comes to a halt; the crazy woman with 6 dogs walks her greyhounds; a man comes out of the building at number 39; the sailmakers' store sign is replaced with 1 that says BABY TOWN; I notice my neighbor in her bra and try to imagine just how happy she might or might not be; I wonder what the shutters on the 4th floor that have been closed for 10 years are hiding; I notice the slaves at the Chinese textile store stirring behind their wire fence; I look up toward the grayness of the gray sky; at number 39 the neighbors on the 7th floor make me smile as they eat their lunch on their little balcony; at number 37 the children on the 3rd floor throw water balloons at passersby and I can't decide whether to laugh or yell at them; I see 1 woman take 100 steps while on her cell phone; a shop owner smokes a cigarette on his doorstep; and maybe someday I'll be lucky enough to directly experience some of the Chinese New Year's festivities whose fireworks I've heard, or else the festival of Janmashtami, or else a Kurdish protest to free Öcalan, the leader of the PKK; someone I know passes by below my window; some Tamils try to enter my building to leave behind flyers for SOS Plumbers, and 1

of them sticks a blade into the door; I'm thinking of something, of nothing, of some nothings; I tell myself that I should
wash this window the better to see my neighbor washing her
clothes; I'm spouting my umpteenth rant against the anarchic
filth of window frames mucking up the uniformity of my
neighborhood's façades; I start thinking that maybe I'm made
of PVC too; a line by Robert Creeley comes to mind and collides with the hope that I might somehow come into some
money; and then I snap out of camera mode, which is so relax-
ing it makes me delighted to be alive. We tell children not to
waste their time staring out windows, as if children didn't have
nothing but time to waste; we advise young women not to ex-
pose themselves the way flies perched on a windowsill do; we
tease the men of the world for standing sentry by their windows when there's nothing to keep an eye out for.

Trajectory
After writing a book on walking every single street of the
10th arrondissement, I've come back home.

Unproductive Assets
As it's fairly difficult to reach, because of my desk's obstruc-
tive presence, I rarely actually open this window. If I decide to
crack it open, and shift the desk to the right, I find myself in a
narrow strait, utterly hemmed in, and have to slide along the
door, squeeze past the radiator, even get around the near left
corner of the desk so I can wriggle into the 28 cm valley that
separates it from the window. It seems like such an enormous,
unexploited space—only ever visited by my vacuum—and
yet, attempting to cross it, I still somehow wind up jammed
against the window, where, as they say in Marseille, I'm
"asquished."

Filthy Panes

The grime on these filthy panes stands out like a reproach; in the sun, the dust keeps breeding and breeding. He grabs a newspaper and some Ajax window cleaner, mixing the black of the window's muck with that of the paper's ink. Soon enough, the newspaper, having become 1 damp black ball, has found its vocation as a dishrag. Then he wipes a soft cloth over both sides of the glass and new rays of light grace the room in thanks. To do so, he had to get up on the rail outside, overcoming his vertigo to experience the particular pleasure in being between 2 spaces, half inside, half outside, standing on the façade, equal parts human and bird.

Another Technique

There's another, less poetic technique of window cleaning, which consists of doing just 1 pane each day. The 1 thoroughly clean window stands out in sharp contrast to the 7 filthy others. In this way, reality shifts from the cloudiness of nearsightedness to a farsighted clarity. The world is remade in 8 days.

The Heavy Blue Denim Protecting Me

Feeling the urge to cut myself off from the world, I yank shut the heavy blue denim that protects me. The curtains that seal off the street have to be thick; ideally, opaque window coverings would also be present to shore up the curtains, as in those respectable houses where rivals are assassinated in the total secrecy afforded by opaque drapes. The piece of denim I use is a single bolt—the better to keep out the daylight. In general, I only draw the curtain when night falls, but sometimes too when my office is bathed in sunlight so bright that I'm blinded. At night, to make sure that nobody can see me from outside, I perform 1 simple test: I turn on the lights, I poke my head between the curtain and the window, and I watch as I wave my hand at myself from inside, staging a little shadow-puppet performance, even having a bit of fun making obscene gestures. If my hand stays invisible, my mind lights up.

Verso

At nightfall, he catches his reflection in the window of the facing building; a hologram on the glass, beyond which seems to be a bedroom, he sees himself pouring himself a glass.

Diplomatic Curtness

I always pull the curtain from left to right, from where my friend the light barely shines to where it pours in. The too-thin rod and the too-heavy weight dragging it down keep the curtain from being easily drawn all the way open or closed; 1 strong yank usually gets the job done, but this overemphatic gesture of mine sometimes pulls the little curtain-rod screws out of the wall. Every time I set the scene, then, I have to be diplomatic: using enough strength to move the fabric, but not so much that it'll bring everything crashing down.

Wanted Dead or Alive

He's had 0 contact with the office's outdoor shutters. They're always open, there on the façade, and he's never had any reason to touch them. Suddenly, though, he imagines these 2 shutters shut—indicating either a place FOR SALE, or an occupant dead. He shuts all the windows—a new experience—then goes outside and looks up from the street. 3rd floor windows all shuttered—but he's still alive.

3rd-Floor Program

This building has 5 floors. You've been put on the 3rd floor. You'll live there happily, not too low down or too high up.

Time will go by. You won't need an elevator. You'll pity the
1st-floor residents, but you'll be jealous of those on the 4th.
You'll get used to it.

Bibliotheca Alexandrina

Now I've come to the other bookshelf, which, as I deal with
an overflow of books, has become an add-on that doubles
my personal Library of Alexandria. Bought for €800 at a flea
market, in the *trente glorieuses* style, standing on 8 rectangular black iron feet and leaving 1 empty 22 cm space above the
floor, it boasts 3 vertical boards holding 6 shelves each, to
which I might add the shelves' little roof terrace.

Continuity

This freestanding addition extends the alphabetical contin-
uum of my library. The last book there was *How I Wrote
Certain of My Books* by Raymond Roussel, and the 1st book
here is Henry Rousso's *The Vichy Syndrome*. Rousseau is the
best-represented author in *R*, the only 18th-century author I
actually like, notwithstanding Sade, whose stately black *S*
adorns the spine of my Pauvert editions. Sachs anticipates Sade,
and Sartre their mutual enemy follows them at a distance. The
letter *T* begins with Tarkos, a poet who died tragically at age
39, the climacteric age at which I, in publishing my book on
Maurice Sachs, could say I was born as an author, and runs on
to the biography of Truffaut, my real-life hero, and the poems
of Tsvetaeva. *U* is a hapax legomenon (the sole instance of a
word in a text) in the person of Ungaretti, whose distichs I often repeat to myself (*M'illumino / d'immenso*). Valéry/Voltaire
could not be more French, and Walser/Woolf could not be
more wonderful. *X* is absent, as is *Y* (I'm not counting that
copy of the *Yi Jing* my mother gave me), and *Z*, which starts
with Zabrana, is as usual filled with many volumes of Zola,

the only 1 of which I've enjoyed being *The Kill*, that novel of flesh and gold that nicely sums up all the human aspirations of these last few centuries of the future.

Quo Vadis?

Despite my steady progress down these literary train tracks, there reigns over this rugged terrain a certain entropic tendency. And so, breaking with my principle of alphabetical classification, this bibliostructure also holds the totality of 1 specific category, the diaries and journals of writers (with internal alphabetical classification, from Barbellion to Woolf), a genre for which I nurse a well-known partiality. The passage of days is also incarnated here by my Quo Vadis day planners, on shelf number 2, which sit in orderly succession from 1997 to the present day in formats distinct from the preceding years' planners as seen in the dentist's cabinet (←LIVING ROOM). This black forest (black, that is, except for the year 1998, which had its leatherette cover thrown into the trash) contains the objective side of my life.

Roof Terrace

Controversial as an urban planner, Le Corbusier, in inventing the roof terrace, was also criticized as an architect; but, from the point of view of interior design, this great pioneer deserves all our esteem. Who hasn't turned the upper surfaces of their furniture into roof terraces? The freestanding bookcase, much as I feared, has had its top colonized by a motley row of books. On the left are my bilingual dictionaries—Bailly for ancient Greek, Gaffiot for Latin, Robert & Collins for English— preceding, contrary to my principles, 6 vertical piles lying flat. Merely looking at this overcrowding is almost as exhausting as my constant pacing; I want nothing more than to get far away from my overfull shelves as quickly as I can, into a thoroughly new and empty space—though not silent, for that would mean my grave.

Spatiogen

Only 2 nonbook items are on this roof. The 1st is a black vase that, like its 2 brothers in the living room and the bedroom, holds 0 flowers. I might joke that I've deflowered it, though nobody ever offered me up their, ahem, flower to begin with. I've hidden this vase behind several volumes to silence any utilitarian objection and so avoid throwing it out, since my aesthetic side would rather hold on to it a while longer. The 2nd is my beautiful squirrel, reclining like a Roman on a couch of catalogs: a stuffed creature that I picked up on the street, probably stolen and then abandoned there as part of the revenge of some opponent of taxidermy, which art makes me think less of dying than of merely keeping up appearances. Its dark-brown fur gleaming, its eyes black marbles, this animal frozen on a branch is grabbing a huge pinecone with its clawed fingers. I didn't pay for the remains of this transfigured rat: I feel as though my rescuing it turned it into a totem.

The only companion animal I appreciate is the cat. I spent 17 years sharing a space with that species, which asks only for gratifying inattention. A cat ratifies an apartment, but I don't know whether a new 1 would get along with this "old mole," as Hamlet called his father's ghost (and a nickname I've happily taken on ever since reading that play).

Anti-Bartleby

Turning around 1 more time in my office where I scriven, I realize that I prefer it, even admire it, less for its harmony—which moving a single piece of furniture would completely undo, and which I'd have to re-create, somehow, if I ever settled into a new place—than for its simple existence: because

I've "had" kitchens before, I've had entryways, and I've had bedrooms, but this is the 1st time I've ever had an office of my own.

Brrring!
Another ring of the doorbell makes me jump. I turn toward the living room—not to go back to the entryway, though, but rather to enter the bedroom.

Bedroom

(11.60 m^2)

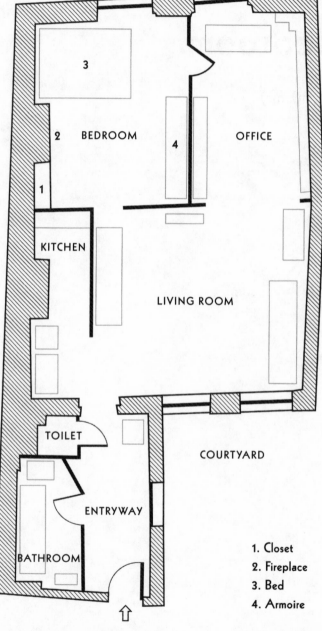

RUE DU FAUBOURG-SAINT-MARTIN

3

2   BEDROOM

OFFICE

4

1

KITCHEN

LIVING ROOM

TOILET

COURTYARD

ENTRYWAY

BATHROOM

1. Closet
2. Fireplace
3. Bed
4. Armoire

Theater

As in some stage performances, there are 2 ways to enter my bedroom: either from the office or from the living room (which is the solution we'll go with). Here a curtain serves as the divider; there, a door. The importance of these entrances is inversely proportional to the consistency of their material. If I enter through the "service" doorway, I feel like a maid; whereas, through the "normal" doorway, I feel like I'm still myself.

Termini

The wall separating the bedroom from the office is probably 1 of those "half-load-bearing" walls mentioned *supra*, but I never intended to knock it down—not before the remodeling started, and certainly not after the incident that educated me in the notion of "half-load-bearing" walls to begin with—because work and sleep are as foreign to each other as day and night, so it stands to reason that any obstacle lying between the office and the bedroom would hardly be in need of removal. This room is solidly demarcated from those that flow into 1 another—the entryway, the kitchen, the living room, the office—and so I must conclude that the bedroom is, along with the toilet and the bathroom, 1 of the apartment's termini.

Undrawn Curtain

1 sea-green velvet curtain hampers access to this intimate room. In order to establish conditions conducive to sleep in my lair, and cut it off from the outside, I draw this curtain at night, and even occasionally by day, when its cameral disorder might appall the living room. Compared to the oak door in the apartment's entryway, the curtain diminishes the sensation of passing through a boundary without quite eliminating it. Such an open system would be embarrassing only in the case of cohabitation; but I break my bread alone. When I'm in the living room, it's not often that the curtain is drawn, because I enjoy the prospect of seeing into other rooms: it's how I make myself feel as though I'm living in a bigger, even panoramic, space. But, then, sometimes I draw the curtain so that I can imagine there's someone in my room, someone who isn't me (which would only be good news).

Rod Happening

This curtain is attached by sliding rings to a rod that could, if pulled on too hard, fall. Which did happen at a party when some women were hoping to change clothes while other guests were already in the living room, and I had pulled the curtain shut to let them preen and primp in peace . . . But someone, evidently intrigued by the noises coming from behind the hanging—and thanks as well to the women's astronomical slowness in getting dressed—tugged heedlessly on the curtain, thereby yanking the rod right out of the wall; in a huge burst of laughter and yelling, the amused guests at my "happening" were treated to the sight of several tight dresses in disarray, while 1 of those dresses' wearers, having barely escaped the rod falling right on her head, begged for some assistance, which I of course hastened to provide—things couldn't go on as they were! The damage could only be undone, however, by my get-

ting up on a Tam Tam stool and reattaching the rod as quickly
as possible, thereby shielding those scantily clad dames from
further upset without making matters worse in the process.
My bedroom, strewn with clothes, had become the changing
room for these models, just as I had become their provisional
dresser.

Spare the Rod . . .

In its precariousness, this light rod system forces me to moderate my actions, to be sparing, a disagreeable deterrent to my
generally voluble impulses. I tend to suffer from the fragility of
such setups, built for far more delicate bodies, be it the door
handle that I tend to pull far too vigorously to the glasses I
come dangerously close to breaking with my clenched fist. My
idea of comfort calls for a particularly Nordic brutality, resulting in sturdy furniture, firm fittings, lots of reinforcement; and
yet I still have to handle everything with care, since I decided
in the end that a dainty setup is simply more elegant. This disconnect between fragility and comfort keeps resulting in the
same accidents; if I consider my apartment to be less than sturdy,
these rods play a big role in that appraisal: that "happening"
was the 3rd time those treacherous objects betrayed me.

The Secret Heraldry of the B——

On the threshold of the bedroom, there remain, nailed to the
left post of the doorframe, the 3 hinges that held the door
that once hung here. I've never seen that door. The preceding
owner had already removed it when I moved in. As for the
hinges, I could have made them disappear, like a construction
foreman gearing up for gut renovations; but I didn't: they hang
there uselessly, unattached, making for a quirky emblem, the
secret heraldry of the bedroom.

Constrained Design

7 paces are enough to cross the length of this 6-pace-wide room. Its modest surface area bothers me less than its unattractive proportions. Relative to other household rooms, bedrooms, considering their purpose, can certainly be small, and might even be more attractive on account of being relatively confined—but the crude geometry of this space has made my design decisions far harder. The problem created by the spatial organization of this room is this: it's a square with only 1 wall, on the right, adjoining the office, completely available (the other 3 bear, respectively, 2 gaping holes—the entrance and the window at the back—and 1 protrusion, namely the fireplace on the left-side wall) for 2 massive yet unavoidable pieces of furniture, the bed and the armoire. I could set the armoire in the space taken by the bed but not the bed in the space taken by the armoire, since the entrance would, in that case, rather than being narrowed, be completely blocked: thus, the entire room must be organized around the bed (which, it's true, is also its raison d'être). My bed can't be put anywhere else, so its volume logically goes in the area between the window wall and the fireplace, although it doesn't completely fill that space; its length, however, goes to half the window's width, preventing the left pane from being opened too easily. The armoire, in contrast, enjoys a broader range of positions along the wall: it's only visible when someone actually enters the bedroom fully, and its shallow depth doesn't take up much of the room, because it's set within a recess. So I've done my best with the double constraint imposed by my furniture and this floor plan.

Square

The bed's gluttonous presence makes it difficult for me to take a leisurely stroll around my square. Meandering toward the window, I have to stop midstream and step right so I don't run into my bed, which blockades that distant shore. Other angles are less tricky. 3 out of the 4 corners are accessible—I can only go partway in some cases: it's easy to make a diagonal crossing from 1 to 3, but not from 2 to 4. At best, I can sketch smaller squares within that of my room by turning inwardly, concentrically, like Josef Albers painting squares within squares. Is this reduction of movement partly why I spend so little time here in the bare center of the room?

Walking Along the Walls

As I enter, I go along the walls, from the left to the right, following the direction in which I write: the wall mirror, the closet door, the fireplace, the bed, a part of the window and its curtain, the electric radiator, the 5th chair, the office door, the garden furniture, the armoire and its double curtain, the Tam Tam stool, the floor lamp.

Mirror Without a Trace

Immediately to the left, on the small part of the wall adjoining the kitchen, stands the mirror, 58 cm wide, hidden in the corner, its full-length 180 cm height approaching mine. It contains me. Firmly affixed to the wall with plastic anchors, it rests on a white wooden bar. I inherited it from the former owner. Most such inheritances evince some element of their pasts, but this mirror has the advantage of retaining 0 trace of its previous owners—including previous Thomas Clercs. (Which is how, when I started this book, my mirror had no mustache.)

I'll Be Your Mirror

Sometimes I walk aimlessly around my place. I'll take 100 steps and finally meet myself in front of the mirror, which is where I always end up: I make sure I exist by making faces, grimacing, or else staying perfectly immobile, impassive, waiting for someone to break through from the other side. Then the glass begins to irritate me: I have to make a spectacle of myself in front of it, as at those parties where I get bored and feel the need to shake things up by acting out. But in the end its steadiness steadies me; I wear myself out while it just goes on hanging where it's always hung.

Mirror Boogie
If a novel is a mirror going along a road, as the aptonymous Saint-Réal had it, then this book is indeed a novel, but a shaky 1. To get an exact reflection, you have to wriggle around in turn.

The Lock of the Law
Forming a corner with the wall is a closet door, in all likelihood a former pantry, which is kept shut with a minilock. Protecting (poorly) a space that holds nothing precious, this tiny lock, which still reeks of the Bazar de l'Hôtel de Ville where I bought it, would be pretty ridiculous if it didn't perform its role with such perfect aplomb. Its smallness is touching, as though it were the last man in town still sworn to uphold the law—like a sheriff shielding his prisoner from a lynch mob.

Casuistry of Closets
This 5-shelf, 30-cm-deep closet houses a hopelessly chaotic world lacking any form. Its concealing function is essential, and opening it reveals its flaws, its unsoundness. But I suppose it's time to concede the futility of that casuistry and open my closet to my readers' inquisitive gaze.

Tied Up
The door discloses an unforeseen element: its inner panel. From a green silk thread kept taut by 2 thin screws hangs a set

of ties. I have a habit of forgetting they're here. Worried they'd just make me look overdressed, I end up avoiding such accessories wholesale, usually to my subsequent regret, because I'm a fan of neither the petite-bourgeois ideology that insists on men wearing finely knotted ties on all occasions nor of the facile nonconformism that rejects this stricture for its unavoidably conservative connotations. Tie wearing is, for me, an occasional joy at best. There are only 3 I actually like: 2 in imitation wool, 1 black and the other sky blue; the 3rd, dark blue, is still in the dry cleaner's cellophane. Imprisoned in this transparent protection, it seems all the more beautiful to me. I adore its sous-vide beauty.

The others are, to me, no more than *possible* ties—such as these 2 patterned silk numbers, dark blue and red, too violently mariachi-printed to be worn, these days, but which I still hold out hope of putting to work again when this style comes back into fashion. As for the rest—the imported ties, which ought to be *de*ported, and then the wholly superfluous 1s, of questionable taste, or anyway a taste that's no longer my own—I'd love, for the sake of cleanliness and simplicity, to get rid of them, so that only what is Useful remains, and yet I don't have the strength to do so. I find myself frozen between the respect I feel is owed such objects and the relief that their disappearance would bring me—staring at these unmoving lengths, hanging there, threatening to outlive me and so wind up in the same consignment shop from which they probably came. I stroke them impotently, as a woman might the detumescent member of a man she barely feels any affection for anymore.

Top Shelf

It's the least accessible 1: to reach it I have to use the 3rd Tam Tam stool, which will appear farther down. There are 4 shoeboxes here, 2 on each side, like headstones or burial mounds, containing the rest of my archives (←ENTRYWAY). Their inventory would provide a complete overview of my social life, but as it isn't my intention to provide a complete autobiography, as yet, I'm only keeping these memorials for conservatorial purposes. Only being stuck at home, sick—such days being conducive to nostalgia, or, in the worst cases, discouragement, or, in the best cases, curiosity or getting to feel like an old man—would ever justify my looking at them. So these boxes will stay shut, sheltered by the text that contains them. My text isn't a text of texts.

2 Burglar's Fingers

1 of these boxes is disfigured by a hole 2 fingers wide, made by the burglar who thought that these shoddy memory boxes might hold some treasure. This crude hole makes me ill at ease: I tried to efface it by transferring my archives into a new box . . . but I've still kept this evidence of the violation of my home as an ever-fresh reminder of the break-in. If he had kept going, scattering the contents of the box on the floor, here is what that lawless bourgeois we'll call a crook would have found: postcards, invitations, announcements, flyers, small whimsical texts, old ID cards, etc. There's a vast abyss between the discrete minutiae of that archive and the unity of this work. Exhibiting these documents would be exhausting; burglary, however, I imagine to be exhilarating.

Hidden Works

2 disproportionate articles fill the space between the shoe-boxes on the left and those on the right: there's a work of art given to me by its creator, Pierre La Police, which I can't unfurl because it's 15 meters long. Titled *Leisure Time*, it's a massive folded-up comic strip, a tour de force only this great cartoonist could have pulled off. I admit I have a strange com-

pulsion to hide this work of art from prying eyes, but then I've already said that my love for art is greater than my need to own it, and that the collector's mind-set is alien to me—a viewpoint that only a sudden change in financial status could alter. Hiding a work of art like this deprives it of its power, 1 way, perhaps, for the writer to exact revenge on the visual artist, whose work asks so little of its audience, in contrast to the book, which asks so much.

A feeling of acquisitiveness is, however, unavoidable for the other object filling this space between shoeboxes . . .

Cash

Containing ugly yellow coins that leave a coppery odor on my fingers is a sordid plastic sachet from the bank: a dusty heap I hope doesn't stand as a metaphor for myself, which may be why I've consigned its dusty traces to silence at the back of this cabinet. Sticking my hand into the bag, I discover that my petty cash comes to just €4.40.

Ready Money

I don't own a safe, and since I trust in banks like an idiot, I don't keep much of a nest egg. Where do I put any extra cash? My wallet usually sits on the dentist's cabinet, but it can move from room to room. For those who prefer their assets liquid, I don't recommend doing what a businessman I know did: slipping bills into books that had titles connected to money, like Péguy's *L'argent*, or Dos Passos's *The Big Money*. 10 years after the switch to the euro, he found some francs hidden in Gide's *If It Die* . . .

Shelf No. 4

Confronted with this shelf, again with heaps of papers and miscellany on each side to give a semblance of order to the documents lying here, I feel a bit ill at its hideousness. To combat this plague, the radical solution would have been to annihilate the contents; the progressive solution would have been to set aside additional storage space; the conservative solution would be called *the status quo*; the literary solution is called *Interior*. To the left are piles of old journals belonging to 2 categories—particularly collector's items and issues in which my own work was published; that "and" isn't necessarily disjunctive. To the right, leaning against each other, 2 copies of my thesis unhelpfully duplicate the 1s already to be found at the bottom of my bookshelves, all of which I keep in the hopes of its eventual publication, a hope that, as year follows year, becomes increasingly hypothetical, possibly even obsolete in the wake of a work on exactly the same subject, *La forme des jours*, arriving in the mail 1 day and giving me the unpleasant sensation of having been shunted aside by some Tommy-come-lately—that'll teach me to keep things instead of making something out of them. Atop these 2 volumes sleep my previous university work, my master's thesis—"The Dilettante Hero in 19th- and 20th-Century Literature" supervised by Michel Crouzet, the preeminent scholar of Stendhal—and my dissertation, "The Literarity of Jules Renard's *Journal*," which was supervised by Georges Molinié, the reigning scholar of stylistics. For me these projects now evoke the same satisfied dissatisfaction I feel toward all such highly specialized work: I came to understand very quickly that my real specialty would be life.

Photo Shop

The space between these 2 piles is filled by a bag of photographs. The time when I took photos isn't quite over because it never really began; I indulge in this middlebrow art purely at random. I do still keep mementos thereof, such as this small blue canvas album in which I intended to paste a photo of myself each year on my birthday (April 27), beginning at 14. I lost the perseverance that would have enabled me to bring this project to full fruition, however, in the intervening time—it would have made sense only if entirely complete, and this "album of a life" now contains more gaps than years.

Photo Finish
Opening this rainbow-striped bag (I put my old photos in a stylish bag the better to create a disconnect between container and contents), I discover some prints made by my aging, sil-vered Olympus camera (← ENTRYWAY). These photos are rec-ords of a past in which I no longer even recognize myself—as if the defunct device that captured them also aged them to almost nothing. I've never wanted to look at these friends and governesses and parents whose presences coincided with the moment of the flashbulb's firing ever again; I just can't shake the fear that the distancing effect these photographs generate would, in turn, contaminate me. The other, more recent photos are the products of Kodak disposable cameras far better suited to my way of taking pictures. Disposability, which frees me from any insistence on quality, suits my vision of technological simplicity. Kodak, alas, is in free fall as of this writing, and the FunSaver with Flash cameras (2 for €15), made in Mexico, are dying 1 flash-spasm at a time . . .

Archives Are Emotionally Endless
It's so frustrating that I don't even feel genuinely uncomfort-able as I lay eyes on this evidence of my life. So I won't force myself to describe these pictures in detail (to you): better to keep these far-too-visual things invisible, considering that I can see in them the principles guiding the assembly of *this* album, where paragraphs have taken the place of photographs: just as a museum's storage rooms aren't accessible to the pub-

lic, refusing to exhibit the entirety of my collection frees me
from the fatal burden of exhaustiveness. In 20 or 30 years, when
I look at these photos again, that action will carry a different
emotional weight—and that's why I think I ought to revisit
this same project many years down the line, just as galleries
promise visitors that all of their many treasures will be rotated
out of, then back onto, display in due time.

Phabricated Evidence

I take out my 4 cameras and place them on the card table now
set up in the bedroom: the 2 identical disposable Kodak
cameras, the Polaroid, the Olympus. Only the last 1 no longer
works. So I take a photo of it with 1 of the disposables as well
as with the Polaroid; then the Polaroid with a disposable, and
the disposable with the Polaroid; then, finally, disposable 1
with disposable 2. In this way I've established some solidarity
between the generations.

A Sickening Piggy Bank

Adding to the crummy jumble of this dark corner is the hyperrealist intersection of an issue of *Pariscope* dating from my
birthday week (in 2010) and a black plastic piggy bank. Grabbing this piglet the very second I finish my sentence, my own
disgusted weariness cries out "Enough!" in the face of my
closet's overstuffed absurdity. This poor piggy bank suddenly
seems utterly senseless, and, as its ugliness no longer strikes me
as especially touching, I decide to pitch it.

The Unbearable Heaviness of Belongings

If, in the process of enumerating my belongings, this text
could also disburden me of them, then I'd be indebted to this
creation of mine; such an impetus to clean up and clear away
every no-longer-necessary belonging could only be for the
best. My dream is of minimalism, but when have I ever fol-

lowed my dreams? So much waste betokens both the misery
of an overabundant society and the difficulty of living an ascetic life: I'm no better than those dunderheads who stuff
their rooms with any old junk for fear of that inverse terror
known as emptiness—I let the same sniggering horror get the
better of me, and so found myself swallowed up by this vast
landscape of rubbish, filling me with the desire to escape to
some secluded hideaway where I can finally live as I'd like. But
enough of talking the talk. If I'm going to walk the walk, I'll
take this gewgaw and throw it out. I'm on the path to freedom now.

Shelf No. 3
It's a neat and tidy shelf, of practically 0 interest: to the left
are the comic books that didn't make it to the bookshelves,
shelved unnaturally (meaning horizontally) along with 2 copies of the 2005 Paris phone book. Being a perfectly outdated
object, this who's who is intrinsically poetic; the fact that it's
becoming an endangered species makes it even more so, and
yet, even still, it remains just useful enough that I've preserved
it here. Oh, how I wish I'd kept my phone books from previous
years! Now I can't even check to see if I really existed back
then. Of course, only a true hoarder would hold on to a life's
worth of phone books—an imperfect monument in 80 volumes.
And yet, reading this old directory, and sometimes gleaning
information from it about people who are now or might as well
be ghosts, gives me more joy than finishing 100 novels (and it
hardly takes much imagination to see the beginnings of a few
new fictions here too . . .).

Bulky, Clunky DVD Player
10 centimeters off sits my DVD player, because there's just no
way to balance this 24 cm × 23 cm device atop an even smaller
TV. To be honest, I don't really like watching DVDs; to my

mind the TV is for TV—that is, for broadcasts. Home the-
aters undermine the present: the TV is less a piece of furniture
than a medium unto itself, and all the derivative products that
have sprung up around it have by now completely overwhelmed the original object.

Inventoried Neutral Mask

This authoritative inventory finds its ironic representation in
the presence, imposing as soon as the closet door is opened, of
a neutral mask. Bought at a joke & prank shop (a specialty of
my neighborhood) for the sheer pleasure of the object, its thin
molded plastic exudes an enigmatic force, an absolute theatri-
cality. A neutral mask intrigues in its inexpressiveness, itself
expressive by sheer subtraction. I don this white mask only on
very rare occasions: staged photographs, erotic scenarios, performances, etc. This membrane, which isn't wholly unlike skin,
suggests the idea of a thin film stretched across all of reality,
a barrier only betrayed by its few apertures (eyes, nose, mouth).
In it I see every self-portrait in 1: a self scrubbed clean yet
shrouded. I recently used this mask onstage, appearing in
front of an audience with my face covered as I declaimed a
poetic response to Valery Larbaud's poem "I always write with
a mask upon my face . . ." which I'd hoped to invert, because
it seems like I'm someone who "always *lives* with a mask upon
my face," a mask that writing should actually tear away. What
greater gesture could there be than to destroy the *hypocrisy of
living*?

The Shelf That Isn't Mine

The central shelf is 35 cm high, putting its shorter neighbors
above and below to shame. Its odor is distinctly feminine: it's
the space I leave for my partner when she comes to spend the
night. Various items that don't belong to me, that I therefore

don't feel I can legitimately describe in these pages, are strewn across this shelf, resulting in a theoretical problem that I hadn't foreseen: I've discovered that not everything I have in *my* home is necessarily *mine*. In effect, if I own all the goods that I've described so far (with clerical precision), the intrusion of these new elements introduces a beneficial disjunction between simple possession and outright ownership.

From the owner's point of view, there's always the option that, although immoral, can't be wholly rejected: simply seizing as 1's own any objects that have been left in 1's domain; a practice I don't think I've often adopted, and even as I wonder where my black cap and my Black+Decker drill have gone, I calculate that the sum total of the foreign goods that have been subsumed into my private domain amounts to: some borrowed, stolen, or unreturned books; 1 earring; 1 secret item entrusted to me by an artist, which I will leave undescribed as I wait to entrust it to another friend. But from the writer's point of view (and those 2 points of view can't be concomitant), the presence of these objects threatens the integrity of my inventory.

In the end, the only items in this shelf's little hodgepodge that could be called "mine" are a container of Uriage lotion and some cotton pads. But if I were to go on describing the other relics therein, I'd feel as if I were betraying secrets that weren't mine to tell, and since there's no reason 1 can't be both a gentleman and a consistent writer, I turn the page on this hoard.

Where the Heart Is

This paltry space often feels like an accusation of emotional neglect. No matter how many arguments I could make to grant her more space here (especially given the closet shelf's central location, which puts its contents directly in my girlfriend's sight), I still can't convince myself to do so. With 2 people in this apartment, I'd go mad; alone, I yearn.

Shelf No. 5

Here we're entering the most explicitly clothes-related shelf, where 2 former shoeboxes hold underwear on the left and socks on the right, with the empty space in between filled by 1 chrome shoehorn.

Interior Man

My briefs are of many brands, so many that it's clear there's absolutely no underlying logic here. I hew to a classic American model, size S, which I like for the simplicity of its line and its wide array of colors; I even have 1 set aside, still in its original packaging. The idea of "clothes set aside" reassures me, just as food set aside in a pantry might, even though I rarely succeed on the latter front. Before I found perfection in an American brand, my preferred pair was a silvery number, its brand Hom, its profile nearly rectangular—an interesting compromise between the boxers and classic briefs that frames its contents in an aura of scintillating autoeroticism. And there are also other specimens of my past life here, such as the burgundy Lycra Jils that I keep for the days I'm playing contact sports. The pleasure of finding 1's brand is the pleasure of a mature man: it keeps me from obsessing over this minuscule detail, and allows me to feel like "myself" (as some silly ad still freighted with some philosophical weight might have put it).

A Theory of Socks

As for my socks, the athletic/dress distinction prevails. My 3 white pairs won't go with anything except my athletic shoes, and what's more pathetic than men who wear dress shoes with tennis socks? The hell they inhabit extends far beyond the visible part of their lower limbs. (The insane Luchino Visconti insisted, after all, that even the unseen underwear in his films be historically accurate.) And yet there'd be no use, in this case, separating these 2 kinds of socks, so they all swim together in this box like fish of different schools in a single bowl, prized as much for their forms as for their colors. While the white streaks attest to this intermingling, the vast majority here are monochromatic black or navy blue dress socks, which I prefer to light or bright colors (except for an emerald pair that gets worn only in summer). I know that these socks made in China though designed in Japan are of average quality; but, far from being a professional shortcoming, cheap mediocrity in the realm of clothing—as the industry figured out long ago—is in fact ideal, since forced obsolescence is the byword of fashion. (Besides, who'd want to wear the same socks their entire life?)

Happy Medium
Considering these average-quality socks, I wonder if the secret isn't, as in so many other arenas, just getting a passing grade. The higher my standards, the greater my potential frustration, and as I've set my sights on Literature, I already have more than enough disappointments in store.

Holes
Stroking these briefs, I notice that practically every 1 is coming apart at the seams; sticking my hand into my socks, I find too many have holes in their toes.

Freud Doll
Between the briefs and socks, in clear plastic clamshell packaging, we may admire my little figurine of Sigmund Freud. I adore Freud (and deplore all those attacks this liberator of

man has been subjected to), and exiling him to my underwear shelf, far from being an insult, is my way of honoring him, by underscoring the attention he focused on the underbelly of practically everything. Every so often, I take out this doll and put it on display. Like a child, I love toying with the placement of things; it's a way of giving my imagination free rein. Taking Sigmund Freud out of the closet means shining a light on the man who showed us that we're all closeted within ourselves. I recently propped Freud in front of my vodka, in a nod to his theories' intoxicating force—but I suspect he shines brighter in the closet.

Disc Jockey Socks

I must now bemoan the presence of certain foreign elements hidden behind my box of socks: a set of LPs I don't care for anymore. That there is no possible organizational justification to this juxtaposition of Jockey socks and vinyl wounds both the heart and the eye; worse, these discs are reprobates—I can't even remember what's back here until I look more closely . . . which I'll do now. So I see, behind the bluish cover of Serge Gainsbourg's *La chanson de Prévert* (double album), a dozen other classics I'd completely forgotten about. I'll just leave this brief selection here since most of my LPs are, as we know, set next to the stereo in the office.

Culture Muffler

The relegation of these albums to the closet follows an internal logic, clearly separating the modern universe from the classical, betraying my musical preference for the former. Barely represented by a dozen works that I never listen to, a half-hearted attempt to experience "great music" that only earned me the snickers of my friend the French composer Jean-Christophe Marti (1964–) back when we were young and considered ourselves the devotees of so many different musical genres, my collection of classical hits is rather disappointing. My misbegotten musical taste, the fact that these classic albums are all hidden by Gainsbourg, who considered his relationship to great art a central problem, reveals my true relationship to culture, which lurches between liberal, postmodern integration of all genres and an inverse preference for the value judgments and hierarchical distinctions of cultivated taste. The great masters of world literature are inarguable, as are Bach or Berlioz, who stand next to horrible old-fashioned Dave and wonderful old Damia at my place. My own problem is that my love for Serge Gainsbourg doesn't have any literary equivalent; I'm only a legitimist in my own realm.

Unacceptable Object

Squatting in the center of this shelf, an *unacceptable object* molders in an Opticiens du Jura bag—a pair of glasses. Just 2 years ago I started having trouble with my vision, so I had to accept that the eagle eyes I'd once taken pride in were turning human. Even as I spend an increasing amount of time reading and writing, my sight has blurred ever so slightly at its edges, almost as if my eyes hadn't quite focused. Faced with this evidence of my ocular aging, I chose the Opticiens du Jura to bear witness to my fledgling farsightedness, not only so as to boycott corporate retailers with 1 of those political microgestures that feel far more effective than merely declaring my principles, but also because the Jura is the original home of the Clerc family: I love connecting the most important of my senses, sight, to my name as well as to my favorite number, 39, which is coincidentally both the *département* number of the Jura and the age at which I published my 1st novel.

I've never put on these glasses. The minute I ordered them, my eye troubles went away.

Sun/Sight

To demonstrate my victory over mere biology, I set my sunglasses atop the corrective glasses in the bag. And, as a further affront, I also keep 2 other pairs, which allow me to look at the world through maple-syrup-colored lenses.

Churinga

Last but not least is a pebble I've transferred from its native habitat on a Breton beach to here, without any real reason. An illustrious poet once wrote about pebbles, and it's perhaps in homage that I've claimed ownership of what a fusty anthropologist might have called a churinga, that totemic object Central Australian indigenous tribes kept to protect their lands.

Bedrock

Traditionally the weakest of strategic positions, the lowermost space, between the bottom shelf and the floorboards, is where all the clutter is stuffed. Some hurricane's been through here (whether a storm system or simply a human being), since everything's at 6s and 7s. In this mishmash are all my shoe-related accoutrements kept self-referentially in a shoebox: 2 shoe waxes (cordovan and oxblood) and 2 tattered graphic tees repurposed for buffing leather, thereby allowing these tatters to enjoy a few beautiful twilight years. This toolkit teeters atop a soft mountain of motley objects: 1 bag full of bags, 1 horridly prune-colored computer bag of uncertain material; 1 small electric heater I could set up in unheated rooms, like my bathroom, or as an extra heating element anywhere else; 1 Wilson tennis racquet I haven't been able to throw away even though I haven't played that sport in eons; 1 pocket-size umbrella that's merely an understudy for my other umbrellas; the metallic base for the shattered entryway light; 1 backpack, justifiable only in the countryside, no matter how often

my countrymen use them in the city; 1 box of plastic badminton shuttlecocks and 1 beachside racquet; 1 unopened
IKEA package holding 1 folded blue canvas bag labeled SKUBB;
finally, the crown jewel of this neighborhood museum, 1
ocelot-fur bed throw, still in its bag, along with a few of the
fur's trimmings.

Wonderfur

The ocelot fur deserves a bit more attention; it was cut from
my grandmother Alice Bovar's fur coat, and my mother had
the idea to turn it into a bed throw by stitching some brown
cloth to its underside. In addition to being beautiful—with its
black spots and bright colors, and all the incomparable softness of real fur—it's saved me from many a chill when I've
pulled it from its niche and used it as an additional, invalu-
able source of warmth. I can't presume it has any monetary
value—it ought to command 100s of euros, but is actually unsellable, as a furrier on the rue d'Hauteville confirmed when
I brought it in for a cleaning—whereas its sentimental value
has long been established by my mother and my mother's
mother.

    The motherly protection of this warm fur warms my heart.
And it's a token of my mother that keeps me cozy when, in
winter's chill, I unfold this beast's hide. 1 other image comes
to mind as I touch this fur, an old memory, hardly maternal,
more conventionally erotic, of my trysts on this animal with a
no less animalistic lover.

Subset

I own 2 more of my maternal grandmother's things in addition to this ocelot fur: the chrome rack in the bathroom, and
the Napoleon statuette. These 3 elements that coexisted at 1
particular time and space, now distant—the apartment she once

had at Porte Dorée—have become a subset of that place, like an entire apartment depicted in a few brushstrokes. Much like the objects in my apartment that move from room to room, constantly changing their placement and configuration (like my watch, wallet, or cell phone), so will the goods now belonging to me eventually be scattered throughout various other homes, my "posterity" creating in turn other subsets, subsumed within other sets of objects from homes that never were mine. Objects may give our abodes their deceptive unity, but they were born elsewhere, they live through eons, and they will endure through the collapse of many other empires.

Coming Out of Hiding

As I shut the door of this closet where my belongings have overcome my attempts to master them, I feel relieved to restore it to its hiding function, a necessity in every home. Lifting the curtain to peek at the wings of my stage set would destroy the (illusory) museum that these spaces otherwise suggest; locking the door with its small latch, I restore this room to its false premise of orderliness.

And then I hear, very weakly, vaguely, from the depths, the voice of Raymond Federman! That young Jewish man who owed his survival in the winter of 1942 to the closet where he was hidden, and who, far from rebuking me for reporting the facts, whispers that I'm right to continue my quest. That my vain self-contemplation shall be forgiven. That life is a political invention. That we all have to empty our closets.

Black White Fireplace

Feeling energized, I make my way to the white-stone fireplace, which protrudes 60 centimeters into the room. I had to have it swept out each of the 1st few winters I lived here (for the sum of €30 each time) to get it to work; after that, I stopped both-

ering with fires; I should really have it swept again (for the
sum of €50) but I no longer feel the same urge to pay my respects to such shrines. Parisians! I know that blazing hearths
hold just the virtues I revere, but I refuse to confer them upon
my own bedroom. This renunciation is more than just an evolution of my theories of interior life. It's a black void.

Lost Fire

If I ever did buy, carry up, and set some wood at the base of this
fireplace, like a ritual sacrifice, I'd only find myself trying to
outlast an invasion of cumbersome logs caked with dust and
soot. And even though I quite like the idea of destruction by
fire—it well suits my dream of negating objects entirely, that
dream I return to each day as I lug a full bin of papers down
to the courtyard—the need to 1st go out and buy kindling
stops me dead: far better, I think, like Bernard Palissy, to burn
1's own furniture. The idea of using my fireplace is so much
nicer than actually doing so. And as I behold its abstracted
power, I make out the 1st signs that my love for my household
is already on the wane.

Fireplace of Consolation

Which doesn't stop me from contemplating it. Its simple form,
its trapezoidal descent toward the darkness of its maw, impress
me more when it's empty than when it's lit. The contrast between the white of its façade and the black of its depths is cold
in its perfection. Instead of ashes, dust proliferates. And, actually, its mantel (112 cm × 31 cm) has a quite practical use.

Postbourgeois Mirror

As in those bourgeois apartments (my own is a pale imitation),
I've very conventionally set a mirror measuring 75 cm × 67 cm
on this mantel. Its gilded frame, with neo-Corinthian moldings,

masks its relative decrepitude: the floral patterns are almost all broken. This noble, ailing mirror reflects 2 aspects of its owner: stability of station, but also diminishment thereof.

The Poetry of Property

I live at the boundary of art and the bourgeoisie, and while I'm not quite sure what this means, I'm writing it down because it came to me, dictated by this fireplace mirror. I'm writing a poetics of property. I am possessed by a lust for possessions; the property code pulsates in every nook and cranny of my average little life.

Mantel Wings

2 sides, 1 vase, and 1 lamp. Use a bit of poetic arithmetic and we've got 3 possible lighting configurations.

April Vase

To the left, a sublime vase, called an April vase, a gift from my friends for my 30th year on this earth, has 25 glass tubes bound by 1 metallic (but malleable) structure allowing for a multiform arrangement. I usually choose that of a bouquet, closed like a fist. I only rarely put flowers in this vase, because I live alone and only have flowers in the house if other people bring me a few. And unlike the House of Lords I might consider those eternal plants 1 finds in waiting rooms, the flowers here make up a House of Commons: any of them can be voted in and just as easily voted out. Flowers are ephemeral. They're impatient; in fact, these 1s here are impatiens.

Perfume Names

Near the vase is a bottle of the cologne I use, its vial embodying the austere and sensual ambiance that a room should exude. Unfortunately there's no fragrance called *ad vitam aeternam*,

so the 1 I'm currently using is called Flowerbomb, by Viktor &
Rolf, which comes in a large oval bottle reminiscent of a gre-
nade, topped by a rose-gold cap whose color complements
that of the eau de parfum it holds. But as I edit these lines, it's
Sables, by Annick Goutal, on my mantel; and then, as I proof-
read them, Musc Ravageur, by Frédéric Malle. The brands have
changed over the course of writing this book. Their scents
layer a whiff of infidelity over everything they touch, so I un-
cork the unadorned vial, bring it to my nose, and think of the
sweet nothings women have whispered to me; then I recork it,
happy that it's half full, worried that it's half empty.

Bedside
The right wing of the mantel, above the head of the bed, holds
a small white-and-green plastic Culbuto lamp shaped like a
teardrop, its base keeping the structure (socket + bulb) level.
The 25-watt bulb burns out slightly too often, and the upper
half has a crack from a fall; these faults notwithstanding, it
insists on being my bedside lamp. I don't keep books on my
nightstand both because I'm a nonconformist and because I
don't have a nightstand, so the fireplace mantel serves in its
stead. These books, about 40 of them in 5 piles, are what I'm
currently reading. There are those at the top that leave, and
those that, at the bottom, stay.

Adverse Sculpture
Invading nearly the entire mantel, these columns of books,
some 20 centimeters high, blockade the mirror's lower 3rd,
making it hard to see myself. This territorial conflict is fought
without mercy: the mirror's false purity on 1 side, literature's
honest impurity on the other, each refusing to blink 1st. I've
baptized this group an *adverse sculpture*. The equilibrium between the books and the glass is fragile; the higher the columns

reach, the closer the mirror comes to disappearing. I have to make sure that this doesn't happen.

Territorial Rivalries

This 2ndary conflict distracts 1 from the deep-seated rivalry between the bed and the armoire for control of the room.

A Bed Secreting Secrets

Aside from Murphy beds in cramped spaces, trailers, or servants' quarters, there's just no hiding beds. Mine takes up a large part of the room but still follows the Chinese art of feng shui. As 1's day is largely determined by the previous night, a better night's sleep calls for the presence, on at least 1 side of the bed, of a lateral wall, following 1's instinct for self-protection. Detached beds remind me of boats adrift at sea. Here, however, 2 sides are protected, 1 by the back wall, the other by the fireplace, so I only have 1 way out. Other users might prefer 2 paths of egress, but that's only necessary when living as a couple and trying to get out of bed without climbing over each other's bodies. I'm a bachelor, but I have a double bed, as I'm by no means a bachelor emotionally; the true bachelor would have a single bed, which would shape his life accordingly. Single-user beds lead to monasticism.

Bed of Fêtes

I bought this standard-size 195 cm × 145 cm bed during my decennial move, as if a new space naturally called for a new bed, and consequently a new life. For purely economic reasons, I made this acquisition at a store on the Place des Fêtes that was offering a package deal on box springs and mattresses. Once it was set up, I was surprised to have made this indisputably "decisive" purchase—especially for a man who devotes 10 hours each day to sleep—in a part of Paris I rarely

visit because of its paralyzing ugliness; but now I see that buying a bed near the Place des Fêtes was an homage to this fundamental object, where the 2 main fêtes of life take place: love
and sleep.

Château de Seix
This bed is raised 20 centimeters above the floor—a choice
I'm not sure I would make again, in my future life. A bed on
legs, aside from the minor inconvenience of thereby offering
dust yet another place to breed, implies a fear of floors quite
detrimental to sleep. It does, admittedly, stave off discomfort
by reducing the spatiotemporal interval between lying down
and sleeping, but for me *falling* onto my bed evokes more
erotic associations than a platform bed might. Does eroticism
need to be elevated? On the contrary, love on the floor seems
more appropriate, more grounded, more fervent than what is
proposed by the 4-legged bourgeois bed—namely, health,
prosperity, honesty, ~~fecundity~~. (I have to cross out what is the
ugliest word in both English and French.)

French Psycho
I've positioned my bed the way they do in love hotels, in sight
of the mirror described *supra*; lying supine, I can't see it, but I
can change my posture and orgasm to this double feature of
sex both realized and reflected. If modesty should narrow my
focus to the act itself, it's easy for me to open the cabinet door
and hide the mirror. But I do so adore the bedside mirror's
eroticism, which lovers, like Patrick Bateman, know can transform the sexual act into an artistic experience! (I'll let him
keep all his other sordid vices for himself, though.) The duplication of the act isn't the act itself; rather, it becomes an image
2ndary to this coital scene, no longer just us but a savage version
of ourselves.

Double Chamber

The bedroom is the most intimate and secluded room, the 1 never explored in strangers' homes or even in the homes of close friends protective of their lairs, the chamber that, as Baudelaire described it, is double; we fill it with our dreams and it is defined by our reality. A friend in my youth, upon seeing the bedroom I had then, once teased me as he entered: "Is this where you make love to your women?" I couldn't tell whether the sting of his sarcasm lay in the word *women*, the word *your*, or the word *this*.

Love in the Afternoon

From the street, the closing of a window's shutters can look mechanical, and yet seeing someone performing this banal gesture, especially in the afternoon, inevitably conjures up an aura of mystery verging on the conjugal. I say goodbye to the teeming world, but I say it out loud, delighting in creating nighttime in daytime. This hammed-up farewell to the world, punctuated with the sharp slap of the wood, is worlds apart from the slow descent of an electrical shutter.

Patchcolor Quilt

My bed is covered with a bizarrely proportioned, not-terribly-thick quilt. 3 slipcovers each play their role with regard to this item, 1 being cotton for summers, another nylon for winters, the 3rd for in between. The 1st, colored yellow/green, has faded (its lemon yellow has become meringue yellow; its green has gone from Granny Smith apple skin to Granny Smith apple flesh); the 2nd is charcoal gray. The middle seasons get a toile floral-print slipcover. Repeating its red & white & red pattern of twisted leaves connected by stems to innumerable branches, this design resembles nothing so much as a dream of wallpaper snaking across the wall. And when I sleep, do these embosoming blossoms bloom in my dreams, unfurling oneiric images?

In her novella *The Yellow Wallpaper*, Charlotte Perkins Gilman describes the mental collapse of a mind overwhelmed by just such an exuberant motif. Was this slipcover decorated to provoke dreams? Is this print on my bed creeping over my mind?

Orientalism

The quilt's arborescence having caught my eye, I am drawn toward the Oriental fabric prints covering the card table I occasionally sit at. I unfold a large cotton cloth bought in Dubai, and I admire its simple, ornamental, Islamic bareness. The interlaced red and green leaves on a white background repeat into infinity. The perfect setting for a nightmare, Dubai left an impression both soft and prickly—not unlike this piece of cotton and its multiplying rhizomes.

Well Covered

In winter, 3 layers aren't too much in a bedroom barely protected by 1 thin curtain. Alongside 2 old cottage-style covers, which I've had since childhood, is 1 large pale-blue wool rectangle, bought used and folded over for double the thickness. In extreme cold, I add the ocelot as well: its hide's soft warmth and its stripes complete the bed's look, which swings between that of a louche porno set (if I may risk this pleonasm) and the claustrophobic atmosphere of a decadence-era Oriental interior (if I dare set down such grandiloquence).

Inglenook

To reinforce the bedroom's role and counteract its gloom, I've decorated the walls of my inglenook with 2 wall coverings, 1 in white cotton, the other in linen, as a sister to the entryway-hallway curtain. Let us not speak; let us hold our breath and look. This sort of alcove, accentuated with the help of a few thumbtacks, delights me as an idiosyncratic creation. Surrounding the bed with a double awning hems in its space a little more;

sometimes women visiting the space ask me why I've decked the walls with these 2 cloths. They may not form a canopy, but they do suggest precisely such an enclosure. Framing my nights, they subdue these walls' cold whiteness with a sense of seclusion. But a faux seclusion, created by mere surfaces, in the bedroom's inglenook.

Double Bed

As the bed defines the bedroom, 2 main activities/passivities define the bed, and commingle as sleep and love. The bed is a contradictory site. Its chief inconvenience for me is in failing to separate these warring functions, which contaminate each other, because desire is oriented toward others and sleep toward 1's self. If I had a bigger apartment (that same old song), I'd love to have 1 room just for sleeping and 1 for making love . . . and yet, even that separate bedroom for sleeping, which every fusionist will instinctively decry, would still be tinged in my mind with a muted eroticism. I can't think of all that many people who actually have a 2nd bedroom, aside from a few characters in American comedies, and other disciples of Sacha Guitry. And while it's true that a bed can lose whatever intrinsic eroticism it once held through the sleep that must eventually follow sex, or through the various other situations to which it plays host, whether dramatic (sickness or death) or sublimative (reading), the fact is that beds will always be the primary site for those 2 primal functions: 2 uses for 1 single space . . . which is 1 too many for me.

As for sex, beds are still the best place for such congress, save perhaps in the eyes of aficionados of those picturesque settings that are to lovemaking what curiosa are to high literature—an infrequent bit of invigorating spice. I've only rarely used my other rooms for erotic purposes; I'd say the bedroom is where we make our best decisions.

Pillowcase

As I make the bed, I pull the pillowcase off my pillow and notice that the pillow itself is pretty stained. The physical evidence of my body. So I cover it again with this new, deceptive pillowcase in soft colors.

Roof, Roof, My Roof . . .

Slipping at night between my sheets, looking out through my bedroom window, the fear of being made to sleep outside—not least because Parisian bedrooms usually look onto court-yards, not the street—makes itself keenly felt. No more than 1 simple wall separates me from the city; but socially, of course, the outdoors might as well be a distant planet. Comfortably curled up in my bed, I know that I've landed somehow on the right side of the world, in contrast to that hobo setting up his cardboard boxes under the revolting arcades of the rue Gustave-Goublier. As the son of a fallen man, I contracted long ago the terror of not having a roof over my head—"Toi, toi, mon toit," the beautiful Elli Medeiros once sang to her lover in a popular French song ("You, you, my roof")—but I always heard the word *toit*, roof, rather than *toi*, you. Is it a stretch to think that I subconsciously preferred the certainty of a shelter that I actually had a chance of claiming for my own rather than the uncertainty of love?

Corsican Proverb Contested by a Homebody

"Better a house full of people than of things." Not necessarily.

Lying Down

Lying down to read, 1 pillow supporting my back + another holding up my head, I'm almost relaxed. I cherish this position, which makes the living into the "pre-dead," enchanted by the human stasis conducive to dreams, and especially daydreams

(I prefer day to night). Various men and women of letters, Beckett 1st and foremost, have assembled and taken up 2ndary residences in their beds—a 2nd residence within the primary 1 (as Woolf put it in *A Room of 1's Own*) of their bedroom. I don't mind setting up a little fort of pillows and blankets and rumpled duvets in a hotel bed, since I can just abandon it afterward, but at home I can't take much joy in sleeping in such a messy structure—why, I wouldn't even be able to find my pen.

Suddenly my covers and ocelot pelt are weighing too heavily on me—I had to compensate for my quilt's extreme lightness, but now I feel imprisoned in my bed, from which it takes such a great effort to extricate myself that I'm worn out.

The Door of Perception

From my position lying in bed, the white door leading to the office, almost always shut, is 2 meters straight ahead. This oak door, with its 2 molded panels, its ceramic lintel and handle, appears 1,000s of times in 1,000s of Parisian apartments. For all its universality, this 1 has its specific imperfections, such as this thin vertical line splitting it down its middle. Like all doors, it might be seen as mysterious, standing between 1's self and the unknown; but as I know where this 1 opens to, it's lost any poetry it might have held. I stare at it steadily, and as if I were on mescaline I notice the delicate play of light filtered through the bedroom window, and the sunlight's streaks like flickering filmstrips or flitting butterflies. The series of continuous, repeated, hypnotic movements, changing and starting afresh, starting afresh and changing, continues into the night when the glare of car headlights comes to etch its own luminous symphony; and these saccadic jumps erase the space around me, so I'm neither inside nor outside, but between worlds.

The Heir's Bedroom
I won't inherit anything from my father, but he bestowed upon me his extraordinary capacity for sleep; from my mother, I just got anxiety.

Insomnia
Night is cut short, I go to the bathroom, crossing the living room's shadows. My place is sunken in a darkness I wish were total but isn't. The office's shutters don't work, and the Freebox's small luminous features make me furious as they stand sentry out there, partially outlining the volumes on my shelves. It's 4:39, and I should take my apartment's nighttime pulse while I've got the chance. My puffy eyes light on the office window. The street is as deserted as a film studio without any actors. Then I slowly make my way back to my bedroom, taking care not to bump into any furniture; a blind person would know his place better than I do.

Destroying a Braun
Time stands still by my bed. Once, for several months, there was a Braun alarm clock here, a black 6 cm × 6 cm square allying beauty in miniature with unticking silence, bought at the MoMA in New York in 2009. Due to some inexplicable technical doom, this device has never worked too well (which is even more maddening than an object that doesn't work at all— arbitrary fickleness being completely unacceptable when it comes to alarm clocks). I'm even more disappointed here, because I was so trusting of both Germany and modern art, and because having a single-function alarm clock at my disposal had allowed me to avoid making use of my cell phone. After all, if the CEO of Braun is selling his alarm clocks at a museum, he must believe that he's making art—and so they should absolutely work. Whenever I opened a design book about the

purity of form, my Braun taunted me, its hands continuing to turn, telling me it's 4:20 when it's 9:45.

So, 1 festive night, I decided to stomp on it, and after I set it on my floorboards, this was easily done.

Joy in Breaking, Pleasure in Destroying

Sometimes, being a martyr to technology, I imagine myself as an annihilator of objects. My resentment finally liberated, I envision the methodical destruction of every machine that's ever caused me indignity and frustration.

Usually, of course, we only manage to break the things we actually like and use—but when that happens, I recommend an immediate counteroffensive, to ruthlessly destroy something that had simply been tolerated before, thus breaking the curse of breakage. Losing a beautiful glass or a favorite piece of clothing can always be offset by wrecking some gadget, eliminating a useless thingamajig (although that means keeping several substandard products on hand for sacrificial purposes).

Nokia Night

Because my Braun is waiting for repairs that will never come, each day I have to revive the "alarm" function on the menu of my black & Orange Nokia, and every morning submit to its harsh little tone with the message "C'est l'heure!" waking 1,000,000 other tertiary-sector agents to their respective destinies. I know there's some chance that the cell phone's proximity to my head every night could prove detrimental to my health, but I still haven't found any substitute for my Braun.

Life's Windows

Leaving my bed where I've lingered too long, I'm immediately drawn to the bright hole it's pushed up against, that hole

we call a window. The rue du Faubourg-Saint-Martin is wide
enough that I don't pay much attention to what I might see in
the building opposite, nor do I worry about what those neighbors might glimpse here in my bedroom. Honestly, being
seen by others doesn't bother me: consistent with my autobiographical conception of literature, I'm on display anyway, and
without any need for reciprocity. I applaud the immense bay
windows of modernist homes, the numerous windows of
Haussmann-style apartments, the general transparency of glass;
what I dread are bunkers, with their little, horizontal, paranoiac arrow slits. The ever-probing urban theorist Mike Davis
wouldn't be happy here; he wouldn't have any seedy underbelly to delve into.

Legal Nudity

Naked at the window, I run into a legal problem. Could some
prudish neighbor sic the law on me for indecent assault? Just
wait: it'll happen.

Jealousy Redux

The bedroom window replicates the office's, so it seems a
waste of time to describe it again: it has the same number of
panes (8); is likewise split in 2 sections; bears the same smudges
on its panes, which, as I write this, still haven't been cleaned;
is finished in the same white laminate that was such perfect
fodder for its detractors when the 1st double glazings broke
up the harmony of Paris's façades.

I claimed that I didn't want to redescribe this window,
but that hasn't stopped me from doing so; repeating what's
already been said has never seemed pointless to me—as in
Robbe-Grillet's *Jealousy*, where the same scenes play out again
and again with only minor variations, and wherein 2 copies of
the same sculpture are found in 2 distinct rooms; I find this

quite beautiful, in fact. What a shame, then, that my own apartment falls so short of such conceptual requirements.

Spot the Difference

2 details help us differentiate between these 2 windows. 1 concerns the view: it's just not the same from my bedroom as from my office, which is a bit further to the south. The other difference relates to the daily opening/closing of the shutters in my bedroom, which sometimes knocks loose the protective slat at the bottom of the window. When it falls, this long strip of polyvinyl chloride uncovers precisely the decrepit strip of wall that it was installed to hide. This dilapidation is a harbinger of further, worse, decay: still, I crouch down and press the strip back against the wall, telling myself that it'll stay, this time. Thus, as in that old game of spot-the-difference (there were always 7), where 2 nearly identical drawings were submitted to our scrutiny, I restore my 2 windows to parity.

Palimpsest for the Future

But before I set the strip in place again, I slip in a piece of paper containing a poem—a secret capital improvement for my apartment. Its future owner won't know it, but he'll be living right next to an autobiographical treasure . . . which I hereby, and gladly, bestow upon him.

A View with a Room

I stand up and, looking at the faubourg Saint-Martin, I think: how wonderful it is to have a forest of windows! Because the sheer pleasure of a vast fenestral range—as seen on those beautiful buildings with long balconies each with 8 or 9 exits—is such a contrast to the unexciting mediocrity of smaller edifices like my own. Odd how property becomes an extension of both dreams and revolutions. I'll admit that my apartment isn't historical: I didn't start a revolt in my living room, or even a literary movement—Mata Hari didn't sneak into my bedroom nor did any Lee Harvey Oswald take aim from my window at any John F. Kennedy. But, even so, this small lodging—practically a concierge's residence—has been filled with a whole life.

Residence

I would have loved for my bedroom to be a beautiful residence conceived by some anguished decorator—*tout comme la Princesse de Castiglione dans ses appartements, ou Frédéric Chopin dans son logis luxueux au Place Vendôme, je me sens comme 1 réfugié.*

Open/Closed

If I open the window, I become public; if I shut it, I make myself private. When I pull in the heavy white wood shutters at night, I'm closing off more than just my room: it's the day itself, and an entire world, that I'm happily silencing and darkening. They're unimportant in the office, those shutters, but indispensable here. Closing them requires taking several firm actions: opening the window, leaning forward, sticking a finger through an iron ring, grabbing 1 of the left shutter's slats, pulling both sides toward me, bracing my elbows against the frame, then fastening everything firmly. This inward movement amounts to a sort of mechanical ballet centered on my pelvic twists. This operation is performed at different times over the course of seasons: it happens very late in the summer, while in the winter I must protect myself against nightfall.

Double Glazing

The 1st night I slept here, I didn't sleep at all. I knew that I'd sleep badly in a new place; I also knew that the rue du

Faubourg-Saint-Martin, a conduit through the heart of Paris, was packed in the daytime, but I never imagined that it could be even louder at night, when there's no traffic, and so cars can just speed right through. Doubly overwhelmed by the fear that I'd cheated myself and could never stand to live here, I tapped at the window glass, which hadn't been changed since the war. The 1st night after I installed double glazing was my true 1st night.

Technical Point

Double glazing is surreal; 2ndary glazing is just supra-real.

Gustave Curtain

Anchored by the usual system of rings and clips, the light yet opaque bedroom-window curtain shields me behind its chocolate-brown color, as oblique as Style itself. I can't dissociate this modest flea-market cloth from the "merino dressing gown" that betrays Madame Arnoux's decline in *Sentimental Education*. Well aware of the slippery slopes of kitsch, not to mention the monetary ambitions that led Arnoux, the proprietor of L'Art Industriel, to abandon his store, the Flaubert-like security guard who led me through the drapery department of the Bazar de l'Hôtel de Ville seemed determined to solve every single 1 of my problems: "Since we can no longer dwell in marble halls and wear the purple, recline on hummingbird-feather divans, enjoy swansdown carpets, ebony chairs, tortoiseshell floors, solid gold candelabras, lamps carved in emerald . . ." but I cut him off before he could intone Flaubert's injunction to "take flight into the ideal" and insisted on being practical: let's *rent* some office chairs, some extra radiators, and curtains without floral prints!

Little Prairie in the House

At the foot of my bed, a nearly empty, virgin 1 m² territory is like a little prairie. There should be other untamed spaces like this in my home, empty stretches for the eye to enjoy. Like the barely known vacant lots of Paris, this miniprairie has unfortunately been overshadowed by the rest of my home rather than showcased in all its untamed beauty.

Sitting Wrong
Here is another chair, the 5th and last of its set, in which I never sit: I only utilize upright and prostrate positions in my bedroom. This duality simplifies the room. The presence of this chair could spark a discussion of whether my bedroom might double as an intimate sitting room, but the bed's entreaties to come and lie down put an end to such conversations with a historically proven efficacy. Sitting here in this chair, I'd feel like I was waiting for a verdict, especially since this chair is set diagonally, in the dunce's corner, right by the 3rd radiator. It would be wrong for me to sit there. So I use it as a place to set my clothes.

In the Corner
Ready to flee this thankless prairie, I succumb to the appeal of the corner. Turning the chair flat against the wall, I stand there. Turning my back to the room, I focus on myself. Spontaneously, I put my hands on my legs. Silence. A welcome, meditative feeling arises in me facing this lifeless little corner, which I immediately depart because I can never stay in 1 church for long. It's cold there.

Wasting Energy
I turn on the 3rd radiator and also open the January window. Cold air and hot air battle. I air out my room but still take advantage of the warmth: these contraries balance out at the cost of an extraordinary waste of energy. Ruination may be pounding on our windows, but at least it's a warm ruination.

Another Angle

I shut the window, I turn around: as my left foot touches
the chair leg and my hand reaches for the office-door handle,
my eye strays diagonally 6 meters off and catches the angle
of the edge of my sink. I'm physically in my bedroom, visually
in my kitchen, virtually in my office, mentally who knows
where.

Junction!

Here we are now in the middle of the bedroom; I take 1 step
toward the shut office door; the junction described *supra*
(←OFFICE) is now manifest. The armoire is 1 meter in front
of us. I sweep my hand over this monument's face and utter a
welcoming phrase to the Penates. They urge me, in turn, to
pause for a minute and drink something in the kitchen, after a
detour through my office, a path I rarely take.

Strait Is the Gate

It's rather difficult to squeeze through the office door, as it
can so easily collide with the left corner of my desk, only 49
centimeters off; but it's wonderful to slip into a room like an
actor onto the stage, through this straitened gate. Another
detail that complicates access to the office: the door is given
to sticking, while the handle is loose; to shut the door, I have
to slam it. This simple solution often ends in a double failure
as the handle then falls out and the door rebounds, hitting
the corner of my desk. Defying this fragile white handle, held
in place by just 2 nails, I've turned its bedroom side into a
purely ornamental piece by draping it with a long azure-and-
silver Charvet bag, which shines its light over all my nearby
furnishings, endowing them with a smidgen of the opulence
of the place Vendôme.

Bad Housekeeping

It behooves me to fix this door handle, but I won't do it. I can't. Inhibition, far stronger than any threat of collapse, paralyzes me. If nails can't set everything to rights, then what can? Better to blaze my trail through some other locus.

Zimmer

So I return through the usual entrance, a glass in my hand, and I install myself at the Meblutil card table that I set up in whatever room I like. Whenever I bring a glass into my bedroom, a glass of wine, for example, I'm not sure whether my bedroom is still my bedroom. It becomes a bar. 1 small red drop falls by accident on my USB drive, and flows onto the cloth covering the card table.

Not in the Cards

My grandfather, a bridge champion, tried to teach me the basics of his game, but, confronted with my unwillingness to understand, he lost patience: it just wasn't in the cards. Still by the card table, I look down at the drying red stain and then, with the weariness of a surveyor near the end of his work, up at the huge armoire awaiting me. I summon up my courage. I press onward.

Garden Bazaar

On the left side of the armoire, a low semicircular piece of furniture (80 cm) catches my attention; it's a veranda planter, in dark-green metal, from the Bazar de l'Hôtel de Ville, that's never held any plant. Still, it holds some traces of its intended purpose, because it never moves, though getting rid of it would certainly bring me closer to the ideal lack of furnishings to which I aspire, and which, in all honesty, I haven't gotten too close to achieving. And, come to think of it, I'm not even positive it came from the Bazar de l'Hôtel de Ville, that department store which inspired the decorative imagination of so many shoppers before renouncing its stature as a high temple of commerce. This 3-level planter is a parasite here in its corner; all it does is buttress a few knickknacks.

Bag Showcase

Its openwork base has become a sort of bag showcase in which my irresponsibility is given free rein: here, derivative folk art (grocery bags) and tote bags commingle almost sexually. Brand-name bags are the stars of the parade, so I've set them on top, with a special place for the 1 bearing a yellow & black rectangle framed by sandy arabesques and the words *Franck & Fils* around its perimeter. It's mirrored by the orange Sentou bag on its right, which hangs from the Charvet while holding a lily-and-pink Diane von Furstenberg. The bags on the 2 lower rungs are 3 in number: a small gray bag I consider my swimming bag; a black shopping bag that's my work bag; a rust-colored bag serving as my weekend bag. (By some miracle, I never have weekends that involve swimming + work, so conflicts don't arise.) I've separated out most of the grocery bags, which are currently doing double duty as soldiers shielding my vacuum cleaner from judgmental eyes (←KITCHEN). Down with all strictly utilitarian bags! Not a single artist's studio could tolerate their wholesale mixture, an ED bag getting frisky with an Hermès bag, a Fnac + a Darty in a La Hune with a Leclerc . . . But in the end, to be honest, there's no special allure to this bag showcase. They're actually all just lying there, on the floor, or just about. They're shapeless and soft. Wait, I'll try sprucing them up.

Object Palette

On a low platform, the painter arranges all the objects that starred in the fresco of his life. Jugs, pitchers, plates, vases, carafes all side-by-side. Duplicates and pointless decorations standing shoulder to shoulder. Then he photographs them. If Matisse were a decorator, he'd simply be known as Hank.

From Dresser to Dressing Room

It takes only 1 step to get from the dresser to the bit of bedroom space that I consider my dressing room. The ideal apartment (which I've given up on) would have, adjacent to the bedroom, a wholly separate dressing room allowing 1 to cleanse the bedroom of every adventitious element, to consecrate it solely to its eponymous activity. Having the armoire in the bedroom makes it stranger, or more familiar, depending on what role we consider clothes to play in the fabric of our days.

Cover These Fabrics

As the armoire is to the bedroom what the bookshelves are to the office, I had them both built by the same craftsman, out of the same light-brown material. But, unlike the bookshelves, my clothes shelves are curtained off, protected from prying eyes. The culture we live in encourages book fairs, but curtains off clothing stores. Detrimental dust and tarnishing light do suffice as justifications; besides, clothes have to retain their element of surprise. And, just think, the curtain necessary to fully conceal my library would be colossal.

Furniture Display

Filling half the wall, the 190-cm-long, 60-cm-deep armoire reaches 2.50 m to the ceiling. An edifice that I honor, as such, conceptual errors and all—the cruelest of which I'm responsible for being its lack of ambition: instead of having it go all the way across the wall, or at least to the office door, I left (oh, why??) an empty 60-cm-wide space from its left edge to the door . . . and what stings all the more is that this wasted space has been contaminated by my bag showcase.

Reasons for Smallness

I have to reconstruct from scratch the genealogy of this failure in westward expansion, which keeps me from being able to fit all my clothing in my armoire (and forces me to use the closet as an auxiliary). At 1st I thought its volume would be excessive, but as it was constructed, I actually asked its builder to make it a bit bigger. Disappointed by the result, I repeated my request, increasing his annoyance and my fees. I had to insist on the 3rd enlargement: I saw in the artisan's unexpected smile his disdain at my owning so many clothes, a prospect that was evidently as foreign to him as owning children's toys would be to me.

Happiness

Happiness is not having children, is not having to have children's rooms.

Capital Improvement

When I leave this apartment, with all the speed of a flame devouring a certified document, I'll leave the armoire (and the bookshelves) to my successor. In legal terms, these 2 pieces of furniture have been made part and parcel of the apartment itself, which is clearly a capital improvement.

I once randomly found myself in a sumptuous apartment. The white living room was adorned with splendid concentric red circles adjoining 1 another. I happened to return to that same apartment several months later. It had changed hands. I asked the new owner what he'd done with the Felice Varini. "Those red things? Oh, we got rid of them."

Dual Matter

2 curtains split the armoire into 2 equal parts: the left covered by a brown cotton curtain (matching the window curtain);

the right by a denim curtain (matching the 1 in the office). There's no special significance in allocating particular colors to particular halves, but there has to be some country or company that champions blue and brown . . . that said, I can't think of any flag or standard made of heterogeneous materials.

Nicer Covered
Although its contents are fundamentally "aesthetic," this massive piece of furniture looks nicer covered: when the curtains are open, it loses its composure.

Left Hemisphere
The left and larger side of the armoire holds shirts, the smaller my coats; the lower space, down to the floorboards, is clearly full.

A Technophilic Arm
I should draw attention to the ingenious device here that allows a person of average height (1.75 m) hoping to grab a shirt not to have to stand on tiptoe (which still wouldn't do the trick) to reach his goal 2.40 meters up. My shirts are hung on a bar with a pull-down arm that just has to be tugged on for the shirts to descend from the uppermost reaches of the armoire down to human height. This mechanism of Germanic invention then returns to its original state, after a gentle push in the opposite direction that slowly brings the shirts back to their perch, as on a crane. This is 1 of those rare technical conveniences that I actually find useful, but this particular apparatus was unfortunately tarnished by an installation error. Since it wasn't set up as carefully as it should have been, I have to yank down the moving arm quickly to make sure my shirts don't fall; when the arm moves too slowly, the hangers laden with shirts all answer *l'appel du vide* and scatter everywhere.

The reason is that it's folded too far back because of the height—greater than mine—of the man who installed it. The large number of shirts hung here keeps me from using this device with the ease it was designed to ensure, so in practice I almost never do. I have to use the Tam Tam stool that always sits in front of the armoire's right side. In other words, this machine, for all its ingenuity, is useless. The only reason to actually use it would be if I wanted to send all my nicely ironed shirts crashing to the floor.

In theory, machines should delight me; in practice, they are the bane of my existence, since I just can't make them work well; like so many other literati, I was raised in a Luddite environment, and its traces linger. Progressivism means overcoming the stigmas we have attached to any opposing religion(s), but my daily life still hews to my inborn tendencies: that is, a murky and superstitious relationship to all technology. Everything I touch falls apart—and the fact that I can't take advantage of this pull-down closet rod, even though I paid for it, merely confirms for me the antipathy in which I am held by all machines.

I, Engineer

Ludism: delight in playing.

   Luddism: breaking machines.

   My ism: playing with machines.

Parade

I don't know how to make things work, so I've focused my energy on words; I don't have a practical bone in my body, so I've become contemplative instead. Sometimes I just look at my shirts and their fine colors, admiring them instead of reaching for them.

Left/Right Shirts

The black pull-down arm hangs vertically from the middle of the nickel-plated bar, and serves to separate my shirts—I organize my things around the defeats I've suffered. This shifting boundary, sliding back and forth, maintains 2 simple, seasonal categories: to the left, summer shirts; to the right, winter shirts. A fairly artificial distinction, actually: the left side really just holds out-of-season shirts, such as winter shirts during the summer, and vice versa. As for the intermediary seasons, they do admittedly muddy this theoretical divide: today, March 19, on the cusp of spring, the summer shirts remain on the left, but are getting ready to sally forth to the right; it's still chilly, but they do want to remind me of their existence. This binary, left/right classification principle therefore makes the left side (the narrower side) the "unused" side, and the right side (the well-stocked side) the current season's side.

If it's relatively easy to shelve books alphabetically, organizing clothes, which fit into so many categories at the same time (cloth, color, brand, type of collar, etc.), calls for a little more flexibility. I own 24 shirts, 15 of them patterned and 9 solid: as I detail this breakdown, I realize that I'd rather it were the other way around, because this current stage in my personal evolution (my euphemism for aging) favors greater rigor, and so drives me toward the shirts of the 2nd category, whereas only a few months ago I was spending my money more . . . decoratively.

Monochromes

Among my monochromatic shirts (ergo, my "favorites"), bright colors predominate, except for 1 black shirt (size 38) that would instantly lose all its sophistication if a womanizer or perpetual partier or sports commentator decided to make it his shirt of choice. (Of course, I do recognize the unfortunate historical connotations of donning a Blackshirt, but then it also seems to me that upon Liberation every true Frenchman's 1st act of freedom would be to construct his or her own style without any concerns, historical or otherwise, aside from being true to themselves.) Also hanging here is a cream-colored shirt with 12 small pairs of initials stitched around the belly, starting with P.S. and J.B. and corresponding to literary and artistic luminaries I've mostly forgotten. The only 1s I'm sure of now are P.S. for Philippe Sollers and J.B. for James Brown, although I repurposed the latter for my own secret use back when I acquired this piece of finery, so that J.B. now means Jeanne Balibar, an actress I adored, although she had no idea about it. This garment is nothing more than a museum piece now, representing the obsolete trend of shirts being worn not tight but rather baggy around the sides; I consider it ugly now, but no doubt future fads will force me to consider it beautiful again.

Blank Regret

My other solid shirts are pink, gray, blue, and mauve. I should state my regret at not having more white shirts (I count only 3): How can it be that the most beautiful style, and the simplest, has become so rare in my wardrobe? And I'm terrified by the absence of this simplicity, which seems to define my relationship to life as a whole—at least when that relationship isn't being defined by my fear of stains.

Disciplinary Eroticism

I used to wear a set of air force shirts, which corresponded precisely to my ideal of simplicity and uniformity: sky blue or white, with stiff collars and epaulets, easy to wash, wrinkle-resistant, drying at record speed, these shirts offered so many benefits that I bought 9 at the unbeatable price of €15 each at the Montreuil market, a purchase accompanied by the violent joy of having broken away from the exorbitance of fashion. In my moments of rational folly, I dream of dressing the same way every day, in a single definitive outfit, easily refreshed by purchasing a few more duplicates, and tempered only by several seasonal variations: air force shirt, jeans, black shoes. This would resolve the eternal question of what to wear, much as Communist China did when it adopted that uniform which made an entire population sexy.

Patterned Shirts

My patterned shirts would seem to reveal a penchant for sartorial gaiety, even though I completely reject that notion: *happy* and *sad* are qualifications that have no place in my conception of clothes, which is defined instead by a severity only somewhat alleviated by color. My shirts, whether striped or plaid, Liberty brand with mauve flower prints or gray scrollwork, are the foundation that allow for the occasional faint glimmer of joy. Less definitive than tattoos, our bodily wallpaper forever whirls around the carousel of fashion. The perpetually changing variety of motifs exhausts multicolor shirts far more quickly than other clothes. The allure of patterns is more obvious than that of the sobriety of solids, but such charm is fleeting. Hysteria ages badly; neurosis endures.

Slightly Too Big

The problem posed by shirts, as with other clothing, is always the same for me: I tend to go for sizes slightly too big, shapes slightly too baggy. And yet my preference is for form-fitting clothes: the closer I get to skintight, the closer I am to perfect ergonomics. For a long while, my favorite shirt was a white size-38 army shirt. But delusions of grandeur led me to the serious error, since there were no more 38s left, of buying several 39s. Only too late did I recognize the dangers of buying a size too large: there's clearly a reason that people who can afford it have their clothing made to measure, but what's less clear to me is why I keep on making this same mistake; perhaps because I'm scared of not being big enough? Which in a literary context might be termed *the fear of being a fop*.

Proportional Lies
Clothes too big / apartment too small.

Down Low in the Armoire
The lower shelf holds my various body-length winter clothes. The instant I approach it, however, the goddess Vanity descends upon me and ushers me onward.

Unburberrying Myself
I have 2 raincoats. 1 is a perfect knockoff of the Burberry style. I rarely wear it, although I love it, consistent with the endlessly frustrating paradox according to which I use what I love as little as possible. I wear this raincoat ostentatiously: the Burberry, identifiable by its distinctive features—half-belt, detachable hood, epaulets, its mythical proportions giving men classic-film-star physiques—is, admittedly, weighted down with associations . . . And it's hard to escape this welter of imagery when wearing a Burberry, because wearing it means clothing myself in an image that I always worry might be perceived as ridiculous. It's not a far-fetched worry, either: on a drizzly day 1 of those perfectly coiffed African men from Château-d'Eau yelled at me, admiringly, "Belmondo!" The secret to successfully wearing a Burberry is that of *unburberrying* myself, which is necessary so that I don't sink into the stylistic anachronism or misplaced heroism of those Jean-Pierre

Melville films where such coats are worn so elegantly along with black Ray-Bans and Stetsons. I have done meticulous research into the dos and don'ts of unburberrying: wearing an Indian-print scarf or a brightly colored shirt is the 1st step; next, to tone down the policeman look, make sure to keep the coat's belt undone; also, so it doesn't look overbearing on someone who just wants to look classy, it has to be worn when in a good mood. All in all, it's best worn when there's heavy rain, when its function augments its status and asserts its authority. The cobalt color on this 1 is the coup de grâce.

My other raincoat, cream-colored, falling below my knees, is less complicated; even on its hanger, its slightly crinkled look makes it much more benign. This intangible difference between a piece of clothing on the rack and on 1's shoulders is 1 of style's greatest charms, and nothing is more astonishing than discovering just how much an item you like genuinely suits you; nothing, inversely, is more disappointing than something that loses its charm as soon as it's on its wearer's body. This raincoat—more "modern" than the Burberry—is easier to wear. On rainy days, I like to alternate between burberrying and putting on this substitute, breaking up my meteorological monotony with this variation in garments that lets me trudge through water just as easily as through different neighborhoods or through different eras.

Quick-Change Act

Sometimes I have to change several times in 1 day, wearing something at night I wasn't wearing in the morning, switching my clothes in the afternoon—and so sing the praises of sartorial interchangeability in the service of our desires, as changeable as our own mental weather. Fregolism is an antidote to the gloominess of life. By contrast, furniture is so stolidly solid.

Bicoatal

My 2 heavy coats are black yet dissimilar. My nice wool coat extends to my knees; it's both soft and warm, shapes my body almost theatrically with its fitted proportions and its sharp collar that, when popped, reminds me of a bat, or maybe of Louis Jouvet. My nice cashmere coat ought to be just as perfectly cut, though, for reasons that are likely to remain a mystery to me (I had it made in Guangzhou for a sum 10 times less than its French equivalent), it arrived, like my shirts, slightly too big. Still, I replaced its fat plastic buttons, which betrayed its global origins, at the Dreyfus market. Even if we must accept that the Chinese have won the war over textiles, the battle for such little details is still being fought. Literature itself, which is by contrast a rather small business, hasn't tried half as hard to seize the global market—but what if, instead of complaining, we literati took some pleasure in occupying this cozier niche?

Site Comments

"Why do you keep saying 'my nice coat'?"

"Because I'm far too sentimental."

Stylish System

My most faithful remaining article of clothing (the others have all ended up in the donation bin at the 10th arrondissement's town hall) is 1 green velvet-paneled fitted and rather light coat—a redingote, in fact—that has, alas, started to show irrevocable signs of wear and tear, especially at the elbows, which looked identical to each other when I bought it but no longer seem to match. Thanks to its soft material, as well as its shape, which the 19th century championed as the platonic form of male dress, this fantastical garment brings together 2 eras, 1 real (that of its acquisition) and the other historical (that of its fabrication). I was happy that distant day in May 1994 when I set aside a considerable sum for this talisman, as beautiful as a woman . . . But when I think of those bewildering movie-star ingenues who demand so much generally fruitless effort for their attention, I know I'd rather spend my time buying clothes like this for myself.

I Stay New

Beau Brummell weathered his clothes to give them some added character. In contrast, it's the gleam of the new that intrigues me, and I like thinking that 1 new entry in my armoire will rejuvenate the rest of it, hoping to keep that newness intact for as long as possible by hiding the recent arrival behind my curtains as well as my dry cleaner's clear plastic protectors—not unlike condoms, which, rather than sounding the death knell of desire, as some claim, sound the charge for making love. I found this fitted coat so beautiful that I waited months before wearing it, unable to stop thinking about how doing so would hasten its degradation. In the end, I've barely ever worn it at all. But what more should I have expected of myself? Even when I was a child, images and words were always more than enough for me; I never was like other people fixated on using—and using up—things.

Dark Side

In nearly identical colors, dark or black, my 6 suits lead me to think, perhaps wrongly, that all it would take to establish equality among men is for them to don these matching uniforms. These garments of mine know I'm looking for a way to reconcile my violently opposed inclinations between conformity and individuality. And if I can't find such a way, my mood will get just as dark as they are.

Suiting Myself

Under their black Bon Marché fitted and zippered covers (which remind me how consummately ironic the store's name is), 2 3-piece suits are sleeping. I sometimes wake them up just to make myself feel different. I'd love to wear suits more often, but something holds me back—not something financial, because there are certainly affordable suits out there (the black 1 and the garnet 1 were €200 each), but rather something in their tone. For some, that tone might seem archaic; for me, it's my epitome. The less that suits are worn, the more they make a statement: acceptable for the occasional event, a risk to my reputation if worn more often. Suits come and go. Their detractors make them out to be symbols of conventionality or coldheartedness, and indeed when all is said and done most people wear them only when they have no alternative. As an outsider who's sometimes outright hostile to these ignorant attacks on my freedom to enjoy things for what they are, however, I take pleasure in wearing suits anytime they're welcome, and I certainly try not to be a snob when I do so. Maybe it's easier to be humble because I know that my ideal suit doesn't exist: I have to consider the suits I *do* own as substandard—so I rarely wear them.

Tomyskin

Reticence seeps through the cloth fibers to my skin. I have to choose. I forget my flesh in favor of fashion.

Structuralist Suitcase

At the very bottom, resting on the floorboards, is my seasonal suitcase, blue and bearing a label that says ÉTÉ, which fits snugly within the armoire. Pulling out clothes for particular seasons is a delicate operation, because the 4 actual seasons of reality have been reduced to 1 binary division—winter/summer—

agreed upon by society. Summer items have a short shelf life, while those for winter never experience this internal exile, being useful for the adjoining seasons as well, and so always stay hung up. This practice (and this suitcase) was handed down to me by my mother, who, when I was young, would always say in May that it was time to "pull out summer" but never in October that it was time to "pull out winter": this oppositional principle functioned only in 1 direction, and maybe I should credit this incomplete practice for my structuralist orientation, wherein everything has its opposite in the realm of signification, and all else results from a single system of subtle differences.

Pulling it open, I see 2 heaps: midsummer clothes (T-shirts, bright jackets, light pants) and "countryside" clothes (pullovers, old pants, defectors that'll show their true colors only outside big cities). It's not often that I go to the countryside, but I still keep these worn-out clothes around, perfect for running through the grass and the wind. Wearing these half-forgotten clothes in nature feels like making amends to an old foe.

Mainstream Summer

Thin shirts, bright jackets, you just don't excite me as much as autumn outfits. Elegance goes on vacation in the summer, when keeping cool is all that our culture demands of us, when lousy design goes mainstream: here, 2 short-sleeved Lacoste polo shirts (1 chardonnay green, 1 burgundy red) and 1 with long sleeves (vermilion) help me pass for normal, since those crocodiles have sunk their conformist teeth into the whole world. I also have 1 XS black polo that isn't too well suited to the sun, unless we round it out with the Tuareg style of full-body desert dress. My white pants come out only when I'm positive it's not going to rain: I've broken this rule just 1 time in my life, and that was 1 time too many. My summer jackets are total shams, pathetic excuses for clothing: 1 is cotton with blue stripes so narrow they hurt my eyes like a Bridget Riley op art painting; the other is white greige, which I've only ever worn briefly, thanks to a friend who informed me that "a white jacket makes you look like a café waiter!" While I don't share his opinion, nor his tendency to essentialize clothing, it should nonetheless go without saying that I have no desire to violate his edict and so find myself being waved at by strangers trying to get their checks.

Packing in Progress

Balanced on top of this suitcase is my travel suitcase. Its color (charcoal) and its brand (Jump) aren't as interesting as its wheels and its 20-kilo allowance. Disregarding all the exotic prospects it seems to hint at, I use it as often for short get-aways as for long trips. The problem with this suitcase is the purported improvement of its extendable handle, which allows it to be towed—a recent and very popular invention. But this handle extends only so far as to make sure that as I pull it along, it bumps against my heels. *Well made* and *badly made* trip over each other.

Well Traveled

A suitcase in full view is always somewhat displeasing (especially if it functions as additional storage, especially when it's plopped on top of a dresser I could be using instead). Extracted from the depths of the armoire, my suitcase stands empty, awaiting its orders. A wheelchair might have its arms out to welcome its user, but suitcases—especially when they're at home and simply being used as additional storage—encase a dreary stagnation that their few airport tags barely do anything to offset. Next to the GALERIES LAFAYETTE label that I left on it because it's red and sets it apart from other pieces of

luggage at the baggage claim, there's also a sticker from MAL-
AISE AIRLINES, an imperfect translation perfectly expressing
my feelings about the current mania for long-haul travel.
Pulling it out of its berth, I lift it easily (as in those B movies
where the star runs with a suitcase in his hands), and set it
rolling on the floor. These casters, which were practically nonexistent before the '80s, have enabled a much greater freedom
of movement, it's true. Maneuver a suitcase through your various rooms (the living room being the most appropriate) and
after hearing all the usual remarks ("Off on a trip?"), you'll
feel like you need to get yourself someplace exotic immediately.

Mobile Home

I won't describe any of my trips. I'm voyaging around my
bedroom, that's all. My suitcase makes me nauseous.

The Racquet Racket

In this suitcase I find a black shoulder bag bought at a mall
in Quentin-en-Yvelines to reward myself after a particularly
crazy day of work; I use it for badminton, that sport I've played
once a decade for the last 10 years. It holds just my Babolat
racquet, weighing a delightful 80 grams: proof positive that
strength likes subtlety. I pull it out of its cover and then am
overcome by an enormous burst of laughter: I've suddenly remembered my friends and me all donning these covers as though
they were the grotesque caps of some imaginary sect, as we all
yell out the rallying cry of "Babolaaat!"

Frame of Reference

I press my face against the racquet and walk through the
apartment. Reality filtered through a net. I fence in everything
around me: to see is to impose a frame across the entire world.

Right Hemisphere
Now I'm ready for the right side of the armoire, which has 3 areas: the upper section with 3 open spaces, the center bar holding pants and jackets, and the lower section with 2 shoe drawers.

Bedlam
The uppermost of these spaces, just under the ceiling, poses a particular problem for those, like myself, who don't have stepladders (and refuse to keep them: my collectivist sentiments regarding subservient objects, from tools [←ENTRYWAY] to stepladders [not here, evidently], are well-known). To really plumb its depths, since all I can see is what's already sticking out, it's not enough for me to stand on a chair; I have to get even higher by setting a Tam Tam stool on top of a chair, though not until I've checked and rechecked how stable my perch will be; still, the moment I've ascended to this 2nd platform, the true precariousness of my situation makes itself felt, and at my 1st—quite possibly fatal—movement, the stool slips, the chair shifts, under my 65 kilos, obliging me to grasp desperately at the edges of my shelves, then at the curtains. The curtain rod comes loose and then the whole ensemble plummets to the floor, myself included, transforming my bedroom into a grotesque sketch of disorder triumphant. I've been defeated: I thought I'd be able to reduce time's erosion of these various objects in my home, but by refusing to own a stepladder I've condemned myself to collapse all the same; I've been vanquished by the need to buy 1, at some point, because not having 1 only multiplies the annoyances of, and hours wasted on, dealing with its absence.

Unread Balzac
What's hidden up here? No real surprises: covers, quilts, and various fabrics in numerous colors from blue to gold by way of gleaming black, as well as a mothball resembling a Christmas

tree ornament—basically a heap of mildly interesting objects that I've found the energy to mention only by thinking of Balzac, the Balzac that I've never read.

The Rolled-Up Poster

This ensemble is rounded out by several rolled-up posters that are here only because there isn't any better place to put them; such posters, lacking any designated space of their own (aside from the walls on which they might, I suppose, be mounted), have to be kept in a protective space, where they'll stay intact, safe from moisture or disturbance. Thanks to my clerical tendencies, I now feel the need to unroll them and see what they depict, because I'd practically forgotten these even existed: here, for example, is an imaginary flag depicting the Star of David superimposed upon the colors of an Arab country in a pacifist statement that struck me as so facile that I just filed it away in this cubbyhole. And then . . . well, there are plenty of other posters here too, but I find that I don't, after all, have the patience to open each 1: to justify this momentary laziness, I'll posit the following aesthetic axiom regarding the perception of works of art, stating that a given piece, made to be seen, only exists in being seen. Like unperformed theatrical pieces, unmounted posters simply don't exist—and so we can safely pass over the remainder.

Sporting Goods

At the edge of the space below, easily accessible, I've set a box of athletic clothes, including 2 near-identical outfits, both for the sake of simplicity and out of a personal preference for doubles—I'd like to write a short story retelling the life of a man who did everything twice. The backup outfit is a pair of tracksuit pants + a T-shirt, both the same brand, but not the same shade of gray (which disappoints me, because I like uniform uniforms), and decorated (unlike the primary 1) with the

1st 10 whole numbers iron-transferred onto the cloth (which are starting to peel away from so many wash cycles), making a conga line (0123456789) enigmatic enough that a friendly girl asked me 1 day during a soccer game, "Is that your phone number?" to which I had only the pitiful riposte "Sure." The other outfit is the 1 I sport more often. The fact that it's almost completely supplanted the original outfit suggests that my preference for doubles is actually 1 for identical duplicates—otherwise I'd wear my "backup" clothes more often than I do. This outfit is made up of a satiny black V-neck T-shirt that dries extremely quickly + a pair of pants made of the same material but in midnight blue, both halves belonging to that charmed category of clothing known as "sportswear," which appellation has allowed a not-insignificant portion of the population to transcend stigmatization on account of their style and be declared masters of elegance thanks to 1 of those democratic reversals the modern world is privileged to effect.

Also among these items is 1 of my favorite pieces of clothing, a sweatshirt with sky blue hood that I use not only for badminton but also in specific weather conditions: when it's mild, gray, and drizzly. The poetry of that particular sort of day—Loire Valley or Île-de-France weather—inheres in this polo, so intimately associated with it, and augments the pleasure of wearing the hood so beloved by monks and rappers. I should add, for self-criticism's sake, that there's also a T-shirt here bearing the logo of the sports club I belong to, which I never wear because I think it's hideous: I detest all forms of servitude, so there's no chance I'd ever wear a shirt I didn't pick out myself—particularly a communal shirt put together by graphic designers. Its fate is clear—a rag for waxing.

Laundry

Thoughtfully set aside here are 9 bath towels and 4 tablecloths making up a "linen closet" already doomed to failure. These poorly folded, never-ironed linens have quickly piled up, making the armoire curtain indispensable for hiding teetering towers of textiles, clean and colorful heaps that look pathetic nonetheless and hardly worthy of Zola's famous White Sale in *The Ladies' Delight*. Really, they're not even remotely spectacular; they certainly don't even deserve to be window dressing in this kingdom I call my armoire.

Sweatspace

The 3rd organizational space in this upper section is at mouth level. Here is where my sweaters sit (12 of them) in 2 piles. There are winter sweaters, like the traditional wool navy sweater with buttons down the shoulder, a gift from my girlfriend, favored by certain kinds of men (usually young, usually cool); though it reminds me of the Breton childhood I never had, and its moist wool is usually scratchy, it's still my favorite by a landslide. My other sweaters, all unapologetically classical, in gray or blue or black wool—except for 1 troublemaker, an electric-blue cashmere number—are all V-necks save 3, which are turtlenecks: a design choice with which I have a rather complicated relationship.

Despotic Collars

The aesthetic of eternally classic turtlenecks, which draw attention to the neck while also protecting it, offers a reprieve from standard-issue shirts and from keeping up with the latest styles. Its stylishness calls to mind both Duras and Robbe-Grillet, the '70s, the lower ranks of the priesthood, and the casually relaxed style of a particular sort of alternative bourgeoisie as depicted in New Wave films; but, my neck being particularly ill-suited to the collar (like all Taureans, my neck is massive), I dread this textile prison, especially when it's wool. The prospect of donning this noose, this ruff of anguish that threatens to choke me in so much cloth, means that I tend to avoid these sweater-gallows, no matter how desperate I am to fit in physically and sartorially. In order to make them tolerable, I have to double them with a looser cotton turtleneck sweater (*infra*) that provides an underlayer and also gets rid of the constricting sensation. It would seem, therefore, that the turtleneck I so revere is by its nature oppressive to my ideas of art and life, as if its charm depended on some degree of physical discomfort, on a threat proportionate to its evident stylishness. There has to be some form for the content of a work of art to affect me, but I have to be convinced that this form has arisen from life itself, much as the torso beneath the sweater gives shape to the sweater's cloth. For me, writing is born of the threat that wool poses to my skin, the fear that it will constrict and compress my body; it makes me break out in sweat and sentences alike. I have to express it somehow, otherwise I'd be curled up tighter than that turtleneck collar, staring endlessly and helplessly at my never-finished work.

Body of the Building
I bring the sweater's seams to my nose. The armpits smell strong. I must have a body. A paint blister bursts on the side wall.

Vice Versa Is as Good as Versa Vice
Another delightful, camel-colored, uncommon sweater (I've ordered these adjectives to underscore this uncommonness) with red piping around the wrists bears the oddity of visible cuts on its shoulders and sides, blurring but not abolishing the notions of vice and versa. I won't claim that the interior and the exterior are interchangeable, but they're as inseparable as the wool is to its knitting.

When *La doublure* Means "The Clothes' Lining"
Raymond Roussel, that author of *La doublure*, double stitched a small square of white cloth onto the lining of his clothes so

he could make a pencil mark there for every use. I haven't gone so far; the need to list my possessions allows me to enumerate them without having to line them.

Surplus

I can see, however, that their role in my book has been mainly to drown me under their mass and so keep me from properly revealing myself: forever delaying my laying myself bare, and so trying, through this continual postponement, to stymie this auto-autopsy. They keep enticing me to try them on, but to do so would be a trap. My struggle to stay focused leads me behind a windbreaker embellished with letters in gold spelling out Marshal Lyautey's precept "Montrer sa force pour ne pas avoir à s'en servir" ("Strength should be shown so it need not be used"). But if I let these clothes have their way, I'd end up disappearing beneath my vestments, since I'd have lost my home to the frenzy of filling it.

When *La doublure* Means "The Understudy"

And every so often my characters stand in for me; all it takes is the right outfit. Which is how this red tartan-print shirt makes me out to be an alcoholic à la Dean Martin in *Rio Bravo*, a role that touches me just as much as do all those failures out there who are struggling to regain their dignity.

The Particular Warmth of Undersweaters

To the right of the sweaters are the 6 lighter turtlenecks made of cotton mentioned *supra*, which I either wear under wool sweaters as protection or with no outer layer at all, weather permitting. They're cheap brands, which *disnoble* my body so accustomed to being draped in classier brands. I love them dearly, and grant them the same affection I hold for special friends or protectors. We have a few clothes friends but *very* few clotheser friends; they're not the same at all. And then, on the far right, are 7 white T-shirts that I only wear, paradoxically, in winter, because their function is to be underwear rather than a way of showing off my muscles. All these undergarments (call them undersweaters if you will, I for 1 plan to) share 1 fundamental quality in my eyes, which is that of human warmth, which is precisely what I look for in my relationships with others, and which I find only rarely. An underappreciated form of dandyism: warm dandyism, call now for your free sample.

Ascetic Tights

Behind this easily accessed row, though still retrievable if I reach all the way in, I've stored my less fashionable underthings. 1st come 4 cotton long johns, very useful in the winter, and which I wear to assuage not only my horror of cold, but also my horror of wool: it's true that I'm terrified of the cold, but I love winter for giving me the opportunity to overcome it, and the challenge offered us by this little-loved season is offset by its aesthetic superiority. Winter spurs man's cleverness. Long johns make me look like a "French kickboxer" if I wear them on their own—which I never do. Their silliness is poignant but remains unseen; I may be old-fashioned, but never retro. Tights remind me of 2ndary glazings; they halve the chill of reality.

Duke of Disguise

2 shoeboxes full of trinkets round out this ensemble, each 1 adding a little something. Here the boundary between vestment and accoutrement is hazy: 1 red swimming cap resembling a yarmulke, 1 black & white vest typical of corrida aficionados, the string tie Robert Mitchum wore in *The Night of the Hunter*, 1 itchy lumberjack's cap, Robert Vaughn's black leather gloves from *The Magnificent 7*, 1 wool hood with pro-

tective neck drape, 1 army jacket bought at the flea market having recently been seen on the backs of many penniless civilians, and the bow tie worn only 2 times in my life, with very specific outfits. I was a decorator, and now I'm an outfitter.

Full Art

Out of this virtual panoply I extract 16 silk scarves, those thoroughly engineered addenda to Beauty: purple square, yellow Broadway bandana, gray Lyon bandana, olive satin, appealing amanita, crimson monkey, Chaulet black, mustard pear, pergola blue, field grape, satinella, Chiang Kai-shek red, moldering bilberry, veranda green, black-speckled prazepam, late-harvest banana.

Ostentatious Fashion Model

Thanks to my particular way of refusing to submit to the scarcity economy, this neckwear assortment (which a slave to fashion might consider meager but a more honest man would call ridiculous) is regularly updated: less often than groceries, more often than furniture. 1 might assume that I've accumulated these thingummies to fill the ostentatious emptiness of the mini–leisure class to which I belong—an unpleasantly accurate theorem that is by no means short of proofs: plenty of other people, be they women or firemen, lions or seamstresses, dandies or floozies, do the same, all of them staving off that realization they'll soon return to dust by digging up and cashing out their matured bonds. Accusations of wild consumerism and over-ostentation don't interest me when it would be more appropriate to aim them at the entirety of this sinister, egoistic, and mediocre era. My possessions whisper to the fashion model in me: We don't want to live Zen. (And neither, indeed, does the fashion model . . .)

Box of Opulence

Within the gleaming machinery of this apartment, the armoire is a world within a world, a box enclosing an attempt at opulence. Bereft of Comfort, deprived of Space, I use Clothing as my means of escape.

Modern Jacket

On the armoire's chrome bar are, among various tops, my jackets: starting with the more modern variety, we have 1 denim with a lush faux fur collar, which strokes the neck with its hirsute caress; 1 khaki bomber jacket inflecting its militant style with a downy lightness; 1 black Harrington, popularized by the British proletariat, which I wear only on Monday nights; 2 extra-light jackets that are both inflammable and nonflammable; finally, 1 dark-blue (but not shiny) puffer jacket perfect for extremely cold days, its hood stuffed into a sausage-like collar—the only argument that convinced me to part with my money and my dignity for this monstrosity was that "it'll make you look more modern."

Imperfect Jacket

And now comes the more classical sort of jacket. Some of my suits call for a night-blue blazer that I've had taken in at the sleeves, and which has a manufacturing defect: its polyester padding pinches. Even having accepted that perfection is an empty ambition, I still can't look past this jacket's inferiority: I'm always finding something wrong with it, some infuriating detail, like its single inside pocket.

Can't Quite Put My Finger on It

I'm pointing now, threateningly, at the jackets I'm not so sure about—this 1, in narrow-striped, deep-blue dyed wool, I liked so much I bought 2 of it (S and XS), whereupon I inexplicably stopped liking it—maybe it was that acquiring it had destroyed its uniqueness; that stiff cotton 1 makes me look like a Ric Hochet–style comic book character—and I feel the urge to go and repeat this dangerous act in every other part of the apartment I'd like to clear out properly.

Paying the Piper

But I have to finish my work, even as it grows more and more omphaloskeptic, and, as I run through all these items, accessories, and brand names, erase all trace of my former penury. I don't care whether this abundance of objects makes me seem as though I've allowed myself to become corrupted by virtue of a lofty philosophy of habitation and appearances, when what I'm really doing is simply trying to bury the era during which, deep in debt and unable to live the materialist life, I couldn't even give myself (any) credit.

Jacketed in Paris

I wanted to please, to declare my love for the world (the world isn't the same as society). Because women have to be won over, let's dress up—let's suit up, in fact, just like everyone else (well, practically everyone—there are always a few heretics out there), hoping that this attention to the way I look will win me their favor as they judge my interior by my well-groomed exterior, in opposition to that old proverb about monks not being made by their habits. I bought my clothes in Paris. I've put on jackets. I've charged my suits with the responsibility of charming my conquests—a resounding failure. "That's not how it's done," 1 of my friends said, apparently oblivious to the irony of his passing judgment as he reached new depths of inelegance by moving into a pathetic studio.

What Hangers?

On the bar, without any segue, come my pants, hanging by their feet from clip-top hangers. They're hung 1 or 2 from each hanger, sometimes 3 for thin linens; it would be ideal for each hanger to correspond to a single pair of pants, but space (certainly) and negligence (perhaps) has kept me short of this goal. My 12 wooden hangers intermix with their plastic and brass homologues from various commercial establishments. The hanger, in all its inherent neutrality, intrigues those of us who are intrigued by organization. Hangers have a particularly pure functionality that allowed me to, if you remember, experience an artistic revelation . . . (← LIVING ROOM)

Pants Hung Low

This horizontal armada of pants hanging bottom-up produces a graphical relationship like the x and y axes of a graph. Just as the Hanged Man from the Tarot of Marseilles, far from suffering, smiles at the world upside down, this long series of trousers hangs here with all the insolence of people who can walk on their hands. They're in good company, after all: this rack doesn't have 1 hanged pair of pants, but rather 22.

Object Choices

In my armoire, every piece of clothing yells "Pick me!" They all preen on their hangers, bemoaning their disuse to the body that, standing undressed before them, could redeem them. Both factions wait, watch, hem and haw, before succumbing to a reciprocal union. Is it possible for the crook of a hanger to lure me with its dangling bait as if it were a fishing hook and I a fish? But I'm the predator here: I touch them, I rummage through them, I take my time to choose my prey and capture it. Then the empty hanger rocks back and forth, clinking delicately.

A Throw of the Dice Doesn't Abolish Chance

My apartment is disparate but clothing wants to be uniform. Every morning the winning outfit amounts to a throw of the dice. I have to play quickly, wedding a top to a bottom that might go well with it. If I waver, I lose my place, I lose the game.

Jacket Uncertainties
My long-sleeved, gray wool 6-button jacket prolongs my hesitation, hanging lonely as 1 cloud. Just as the mustache I'm currently wearing situates me uneasily between Roussel and Mesrine, this jacket makes me waver—depending on whether I wear it open over my turtleneck or buttoned up tight over it—between looking like the fed-up son of a stockbroker and projecting the false amiability of a '70s killer offering you a drink.

Working-Class Jeans
The dandy who wants the aristocratic pleasure of displeasure pulls on a pair of jeans and finds himself sporting a working-class desire to please.

Tone-on-Tone
This outfit is somber: I can't keep it a secret anymore that these dark colors, my short hair, these turtlenecks, these straitlaced suits, and these inky pants all just serve to rekindle those puritan sensibilities I thought had long been extinguished in me. It's true that there are some glimmers of color flashing in this gray-black sea: some light-blue, regal trim, some gleaming yellow velvet, a rainbow of sky blue, green, saffron, waterlily, pink, and, in a last gasp, red. But the occasional variegated diversion in my wardrobe gets me nowhere, ultimately fooling no 1.

REDRUM
Trap a hyperneurotic man in a red room, and he'll quickly go insane. How could I have ever worn these raspberry-pink pants? I keep them around only because of their criminal color. I still

have the utmost respect for the faded, accidental pink of 1 beloved shirt, however.

Clue

Miss Scarlet, in the bedroom, with the rope!

Siege Mentality

I'd rather define myself with costumes, disguises, and false outfits than strip down to my bare skin. But this display just keeps on spooling without stopping. My hordes overwhelm me. I'm stuck in a siege mentality. Bloodstained clothes dance before my eyes. What did my great-grandfather wear the day he died? And his wife—was she dressed to the 9s?

Step by Step

We are struggling our way through my wardrobe as we might through snow, sand, or sawdust—step by step, centimeter by centimeter.

Restrained Movements

I have to get down on the floor to reach the bottom of the armoire, where I keep my shoes, and a bend of the knees does the trick. Every time I fish for shoes, I squat rather than kneel, to stave off lumbago. That's the game: how best to deviate from my normal posture. I've practiced every time I need to look at these shoes, just as gunmen in Westerns have mastered pushing doors open with their feet to keep their hands on their pistols. There are 2 drawers here with holes instead of knobs; I open them with my fingers, but shut them with the tips of my shoes. This measured movement is not without its consequence, which is that the drawer's circumference is dotted with small black scuff marks. I love traces of this kind, which mark every home: indelible proof that people have lived full lives here.

Basketball Shoes

The lower drawer holds the least cool shoes—that is, athletic shoes. I wear them only once a week; their ugliness is therefore untouched (as is their whiteness, which stands out against the black outfit I wear when hitting shuttlecocks)—a massive, overstuffed ugliness that pads my feet so nothing can harm them; they have absolutely 0 physical defects except for being knockoffs made in China. In contrast, this pair of Spring Court tennis shoes delights me, pulling off the miraculous feat of reminding me, all at once, of my childhood, my adolescence, my young adulthood, and my maturity—in short, my entire life, from the '60s to the present day: the brand disappeared from our cultural consciousness at 1 point before reappearing to extraordinary acclaim—it must have been revived by my generation. Exuding a particularly French elegance, from a gentler era, when sport was just 1 activity among many others and not a burgeoning industry, let alone a global phenomenon, their whiteness remains thoroughly white, demanding care that I'm not well equipped to provide: I'm unappreciative and lazy—far better at making public apologies. I also have some red Converse high-tops that I bought for no better reason than that they were trendy (even though I'm supposedly blessed with fashion-agnosticism), and which I'm sorry I ever bothered with, because they simply don't suit me. But the longer this trend persists, to the point that it threatens to become a style of its own, the more these basketball shoes transcend the already porous boundary between fleeting trend and serious style, forcing me to concede that Converses suit other people the way Spring Courts suit me. I hurriedly put them in a plastic bag that I'll only bring with me when I go hiking and nobody can see me wearing them.

Dirty Occident

I don't like being barefoot at home, in the Oriental style, because the proof of my floors' false cleanliness gets imprinted on my soles. To sidestep the shame of dirtied feet, the Occidental tactic is to dirty 1's floors further with dress shoes and call that "normal." We might think about it the way Stalin did: it may be shit, but it's *our* shit. How odd that a communist gave us the best definition of property.

Walking Around the Room

Each morning I choose between 2 indoor slipper options: a pair of gray Moroccan babouches, thusly repurposed, or a pair of black espadrilles, which I use to make believe that it's still summertime. In both cases, as I walk off in them, I opt for a sort of intentionally outrageous movement, which consists of dragging my feet as much as possible, making a disagreeable, dissonant noise against the parquetry: it's my counteroffensive against the cult of the slipper. Between the clink of boots and the silence of slippers (Heidegger forced visitors to his hut in the Black Forest to wear the latter), there's almost a harmony.

Cabinet of Quotations

A recess in my armoire serves as my imaginary repository of quotations, and in my mind I pull out, among the fabrics, Marshal Lyautey's philosophical and decorative line that served me *supra*, as well as a line from Michel Foucault, which will serve me *infra*.

Dressing Up and Up and Up

The upper drawer holds my dress shoes. 7 pairs, soirée-ready. They gleam.

Black Troops

My compatriots tend to wear black boots, and I myself have 5 pairs. They allow us the joy of lacing past our ankles; a joy great enough that having to wear shorter shoes on nice days after so many wintry months stirs up a feeling of hyperthinness that all lovers of boots know intimately. My favorite Mansfields with square toes, which I wear too often, are falling apart: the tips are dented, there are plastic joins in the heels, cracks in the leather, scratches covered by layers of wax. Leather fetishists aren't known for their subtlety, whereas the damaged leather of this civilian's boots is more allusive; its eroticism is merely hinted at. I like this caddish look, which has been sexualized by the *tifosi* of Fassbinder's phantasmagorias just as much as by crude hairdressers with sensuous pouts.

Politics of Incompleteness

I set out the shiny dress shoes for evenings alongside the less glamorous boots serving as my day-to-day pair for inspection. The contrast amounts to a new iteration of the old class struggle. Then I yank all my pairs of footwear out of the drawer and, embarking on a thorough uncoupling, take each left shoe and recouple it with another pair's right shoe. Before long, the floor's strewn with a mongrel horde in which all established patterns have been broken. These mismatched couples give my full assortment of shoes the allure of a newborn democracy.

Thin Lace

An eagle-eyed inspection of my shoes reveals that several pairs no longer have their original laces. But who would notice that this black lace isn't exactly the right fit, that the brown lace is slightly lighter on 1 side, slightly darker on the other? My footwear is no longer pristine—the system's been infiltrated by replacement laces.

Delayed Tassel Loafers

I used to always feel contemptuous of those conceited schoolchildren parading around in their tassel loafers, the most bourgeois of shoes, but now, as I've finally come to appreciate their utter simplicity, I can't be sure I wasn't misjudging this footwear's social status all along. The sheer respectability Dewar & Gicquel brought them by sculpting them in 150 cm × 140 cm × 180 cm marble has made it that much harder for me to sneer at them.

Heraclitean Shoes

Authors' shoes always hint at their overinflated egos: I guess I should complain that this brown size 11 makes my foot too long, a morphological detail that's only done me harm, since it keeps tripping me up, and all this even though I measured my foot 7 times. Heraclitus insisted the sun was the width of 1 human foot . . . and, in fact, if I pick up the shoe that was lying on the floor and hold it up to the window, it does seem that I can blot the sun out completely . . . and so savor culture's majestic humiliation of nature!

Foucault Clarks

As for my other nonblack pair, which are dark-brown calfskin Clarks, I don't wear them anymore. Their style, paralleling my espadrilles and Spring Courts, rounds out a sentimental '60s-era triptych. I'll omit them from my chronicle, showing them some unearned respect (respect is just a simulacrum of love), rather than submit them to any inclemency here. After all, they can be worn only in dry weather, which we rarely get at Parisian latitudes, so I just keep them out of life's warpath entirely . . . and Michel Foucault's haunting line, "Those I love, I use," pops out of the drawer like a jack-in-(or out-of-) the-box.

Ingress & Egress

We talk about ingress and egress when we consider the layout of rooms. Books and furniture hardly ever leave, whereas clothes breach the inside/outside interface. And so they come back filled with both wisdom and folly: my boots have learned to make quick getaways; my suits have suffered sarcasm and envy; my navy sweater has breathed the air of urban thorough-fares; my blazer has shielded me from inevitable passersby in the city; my hat has allowed me to play the gentleman out in the countryside; my fitted coat has survived 3 breakups and accompanied me back home every time.

Failing to Give Up the Ghost

The longer I think about my clothes, the more I see what a ghost I am. I've made my clothes my allies because we have so few allies, yet these aliens have only alienated my spirit. On the assumption that I'd become more individualistic through their intervention, the converse has obtained: they've forced me beyond the welter of possibilities they offer into a sort of impersonality, the distance growing more and more terrible as I, too, become terrible. By multiplying my provisional incarnations, they reveal my essential emptiness. I hear Édith Piaf's plea to a ragman to dredge up her lost heart among so many old clothes reverberate in my head full of dust and references, and I realize that the only outfit I absolutely can't bear to wear is that of a writer—which is, alas, my own skin.

Brands down the Toilet

Agnès b., A.P.C., H&M, José Lévy, Lacoste, Monoprix, Uniqlo: they'll end up going down the toilet, all the furniture to the flea markets, all the books to used bookstores.

Vanitas Vanitatum
I now have more shoes than space for them in my armoire: I have to leave 2 pairs out. What should be hidden, no longer is. Everything's overflowing; I push the drawer in with my foot and shut the armoire.

Slowly Shut
Drawing the 2 curtains together very slowly, I hasten the downfall of all that is novelistic.

3rd Tam Tam (White)
Set in front of the closed armoire, my 3rd Tam Tam stool is waiting for its moment in the spotlight. This white 1, identical to its red and black brothers, serves as footboard or pedestal for waxing shoes. Due to a manufacturing error that I didn't notice immediately, its 2 components don't fit together well, and it's impossible to use without these elements coming apart. I'll get rid of it as soon as I can.

Ruinous Parvenu
As I come to the end of this survey, I'm seized by a brutal disgust in front of the inert mass of all these things to which I've tried to give some life and light. I'm beginning to want to see the ruination of everything here, even the building around me; what I feel is the relic of some respect I once held for the past. A respect that's only grown more and more absurd as mediocrity and dilapidation have taken root in this space. There's something vile about living in old things that are nonetheless devoid of history.

A Real Estate Expert's Visit After the Next Crash
"Monsieur, your 50 m^2 apartment has tripled in value since you bought it on September 11, 2001."

"And I can provide a complete inventory!"

Assailing Surroundings

It's taken me such a long time to make my way around my apartment! But 3 years is 3 times less than Ulysses took returning from Troy. Ulysses didn't want to get home, and I, assailed by the prospect of heading out, I plead not to have to leave.

Blocus Solus

Not leaving my apartment for all these years, staying caged like a rat, cloistered, was my homage to all those other shutins I could name, for whom leaving home amounted to an impossible feat. Unable to poke their noses outside, this outside that threatened to crush them, they whiled away their days, unable to lose themselves even in decorating, painstakingly, the voids they called their homes.

Scorning the Light

My bedroom lights should be turned off. Near me is the room's 2nd light source, a vertical 1.80-m-high Ikea floor lamp that can be put wherever the shadows of a poorly lit room congregate. Along with the HP printer (←OFFICE), it's 1 of my place's numerous poorly made knockoffs, and, indeed, I scorn this lamp as much as I hate my printer. Really, though, it's my own weakness that I scorn, since I've never managed to get rid of the thing. It belongs (belonged) to the previous owner of this apartment, and before that must have come from some junkyard, with its long crooked pole that isn't properly screwed in, its white plastic shade with its circle of dust, its gray base filthy with stains, and its twisted black cord like a crummy theater prop—none of which, clearly, has kept it from becoming a star on stages all around the world: through the window, I can see its replica in my neighbor's apartment. Only the optimal angle of its illumination saves it from being chucked onto the sidewalk. When I move out of my place, I'll leave this floor lamp for my successor, repaying the favor my seller believed she was doing me. As I make my way beneath its 100 watts toward less notional realities, I see myself in a harsh light; this entity illuminates another (and another and another and another). What it highlights is that my apartment doesn't completely belong to me, nor I to it.

Packing My Bags
I pick up the Oriental silk screen protecting my card table, and the table itself, its 4 legs folding neatly under its top. The volume it delineated merges into the rest of the apartment's volume.

Camera Obscura
I hit the floor lamp's button, then flick the wall switch. The curtains are drawn. The room is dark, though the living room projects a hint of luminescence. I listen to the space's inhabited silence, and then its 1,000 small noises, among which are those I make myself. I wait for something to happen.

The Doorbell Rings!
I enter the living room, glancing conscientiously at the corners. Did I make a mistake, earlier, not answering? Pale light streams in from the courtyard. On the dining table, white sheets are stacked high. I take my pen, I sit down, read the final page, add some words.

The World as Will and Idea
And, penning these lines, I realize for the 1st time that when I die I don't know who will inherit this world I call an apartment. I have no idea whether this text might have any legal weight; just in case, I might as well use this opportunity to name my heirs and assigns: I hereby bequeath my apartment,

in the event of my death, to the person to whom I dedicated this book.

Doorbell
The doorbell rings. I go. Peephole. Nobody. I grab my keys. I open the door. The 3rd-floor hallway. Empty. A glance. The stairwell. "Anybody there?" I can't have been dreaming. I go up some steps. I go back down. I'm in front of my open door.

A Note About the Author

Thomas Clerc was born in 1965 and is the author of several books, including *The Man Who Killed Roland Barthes*, a collection of short stories for which he received the Prix de la Nouvelle of the Académie française. Clerc teaches at Université Paris Nanterre, where he specializes in contemporary French literature.

A Note About the Translator

Jeffrey Zuckerman is an award-winning translator of numerous French authors, including Marie Darrieussecq, Ananda Devi, Antoine Volodine, and Hervé Guibert.